M000271925

To Amanda,
Great work! Thank you.

Rhode Island Civilian Conservation Corps Camps:

HISTORY, MEMORIES, AND LEGACY OF THE CCC

[signature]

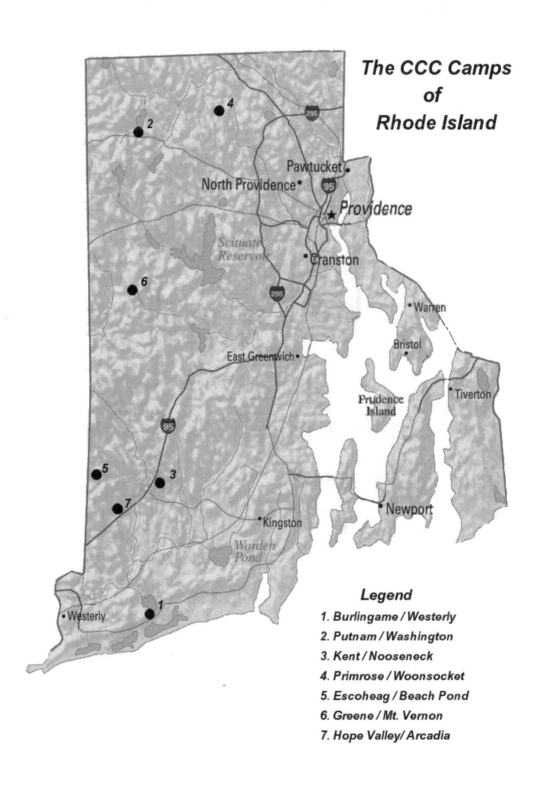

The CCC Camps
of
Rhode Island

Pawtucket

North Providence

★ Providence

Scituate Reservoir

Cranston

Warren

Bristol

East Greenwich

Prudence Island

Tiverton

Newport

Kingston

Worden Pond

Westerly

Legend

1. Burlingame / Westerly
2. Putnam / Washington
3. Kent / Nooseneck
4. Primrose / Woonsocket
5. Escoheag / Beach Pond
6. Greene / Mt. Vernon
7. Hope Valley/ Arcadia

Rhode Island Civilian Conservation Corps Camps:

HISTORY, MEMORIES, AND LEGACY OF THE CCC

Martin Podskoch

Edited by David Hayden

Podskoch Press, LLC
East Hampton, Connecticut

Rhode Island Civilian Conservation Corps Camps:

HISTORY, MEMORIES, AND LEGACY OF THE CCC

Published by
Podskoch Press, LLC
43 O'Neill Lane
East Hampton, CT 06424

podskoch@comcast.net
www.martinpodskoch.com

Copyright 2020, Martin Podskoch

All rights reserved under International and Pan-American Copyright Conventions.
No part of this publication may be reproduced or transmitted withoutconsent in writing from the publisher.

ISBN 978-0-9971019-3-5

Manufactured in the United States of America

654321

Cover photos courtesy of Lorenzo H. Frisiello & Kathleen Duxbury Collection,
John Cinq-Mars, Robert Bisaillon
Design & Layout Amanda Beauchemin of Ford Folios
Maps by Paul Hartmann

TABLE OF CONTENTS

FOREWORD

Albert "Al" Klyberg at Kelly House Museum in Lincoln where he worked for the
RI DEM as a Ranger and as a researcher/writer. There he gave tours to visitors
and also arranged and developed programs for school and other group tours.
Kevin & Beverly Klyberg

[Author Note: Albert Klyberg, Director of the Rhode Island Historical Society (1969-1999), first started researching the History of Rhode Island's Parks about 2005 when the RI Department of Environmental Management asked him to create a booklet for the 100th anniversary of the Parks of Rhode Island in 2009. In 2013 he worked to flesh out the story of the CCC camps on RI and the next summer he walked around the areas from Woonsocket to Westerly with his camera, looking for remnants of the CCC camps and their projects. He found a few picnic shelters, outdoor fireplaces, and buildings still intact, but the rest have fallen into disrepair or no longer exist.]

The following is the Prologue to Klyberg's CCC project.

Writing the "history" of something as recent as eighty years ago is not as simple as it might first appear. First of all there is the name, itself. The familiar moniker of the famous jobs program of the 1930s is the 'C.C.C.' However, this acronym did not exist at the outset of the program. One has to look for references to the 'E.C.W.' which stands for the Emergency Conservation Work if you seek to start at the beginning. The ECW eventually evolved into the CCC, but not at first.

There were seven such camps in Rhode Island that were designed to deliver reforestation and fire protection to Federal, state, and private lands. Two of these camps were converted into state park improvement camps. There were also a couple of occasions when the original camp was closed down and another camp took its site. No more than six, however, operated at any one time; sometimes there were only four. Seven distinct companies of CCC operated here. The official time frame of the CCC program was from mid-1933 until mid-1942, though much of the energy tailed off by the end of 1941 with the break-out of World War II.

The program to place unemployed youths on work in forests and parks was authorized shortly after Franklin D. Roosevelt was inaugurated as 32nd President in March of 1933. Within the month of March, the program got under way. By the end of May, recruited enrollees, who had received their orientation at Fort Adams, were sent to Burlingame State Park/Forest Reservation. A month later, in June, the second camp was running at the George Washington Memorial State Forest in Glocester, RI. Another emerged on Nooseneck Road, site of the present Lineham School in West Greenwich.

To set the stage properly for this story, it's necessary to back up a bit and focus on the state forest. (This seems to be the problem with beginnings; there always seems to be a beginning before the beginning. Only the first chapter of the Bible, Genesis, seems to have gotten it right, "In the Beginning was the Word…") In the case of Rhode Island, were it not for the Edgewood Woman's Club in 1931 and an anticipated national celebration in 1932, marking George Washington's birth, there would not have been a state forest for the CCC to work in.

In 1924, President Calvin Coolidge signed a bill from Congress establishing a George Washington Bicentennial Commission to carry out appropriate commemorative activities during the 200th anniversary of Washington's birth. The anniversary would be in 1932, so, the Commission had eight years of ramp-up time to celebrate the memory and achievements of G.W.

In Rhode Island, a ladies' civic group, the Edgewood Woman's Club (estab. 1903) came up with a plan not just to plant individual trees, but to acquire and set aside an entire forest. The exact source generating this idea is still elusive, but there is no doubt as to the attention and to the energies these women focused on the task. Before they were done, they made this project a truly community effort with wide appeal and great results.

Providence Journal news articles for early 1932 (beginning around the actual anniversary of Washington's birth) document a growing support among other civic-minded and patriotic groups to support such an effort. Organizations were offered the chance to contribute funds to buy sections of a 140-acre parcel of woodland on the Putnam Pike near Bowdish Reservoir in Glocester. By April of that year the sale was secured and the call went out for additional funds so that nearby wooded properties could be added to the forest. Within a short time the size of the forest grew to 244 acres. Today, George Washington Memorial State Forest is 4,000 acres and contains within it the Casimir Pulaski State Park and Recreational Area.

The idea was that because the state itself could not buy the land (budget restraints or state law prohibitions), civic groups would do it for the state and make it as a gift as part of the Washington Bicentennial, hence the name, George Washington Memorial State Forest. (The terms state park, state reservation, management area, and state forest appear interchangeably in annual reports). The department of state government which would manage the site was the Department of Agriculture and Conservation, not the Metropolitan Park Commission, which had run the state parks and beaches (reservations) located in a ring in an eight-mile radius of the statehouse, but was sun-setted in the reorganization of state government on the first day of the 1935 legislative session.

In September of 1931, however, the minutes of the executive board of the club reflects its interest in purchasing land in Glocester for forest purposes and, also, that other similar organizations, like the Girl Scouts, Camp Fire Girls, and the Daughters of the American Revolution had joined the cause. By December 1st, club minutes noted that $75 was in the fund, and the intention was to purchase four sections of land owned by Mr. and Mrs. Adelbert Reynolds of Glocester. To spur a wider public interest in the project the club arranged for an exhibition to be held in the banking rooms of the Rhode Island Hospital Trust Bank in Providence the week of March 4th, 1932.

As of the following week, March 8th of 1932, the fund had grown to $562.23, and, as of April 5th, it had nearly doubled to $991. Mrs. Robinson Peirce was appointed club representative for passing the deeds to the land to the Rhode Island Department of Agriculture. The resolution of the club was that the land was to serve as a 'demonstration area' of best re-forestation practices at the time. Rhode Island Governor, Norman S. Chase, was on hand for the occasion.

Within weeks of this outpouring of private philanthropy, Wickaboxet Farms of West Greenwich donated a second forest of 288 acres. Although there had been a forest agency in state government since 1907, about the time of the Metropolitan Park Commission's establishment by law in 1904, it wasn't until 1932 that the state had its very own forest; and now it had two.

The stage was now set for the CCC of 1933 and Emergency Conservation Work to work on projects on state forest land.

Each camp and company term was for six months. There were up to 200 enrollees for each term, but the 18-year-old to 25-year-old participants were allowed to re-enlist several times until they landed a permanent civilian job. The administrative staff drawn from the U.S. Army, U.S. Forest Service, and National Park Service, along with trainers (called LEMs, or local experienced men) raised the average total of a camp to 250. Therefore, it's difficult to get a firm fix on the actual number of individuals who went through the program, but somewhere between 12,000 and 15,000 single, unemployed men from Rhode Island were in the CCC. Not all were based in Rhode Island; some served in Maine and Vermont.

Other Ocean Staters went out west. Although the focus on the jobs plan addressed the younger un-employed, the program expanded to admit veterans from World War I. One such 'V' company served in Rhode Island, first at the Arcadia/Hope Valley camp, and later at George Washington Memorial Forest, where they built a trail linking G. Washington to the new Casimir Pulaski area.

The CCC jobs program was one of the most popular of the New Deal efforts to lift one fourth of the nation's work force out of unemployment. There were others, like the WPA program that did public works, often side-by-side with CCC such as the highway road-side picnic groves, or in city and town parks.

Finding and photographing the surviving examples of the park and forest work of the 1930s was the focus of this season's work in 2014. The project product takes the form of the following written report and a PowerPoint program depicting what turned up in the trek of sites from Woonsocket to Westerly.

The season's work was not a lonely walk in the woods; I had many guides who donated time and advice. Among those in whose debt I am are Marty Podskoch and Mike Wilk who guided a full day overview from Primrose in North Smithfield, to West Greenwich, where Town Administrator, Kevin Breene showed us the Camp Kent site and Dawley Memorial State Park, and then on to Mt. Vernon to meet with representatives of the Foster Preservation Society who explained that Camp Greene was not in Coventry, but rather in Foster. Lastly, that day we went on to Glocester and met with Paul St. Pierre of Forestry who showed us a number of buildings still in use at the George Washington Memorial State Forest, including a spectacular structure performing its original purpose as an education meeting place.

I had learned of Marty Podskoch's work in CCC history from a notice of the Westerly Historical Society for a talk last winter. Marty has written several books on the CCC, mostly on their work in the Adirondacks. Now, he is focusing on Connecticut and Rhode Island. Mike Wilk was his guide in Rhode Island. Mike's dad served at Camp Kent, now the site of the Lineham School in West Greenwich. At our first stop in North Smithfield, Betty Cesario gave us a tour of her family farm, site of the Primrose Camp. Alas, all that remains is a two-story fieldstone fireplace of one of the program buildings.

The Foster visit was similarly without any remainders of the camp, but one of our guides, 90-year old George Newman, was a veteran of the CCC and had supervised the erection of several fire towers before becoming a long-time employee of the state forestry division.

[Author Note: Albert passed away in 2017 before publication of this book and I am honored to include his voice in spreading the word of the vital work of the CCC in Rhode Island.]

Al Klyberg talking with students from Worcester, MA at the site of the Kelly Mill in the Blackstone River State Park. Beverly & Kevin Klyberg

Al Klyberg talking to a group outside of the Captain Wilbur Kelly House Transportation Museum in the Blackstone River State Park. Beverly & Kevin Klyberg

This book is dedicated to the three million CCC men who worked in the United States and its territories on conservation projects such as planting trees, building state and national parks, fighting fires, building roads and bridges, helping farmers and ranchers prevent erosion, and aiding citizens during disasters.

PREFACE

My interest in the Civilian Conservation Corps (CCC) began while gathering information in the Adirondacks for my fire tower books during the summer of 2004. One day I visited Joanne Petty Manning of Saranac Lake whose father, Bill Petty, had been the District Forester at the DEC Office in Ray Brook and had a large collection of photos and information on fire towers. She brought out a large box of photos and in it was a packet of six or more photos that didn't relate to the Adirondack fire towers.

One showed a large group of young men posing for a picture. The men wore dungaree shirts, pants, jackets, and a variety of hats. Some were holding shovels. Other pictures showed a group of guys leveling a dirt road, young guys planting trees, boys eating at picnic tables with tents in the background, and a group photo of older men posing for a picture. Joanne told me that these were of the Civilian Conservation Corps and I decided to copy them just in case I needed them in the future.

My northern Adirondack fire tower book came out in the fall of 2005. This was my third book on the men and women who worked on the fire towers of the Catskill and Adirondack mountains. I wondered what I'd do for my next book. I remembered Joanne's photos of the CCC and then I knew what I wanted to work on. I had just finished writing about the men and women who worked in fire towers saving the forests from fires now I'd write about the young men and veterans who worked in the CCC who built up our forests and state and national parks.

I began searching for information on the CCC of New York by giving talks throughout the state and writing newspaper stories about the CCC camps. Gradually I was able to locate many former CCC enrollees and their families. After six years of work and over 100 interviews, my book *Adirondack Civilian Conservation Corps Camps: History, Memories, & Legacy of the CCC* was published in 2011.

In the mean time I had moved to Connecticut in 2005 and it dawned on me that I should also gather information on the CCC camps in Connecticut. I had to find the men who were still alive in my new state. It also required a lot less driving.

At the end of 2007 I began calling libraries, historical societies, and senior living communities to see if they would be interested in giving a presentation on the CCC camps in Connecticut. I also sent news releases and photos to newspapers describing my search for information and photos concerning CCC camps and asking readers to contact me.

The response was tremendous. Many of the old Boys or family members contacted me and shared their photos and stories. I either went to their homes or called them on the phone for interviews. By the end of 2008 I had given 56 presentations and I was on my way for a second book on the CCC.

There were times of frustration when I was told: "Oh, if you were only here a month or a year ago when Joe was alive. He had great stories." Then there were the times a son or daughter told me: "I only wish that my father told me about his days in the CCC. I don't even know what camp or state he was in."

After almost eight years of research, my book on the 25 CCC camps in Connecticut was published in 2016.

But my interest in the history of the CCC did not end. I turned to the history of Rhode Island's CCC camps when I met Mike Wilk on April 18th, 2009 at one of my CT CCC talks at the Sterling Historical Society in Connecticut . Mike asked me if I had any information on CCC camps in Rhode Island because his father worked in one. He wanted to find it and see if he could get more information on the camp. I told him I knew nothing about them and suggested he write to St. Louis where the Army records were kept on CCC enrollees. He should ask for his father's "Discharge" papers. The papers would tell him where his dad was, when he joined, what he did, and when he was discharged. I figured I was so busy doing research on Connecticut camps that I'd never get to doing a book on RI camps.

In 2009 Mike did get his dad's discharge papers and now tried to find Camp Kent in Washington, RI. His goal was: "to find the location of the former Camp Kent and walk the grounds which my father walked in 1933."

It was not until 2013 when he was able to read some articles in the Providence Journal that found out his dad's camp was at the current site of the Lineham Elementary School on Nooseneck Hill Road in West Greenwich.

I began giving talks at libraries and historical societies throughout the state and I was able to get more information on the camps. After a talk at the Westerly library Al Klyberg contacted me and he wanted to see if he could travel with me and visit the seven CCC camps.

On May 30, 2014 Mike Wilk and I met Al in North Smithfield and visited the site of the Primrose camp. We then went to West Greenwich, where Town Administrator, Kevin Breene showed us the Camp Kent site and Dawley Memorial State Park. Then we went to Mt. Vernon to meet with representatives of the Foster Preservation Society who explained that Camp Greene was not in Coventry, but rather in Foster. We also traveled to the sites of the Hope Valley camp in the Arcadia Village and then to the Burlingame and Escoheag camp sites. Lastly, that day we went on to Glocester and met with Paul St. Pierre of Forestry who showed us a number of buildings still in use at the George Washington Memorial State Forest. What a great day to learn so much and visit all of the Rhode Island camps.

It then took me six more years of research and writing to complete this book. It is not a comprehensive history of the Civilian Conservation Corps but the history of the seven Rhode Island CCC camps and the stories of the young men who left their homes to earn $30 ($25 went home) a month to help their families survive during the Great Depression. The reader will see how these young men developed a sense of worth. Many had only an eighth grade education and were wandering the countryside and city streets in search of a job. Once in the CCC they felt important. They learned how to take orders, developed a love of nature, and learned a trade, all of which gave them a sense of self-worth. They knew they were helping their country and their family.

As you drive through the Rhode Island countryside you pass by the lofty plantations of white pines that were planted by the CCC during the 1930s. You will also pass by and maybe camp at the many state parks that were established or developed by the young enrollees or the Spanish American War and WWI veterans.

Now sit back and enjoy an illustrated chronicle of the CCC boys who worked in the state parks and forests. You will also find the stories of Rhode Island's young men who were sent to Western states and found adventure there.

Marty Podskoch

podskoch@comcast.net • www.martinpodskoch.com

Marty Podskoch and family at home on Lake Pocotopaug in East Hampton, CT. (L – R) Seated: Lydia & Kira Roloff. Standing: Kristy & Matt Roloff, Ryan & Jenna Podskoch holding Anna & Lily, Lynn, Marty and Matt Podskoch

CHAPTER 1
RHODE ISLAND CCC CAMPS – THEIR HISTORY

One of the most important events in the history of the United States was the election of Franklin D. Roosevelt (FDR) as President during the Great Depression. With over 13 million unemployed FDR promoted many relief programs that created jobs for the unemployed. The Emergency Conservation Work Act, better known as Civilian Conservation Corps, was the first such program passed by Congress in 1933 during Roosevelt's first "One Hundred Days" and is also considered his most successful program and certainly his most popular. During its nine years 3 million young men worked conserving our natural resources throughout our country and possessions.

Conservation was important in the Roosevelt family. FDR and his cousin Theodore "Teddy" Roosevelt had a deep love for conserving the land and forests in the United States. Both were governors of New York State (NYS) and presidents of the United States.

While President (1901-1909), Teddy helped preserve approximately 230,000,000 acres in the United States. In this new land the government established five new National Parks, 16 National Monuments, 51 Wildlife Refuges, and huge reserves and National Forests.[1]

Gifford Pinchot, a college trained forester, influenced both Teddy and Franklin. Pinchot urged the use of scientific management of the natural resources of the West and worked to prevent developers from destroying the land. Teddy appointed Pinchot to head the new U.S. Forest Service.[2]

When FDR became President in 1933, Pinchot warned him about the depletion of our forests and impressed upon him the importance of purchasing large tracts of privately owned forest lands. When Congress passed the Weeks Act in 1911 it enabled the government to purchase private land. This made it possible for the creation of the national forests east of the Mississippi. Pinchot also urged FDR to purchase the 50 million acres of recently abandoned farmland east of the Mississippi and employ men who were on relief to reforest these lands.[3]

FDR grew up at his family's estate, Springwood, in Hyde Park, NY where he enjoyed roaming the forest and hills near the Hudson River. Later he went into politics and was elected to the state senate in 1910. Here he became the Chairman of the Committee on Forestry. FDR took over the family estate in 1910 and the following year he hired a forester who developed a management plan for Springwood. In 1912 he had a few thousand seedlings planted, the first of some 550,000 trees planted over the next forty years.[4]

In 1928 FDR became governor of New York and advocated for government intervention during the Depression. FDR developed relief programs for the unemployed. One program gave 10,000 men jobs working in the state forest and parks. They built park buildings and roads, planted trees, and did erosion control projects.[5]

During his years as governor FDR encouraged the state legislature to pass laws promoting conservation and development of the state forests. In 1931 FDR proclaimed Conservation Week. His press release stated his goals: "...to bring to the attention of the people the great public benefits that are dependent upon the wise use and perpetuation of our forests, the protection of the birds and animals that they shelter, and the safeguarding of our water from alienation and pollution."[6] FDR encouraged the state to purchase substandard farmland and then reforest the land. In 1931 the state legislature approved a $19 million bond issue to purchase submarginal farmland. The Conservation Department supervised this program and purchased farms that had at least 500 acres. In 1932 the state hired 10,000 temporary workers from the relief rolls to plant trees. The land was reforested and helped in preventing soil erosion and provided forests for future timber production.[7]

The Great Depression

The Great Depression was a traumatic period for millions in the United States. It began when the stock market crashed on October 27, 1929. Many economists thought it was merely a bump in the market but the slow economy dragged on. President Hoover believed that

During the Depression many people were forced to live in shanties. Library of Congress

local governments and private charities should provide relief to the unemployed and homeless and not the federal government. Breadlines and Hoovervilles (homeless encampments) sprang up around the United States.[8]

There were nearly 2 million unemployed men and women who wandered the U.S. on foot and freight trains, lived in caves and shantytowns in search for a job and security. In this group were a quarter million called "the teenage tramps of America" who were in the same search to find security.[9]

In 1932 George Rawick, an American academic, historian, and socialist, best known for his editorship of a 41-volume set of oral histories of former slaves, titled The American Slave: A Composite Autobiography, estimated that one in four of the youth between ages 15-24 were unemployed. Of this age group only 29% did part-time work.[10]

The U.S. was not only facing a financial catastrophe but an environmental crisis as well. States were unable to control the frequent forest fires and the diseases and pests that decimated the forests. Poor farming practices, overgrazing of public lands, and over-cutting of forests led to erosion of topsoil. Streams became uninhabitable leading to the decline of fish. Frequent flooding occurred.

During the 1932 election the Democratic Party nominated Franklin D. Roosevelt. His slogan in the campaign was a "New Deal" for America. He promised to work to reverse the economic collapse that Hoover failed to achieve. With over 20% of U.S. workers unemployed, FDR pledged to help the "forgotten man at the bottom of the economic pyramid."

Americans were looking for a change in leadership and in November they chose Roosevelt over Hoover by a landslide vote, 22,821,857 to 15,761,845. FDR was sworn into office on March 4th, 1933. After FDR was sworn into office he decided to forego the traditional balls and celebrations and sat down with his cabinet and began working on solving the economic crisis.

Hundred Days & Emergency Conservation Work Act

On March 9 FDR declared a "Bank Holiday" that closed the banks for four days to help stabilize the financial system. Then FDR and Congress passed the Agricultural Adjustment Act, a farm relief law that paid farmers subsidies for not planting part of their land and reducing their livestock. Its purpose was to reduce their crop and raise its value.

On March 21, 1933 Roosevelt called the 73rd Congress into Emergency Session to hear and authorize his program. He proposed to recruit thousands of unemployed young men, enroll them in a peacetime army, and send them into battle against the destruction and erosion of our natural resources.

"I propose to create a civilian conservation corps to be used in simple work, not interfering with normal employment, and confining itself to forestry, the prevention of soil erosion, flood control and similar projects. I call your attention to the fact that this type of work is of definite, practical value, not only through the prevention of great present financial loss, but also as a means of creating future national wealth."[11]

Organized labor unions were concerned that the CCC would lower wages. They were also worried if the Army was involved in running the program it might lead

President Franklin D. Roosevelt signing the Emergency Conservation Work Act. CCC Legacy Archives

to regimentation of labor. Others feared the CCC would take jobs from men working in the forests.[12]

On March 27 FDR introduced Senate Bill 5.598, the Emergency Conservation Work Act (ECW).

It went through both houses of Congress and on March 31, 1933 FDR signed the ECW Act, more commonly known as the Civilian Conservation Corps. This provided work for 250,000 unemployed young men ages 18-25. FDR brought together two wasted resources, the young men and the land.[13]

By the end of the "Hundred Days" FDR had pushed 15 major bills through Congress, such as the Federal Emergency Relief Administration (FERA), which provided funds for grants to states to establish relief programs, the Tennessee Valley Authority (TVA), which provided hydro-electric power, flood control, and soil conservation to seven southern states, and the National Industrial Recovery Act (NIRA), which stimulated industry and established labor standards.[14]

Organization of the ECW (CCC)

On April 5, 1933 FDR signed Executive Order 6101 authorizing the ECW (CCC) program and appointed Robert Fechner director. He was a vice-president of the American Federation of Labor. James J. McEntee became his assistant.

FDR established an Advisory Council composed of representatives from the Secretaries of War, Labor, Interior, and Agriculture. These agencies worked together with Fechner in performing miracles in organizing large number of enrollees and camps throughout the 48 states, Alaska, Hawaii, Puerto Rico, and the Virgin Islands.

The Army mobilized the nation's transportation system to move thousands of enrollees from induction centers to working camps. This was the largest peacetime mobilization of men the United States had ever seen. Most of the young enrollees came from the East while the majority of the projects were out West. The Army used its regular and reserve officers, together with regulars of the Coast Guard, Marine Corps and Navy to temporarily command camps and individual companies.

The Departments of Agriculture and Interior planned and organized work projects.

The Department of Labor, with the help of state and local relief offices, selected and enrolled the young

ECW (CCC) Director Robert Fechner (5th from left with dark coat) visited many camps throughout the U.S. Here he was at the Paul Smiths camp in the Adirondacks in 1933. Workers are busy building camp. NYS Archives

men. Each state had a quota for enrollees based on population. The qualifications for the junior enrollees were: single, male, 18-25 years of age, unemployed, on the relief roll, healthy, and not in school. They signed up for a six-month period. Later enrollees could re-sign 3 more times for an additional 18 months. They were paid a dollar a day. The enrollee received $5 for spending money and the government sent $25 directly to the parents each month. If the men found employment they could ask for an honorable discharge.[15]

Only 37 days had elapsed from Roosevelt's inauguration on March 4, 1933. Henry Rich of Alexandria, VA was the first enrollee on April 7. Ten days later Camp Roosevelt, the first CCC camp in the U.S., was established near Luray, VA in the George Washington National Forest.[16]

FDR promised to have 250,000 men in camps by July 1. All the agencies and branches of the federal government cooperated in implementing the program. His goal was achieved in July and junior enrollees (ages 18-25) were housed in 1,463 CCC camps. The total enrollment by the end of the year was half a million men.

In the July 8, 1933 issue of the weekly CCC newspaper, "Happy Days," FDR welcomed the CCC enrollees:

"I want to congratulate you on the opportunity you have, and to extend to you my appreciation for the hearty cooperation which you have given this movement, so vital a step in the nation's fight for progress, and to wish you a pleasant, wholesome and constructive stay in the CCC.

"I welcome the opportunity to extend a greeting

The Army organized and supervised the CCC camps. Putnam/ Washington Captain T.E. Lorenz is visiting Roland N. Bisaillon, attendant at the camp Dispensary/Infirmary. Robert Bisaillon

CCC Director Robert Fechner (center) and President Franklin D. Roosevelt are surrounded by CCC enrollees when they visited Shenandoah, VA on August 12, 1933. CCC Legacy

to the men who constitute the Civilian Conservation Corps. It is my belief that what is being accomplished will conserve our national resources, create future national wealth and prove of moral and spiritual value, not only to those of you who are taking part, but to the rest of the country as well.

"You young men who are enrolled in this work are to be congratulated. It is my honest conviction that what you are doing in the way of constructive service will bring you, personally and individually, returns the value of which it is difficult to estimate.

"Physically fit, as demonstrated by the examinations you took before entering the camps, the clean life and hard work, in which you are engaged, cannot fail to help your physical condition. You should emerge from this experience, strong and rugged and ready for entrance into

the ranks of industry, better equipped than before."

Afro-Americans were also accepted into the CCC because the law creating it barred discrimination based on race, creed, or color. The unemployment rate of Negroes was twice that of whites. The CCC administration became frustrated when several southern states like Georgia, Arkansas, and Florida refused to enroll few or any Afro-Americans in 1933. When the federal government threatened to withhold state quotas of CCC camps they gave in.[17] Discrimination, however, led to separate Negro camps with white Army officers in command. Only when there weren't enough Negroes for a company were they integrated with whites. In Rhode Island the camps were integrated but in nearby New York there were separate "black" or "colored" camps.

In April 1933 there were two modifications to the ECW. On April 14th the program included the enlistment of approximately 14,000 unemployed American Indians.[18] There were only a few such camps and they were on the Indian reservations. Most of these enrollees were married and lived at home. By 1942 over 80,000 Native Americans had worked to reclaim the land.

Another change in the program was the hiring of approximately 25,000 local experienced men (LEM). At first they were called "experienced woodsmen." For every camp with 200 enrollees the camp could hire 16 local experienced men.[19] These men were experienced in carpentry, logging, masonry, etc. They trained the young enrollees in skills that many would use later in life. They also taught the workers proper use of tools, safety skills,

The Bonus Army composed of veterans of WWI first came to Washington in the summer of 1932 and lived in tents. They demanded a bonus that had been promised to them in 1924. Since many of the veterans had no jobs, they said they couldn't wait till 1945 to receive the money. They wanted it now. Library of Congress

discipline, and cooperation. The LEM program benefited the local communities by giving jobs to the unemployed whose salaries pumped money into the local economy.[20]

A third modification of the program occurred when veterans were admitted into the CCC. Their average age was 40. Many were unemployed and filled with despair during the Depression. Many had physical and mental impairments from WWI. They first became a problem to the government during the spring and summer of 1932 when they came to Washington D.C. and demanded a bonus that was promised them when they received Service Certificates in 1924. The government responded by saying they had to wait till 1945 to cash them in but the unemployed veterans wanted to be paid right away. When this "Bonus Army" refused to leave the city, President Hoover had General Douglas MacArthur and the Army drive the veterans, their families, and friends out of the city and burn the protestors' shelters.[21]

The Bonus Army came a second time to Washington D.C. in 1933. FDR's reaction to the Bonus Army's march was different. He didn't send the Army but instead sent his wife, Eleanor. She listened to their concerns and told her husband. On May 11, 1933 FDR issued an executive order authorizing the enrollment of approximately 25,000 veterans of WWI and the Spanish American War. There were no restrictions as to age or marital status and the men were housed in separate camps while working on conservation projects suitable to their age. By the end

of the program nearly 250,000 veterans had participated. Veterans received a dollar a day but ¾ of their monthly salary went to their dependents. If they didn't have dependents it went into an account that they received when they left the CCC.[22]

CCC Begins in RI

Historian Albert Klyberg described the early days of the CCC in RI: "Initially, Rhode Island was authorized to set up two Emergency Conservation Work camps. At 200 enrollees per camp that would account for four hundred jobs from the 2,000 applications in the first week. The jobs were for only six months duration, at a dollar a day.

"In the employment enthusiasm/excitement– almost euphoria – caused by the announcement in Washington, D.C. on the 31st of March, 1933 of the jobs bill to set unemployed single men to work in the forests of America, coupled with the notice in Providence, a week later, that enlistments were open, Governor Green set out to produce a third CCC forestry camp since the first two were so oversubscribed that Rhode Island enrollees were being sent off to Maine and Vermont to work. Two thousand hopeful young men had mobbed the facilities at the Providence Federal building filing their applications. Police had to be dispatched to quell the scene.

"Three days later, on April 8, there were two more announcements in the press. One was that the recruits would undergo training at Fort Adams before being dispatched to the woods, and that between 1,500 to 2,000 single men were scheduled to get forest jobs. Fort Adams itself had only a week to get ready to receive recruits. Since Rhode Island had just acquired its own forests less than a year before, there was a delay in setting up some of the projects, so, in the interim, Rhode Island enrollees were dispatched for a while to projects in Maine and Vermont. The Maine destination was the Rangeley Lakes region, and the particular company designated for this assignment was the 144th. This outfit in CCC records is listed as a Maine unit; a Rhode Island contingent was simply assigned to it, as was the case for the 146th in Vermont.

"The first contingent to be processed at Fort Adams arrived on April 25. On May 7th, President Roosevelt approved the Burlingame Reservation and the newly established George Washington Memorial Forest as

During the summer and fall of 1933 CCC enrollees lived in Army tents. It was not till the fall that the wooden barracks were completed. This is the Primrose/Woonsocket camp. *Lorenzo Harry Frisiello & Kathleen Duxbury Collection*

CCC camp sites. As early as May 18th, Governor Green was arranging for a third camp in West Greenwich, on Nooseneck Hill Road.

"By the end of the month, the U.S. Army was laying out the camps at Burlingame, George Washington, and Nooseneck. At first these sites consisted of surplus army tents from the First World War era until permanent wooden barracks and other structures could be built. In addition to the U.S. Army personnel designing and supervising the creation of these camps, civilian mentors, Local Experienced Men (LEMs), were hired to teach construction and forest management skills. There were eight LEMs for each camp. By May 26, the Journal reported that, 'Rhode Island forest army whips Watchaug pond camp into shape.' At that point the entire program was just two months old.

"Records indicate that very few of the enrollees had any experience living in the out of doors. Names and addresses from the early camp rosters show most of them hailed from the streets of Providence, Pawtucket, Woonsocket, and Central Falls. Until they could build their own wooden camp buildings, they lived in the tent city. They were as 'green' as the forests. Each day, each week, was a new experience, but it was the first time in a long time that any had a job. In most cases, it was their first job. They were busy from dawn to dusk. They were being trained in tasks for forestry work, for the building trades, and they were clothed, fed, and housed—even though they had to build their own housing.

By the end of 1933 there were three camps in Rhode Island: Westerly/Burlingame in Charlestown, Kent/Nooseneck in West Greenwich, and Putnam/George

Washington in Glocester.

Early Years

The CCC was popular throughout the U.S. A poll of Republicans showed that 67% supported it, and 95% of Californians approved. Even the Chicago Tribune, an enemy of FDR, and the Soviet Union praised the program. A Chicago judge thought the CCC was largely responsible for a 55% reduction in crime.

By April 1934 the program had almost universal support. The $25 monthly allotment to the enrollees' parents improved the U.S. economy. Families could now provide a better life for their children. During the fiscal year 1935-36 the federal government sent to families throughout the U.S. approximately $123,000,000. At first enrollees were limited to working one 6-month enlistment to allow others a chance to sign up and take advantage of the opportunity to work. Communities near the CCC camps benefited economically, too, because the enrollees pumped into the communities approximately $5,000 a month with their purchases at local businesses.[23]

Word about the camp's positive effects spread throughout the nation. The young men were working hard, eating well, gaining weight and strength, and improving millions of acres of private, state, and federal lands. They built new roads, strung miles of telephone lines, fought fires, cleared forests of dead trees, and planted millions of trees. Newspapers published their accomplishments and many who opposed the program were won over. FDR decided to extend the program for one more year.

A group of Army officers, educators, foresters, and the camp superintendent at the Primrose/Woonsocket camp. *Lorenzo Harry Frisiello & Kathleen Duxberry Collection*

By 1935 the CCC program was enjoying one of its best years. The enrollees were no longer living in cold, drafty tents and wearing poor fitting uniforms. Senators and congressmen realized the benefits to their constituencies and urged Director Fechner for more camps in their states. By the end of 1935 there were 2,600 camps, some in each of the 48 states. They performed over 100 types of work. Local men worked as superintendents, foremen, blacksmiths, tractor operators, and mechanics and most of the salaries were spent locally and so benefited the whole area.[24]

The number of enrollees doubled since its beginning in 1933. There were now 505,782 men and more than 100,000 men who were officers, supervisors, foresters, education advisors, and LEMs.

In 1935 the number of Rhode Island CCC camps went from three to six. Since the Kent/Nooseneck camp closed, there were really only four new camps: Hope Valley/Arcadia, Greene/Mt. Vernon, Woonsocket/Primrose, and Escoheag/Beach Pond. The Woonsocket/Primrose Camp Company #1161 would do work in the Blackstone Valley in the northeastern section of the state.

There was also a change in governing the work of the CCC in Rhode Island in 1935. Historian Albert Klyberg stated: "On the first day of the RI General Assembly in 1935 the entire scope of state government was reshaped as some 80 boards and commissions controlled by legislative committees were scrapped in favor of nearly a dozen new state departments under the direction of the Governor. The former Metropolitan Park Commission which ran state parks and beaches was folded into the new Department of Agriculture and Conservation, along with the former Bureau of Forestry. A new division was created in the Department to be known as Division of Forests, Parks and Parkways. The direction of the Emergency Conservation Work of the CCC was combined between forestry camps and park camps, and four more camps came on the scene, while one of the original camps, Camp Kent in West Greenwich on Nooseneck Road was closed."

In 1935 the CCC continued to be popular. Congress voiced their approval and extended the program to increase the enrollment to 600,000. This included enlarging the supervising staff to 6,000 Army, Marine, and Navy Reserve officers. The CCC expanded the age requirements for enrollees from 18-25 to 17-28 in order to fill the larger quota. This made at least 40,000 youths aged 17 eligible.[25] There were many young men who lied about their age or applied using their older brother's name. Now they could apply legally.[26]

Number of Camps (June 30, 1935)[27]

California	155	Colorado	31
Pennsylvania	133	South Dakota	31
Michigan	103	Indiana	29
Wisconson	103	Nebraska	27
Illinois	88	New Jersey	26
Missouri	88	Louisiana	25
Idaho	82	Alabama	24
Oregon	75	Florida	23
Minnesota	74	New Hampshire	23
New York	69	Oklahoma	23
Washington	69	South Carolina	23
Virginia	63	Arizona	22
Massachusetts	58	Connecticut	21
Tennesee	57	Wyoming	20
Texas	55	Maine	19
Arkansas	50	North Dakota	19
Iowa	41	Utah	19
Ohio	40	New Mexico	17
Kansas	39	West Virginia	17
North Carolina	38	Maryland	15
Vermont	37	Nevada	14
Kentucky	34	Rhode Island	7
Mississippi	34	Delaware	3
Georgia	33	Dist. Columbia	2
Montana	32		

Charles Price Harper in his book, The Administration of the Civilian Conservation Corps, wrote that on September 30, 1935 there were 2,110 camps in all the U.S.

In the U.S. Territories, here are the number of camps from 1933-42: Puerto Rico 12, Alaska 7, Hawaii 6, and Virgin Islands 2.

The government set a goal of enrolling 600,000 men for 1936 but a new FDR advisor, Harry Hopkins, impeded the attainment of that goal.

In 1935 FDR had selected Harry Hopkins, former head of the Federal Emergency Relief Administration, to be the Director of Work Projects Administration (WPA). Hopkins created new rules for the selection of enrollees. These rules were based on relief rolls and ignored the quota systems previously used in the states. Director Fechner did not agree and protested. This caused confusion and delays in the enrolling process. By September 1935 only 500,000 men were enrolled. This number was never reached again during the duration of the CCC. Near the end of 1935 another problem faced Fechner in attaining 600,000 enrollees. FDR secretly told him that since an election year was coming, he wanted to balance the budget by a drastic cut in the number of enrollees and camps. This plan eventually caused Roosevelt problems in 1936.[28]

Middle Years

In January 1936 when Roosevelt announced the elimination of 489 CCC camps nationwide.[29] This reduction resulted in a huge outpouring of disapproval that reverberated throughout the nation. The politicians on both sides of the aisle in Congress showed their disapproval. They knew the CCC program was successful in creating jobs and helping their constituents in the communities where the camps were established.

FDR refused to listen to the protests and announced a reduction in enrollment to 300,000 men and 1,400 camps.

Citizens responded with an outpouring of letters to FDR. Even Democratic members of Congress protested the reductions. Finally, FDR and his advisors cancelled their proposals and kept the same number of CCC enrollees and existing camps. The CCC program continued to produce successful work during 1936 despite these governmental hassles.

In 1936 the CCC was not only popular with the Republican presidential candidate, Alf Landon, but it had a 67% approval of the registered Republicans.[30]

Although the ECW was originally called the Civilian Conservation Corps it did not become official until June 28, 1937 with an act of Congress.

"The new year of 1937 produced shifts and changes in the CCC, not only in Rhode Island, but also nation-wide," wrote Albert Klyberg. "Although

Franklin Roosevelt achieved a landslide re-election vote in November of 1936, the United States Congress, as well as many business groups, were weary and wary of the continued level of 'emergency' expenditures to relieve unemployment and stimulate the economy. The alphabet-like programs aimed at getting people back to work through public works programs had produced many gains but were always seen as 'temporary/but necessary' interventions by the Federal government, and calls came from all directions to balance the national budget."

In 1937 FDR decided to cut cost by reducing government spending to the states. This resulted in states reducing the number of camps working on park, forestry, and fish and game projects.[31] The number of state camps in Rhode Island was reduced from six to four camps by the fall of 1937 with the closing of the Greene/Mt. Vernon and Primrose/Woonsocket camps.

Later in 1937 Congress responded by extending the life of the CCC for three years and separated the CCC from the federal relief organization by establishing it as a regular government bureau.[32]

The enrollees received a present from President Roosevelt in 1939, new uniforms. Since its beginning in 1933 the enrollees used WWI Army surplus uniforms. On FDR's visit to Warm Springs, GA in 1938, he was upset to see the CCC men wearing poor quality uniforms. He felt this shoddy clothing weakened the men's morale. FDR had the Department of Navy design a new forest green uniform that became widespread the following

CCC enrollee (L) admiring his friends new 1939 uniform. Gary Potter

year.[32]

Despite the popularity of the CCC, Congress decided not to make it a permanent government agency. For the next two years Congress funded the program as an independently funded agency. Perhaps it was because Congress thought it was a temporary relief program to help with the Depression.

Historian Albert Klyberg stated: "Just as the year 1937 ended in a loss of one-third of the CCC in Rhode Island, the year 1938 provided its own upset in the form of the great September hurricane that drove a twenty-foot wall of water up Narragansett Bay and toppled thousands of trees. Loss of life and property damage convulsed every aspect of state life. Instead of the focus on fire-fighting and tree protection, the agenda for the four remaining CCC camps was recovery and the rescue of 84 million of useful board feet of downed lumber. The first jobs of the enrollees was road clearance and restoration of power line service. Then they attacked the devastation in the forests and parks. The recovery took at least nine months, using 2,600 WPA workers and 600 young men from the remaining CCC camps."

Later Years

In 1939 Fechner was faced with new challenges. The threat of war in Europe and possible German invasions of England and France. Threats of war spurred the economy to produce materials for our allies. Factories needed workers and the number of CCC enrollees began to decrease.

Roosevelt decided to reorganize several agencies. Congress created the Federal Security Agency (FSA) that consolidated several offices and boards under one director. It brought the CCC into this agency. Fechner was furious. He was no longer the director of an independent agency and now had to listen to the directives of the FSA Director. Fechner asked the President to change his plan but FDR refused. To show his indignation Fechner submitted his resignation but later withdrew it. Many think this conflict with Roosevelt led to Fechner's ill health and in December he had a massive heart attack and died on December 31.[33]

The CCC Legacy Foundation states: "Fechner was the CCC. His honest, day-by-day attention to all facets of the program sustained high levels of accomplishment and shaped an impressive public image of the CCC. He was a

common man, neither impressed nor intimidated by his contemporaries in Washington. Fechner was considered deficient and lacking vision in some areas but his dedication was second to none. His lengthy and detailed progress reports to FDR were valuable information. He was a good and faithful servant who was spared from witnessing the end of the CCC program."[34]

During 1939 there were only three camps operating in Rhode Island: Westerly/Burlingame, Escoheag/Beach Pond, and Putnam/George Washington.

"In the year, 1940, the State of Rhode Island acquired leases from the Federal government for some 10,000 acres of sub-marginal land in Westerly, Exeter, Richmond, Hopkinton, West Greenwich, Glocester, and Burrillville – most of it from north to south as wooded land adjacent to the border with Connecticut," stated Albert Klyberg. "One of these tracts in Burrillville contains Peck Pond, now part of the Casimir Pulaski State Park, joined with the George Washington Memorial State Forest, straddling the line between Glocester and Burrillville. There was much work done there by the CCC camp in the aftermath of the '38 Hurricane. There were six truck trails built there by the CCC and approximately ten miles of road."

In 1940 the CCC was now confronted with the loss of their leader and a President and Congress who were more concerned with the conflicts in Europe than the CCC. Congress appointed Fechner's assistant, John J. McEntee, as its director. McEntee was a very knowledgeable person but did not have the patience of Fechner. The new director had conflicts with Harold Ickes, the Secretary of the Interior, who disapproved of McEntee's nomination. McEntee struggled to keep the program going and received little praise for his efforts.[35] He worked until the program ended in 1942.

In 1940 when France fell to Germany public support for the CCC began to waver as the threat of war increased. Emphasis in Congress was now focused on the defense of our country and mobilizing for a future involvement in war. Demands for ending the CCC increased in Congress.

Despite the CCC difficulties, it continued to be a popular program. FDR tried again to reduce the CCC for economic reasons during the election year of 1940 but Congress refused and added $50 million to the 1940-41 appropriations. The number of enrollees continued to be approximately 300,000.[36]

In Rhode Island there were three CCC camps at the beginning of 1941: Westerly/Burlingame, Escoheag/ Beach Pond, and Putnam/George Washington, but with the increase of factory production the number of camps in the U.S. was reduced to 900 camps and 135,000 enrollees.[37]

Towards the end of summer in 1941 the CCC faced new challenges: the decrease in applicants, desertions, and resignations due to better jobs. There were now less than 200,000 enrollees and approximately 900 camps. The citizens and newspapers who had supported the CCC now questioned its continuation. Unemployment was down and the defense of our nation was of the utmost importance.[38]

On December 7, 1941 the Japanese bombing of Pearl Harbor had a traumatic effect on the nation and the life of the CCC. The U.S. had to focus on defeating its enemy and any projects not directly related to the war effort were considered non-essential and many were dropped. Congress appointed a joint committee to study the various federal agencies. The CCC came under close scrutiny towards the end of 1941 and the committee recommended the abolishment of the CCC by July 1, 1942.[39]

During 1942 the Westerly/Burlingame camp in Charlestown was the only operating camp in Rhode Island.

On March 25, 1942, the ninth anniversary of the establishment of the CCC, FDR sent a letter to CCC Director James McEntee to congratulate him for his work: "There is a real place for the CCC during this emergency and it will be called upon more and more to perform tasks which will strengthen our country, and aid in the successful operation of the war. Many of the young men now in the camps will enter the nation's armed forces. When that time comes, they will be better prepared to serve their country because of the discipline, the training and physical hardihood they gained in the Civilian Conservation Corps."[40]

The CCC plodded on for six months knowing that the end was near. Finally in June the House of Representatives voted 158 to 151 to curtail funding to the CCC. Then the Senate voted on a bill to continue the CCC that twice ended in tie votes. Vice President Harry Wallace voted to continue funding. Then the Senate-House Committee came up with a decision that authorized $8 million to liquidate the agency. Both the House and Senate confirmed the end of the CCC and it became history.

Historian Albert Klyberg estimated that there was somewhere between 12,000 and 15,000 enrollees, including "juniors" and veterans, working in the local and out of state forests and beaches from 1933 to 1941.

To enroll in the CCC, the individual had to be a male, U.S. citizen, unmarried, physically fit, and unemployed. Many were selected from families on public relief. In total, some 15,900 Rhode Island young men enrolled with those qualifications.

When the U.S. entered WWII it became apparent that the CCC program would end. Provisions were made to end work projects. States made provisions to turn over the camp buildings and all operating equipment such as tools, tractors, trucks, etc. to the Army for the war effort.[41] During the war a few of the camps in the U.S. were used as Prisoner of War (POW) camps. Most of the CCC camp's buildings were taken down and used by the state while some were sold to individuals just to get rid of the buildings.

Accomplishments

The CCC, composed of both young men and veterans, played a significant part in saving and restoring our natural resources. Listed here are some of its major accomplishments throughout the U.S.

CCC Programs in U.S. & Territories

- employed 3,463,766 men
- enrolled 2,876,638 Juniors, Veterans, and Native Americans
- enrolled an estimated 50,000 in territories of Alaska, Hawaii, Puerto Rico, and Virgin Islands
- planted between 2-3 billion trees
- constructed more than 3,470 fire towers
- constructed 46,854 bridges
- developed 52,000 acres of public campgrounds
- constructed 125,000 miles of roads
- 97,000 miles of fire roads built
- 7,153,000 man-days expended on protecting the natural habitats of wildlife; 83 camps in 15 Western

states assigned 45 projects of that nature

- 46 camps assigned to work under the direction of the U.S. Bureau of Agriculture Engineering
- more than 84,400,000 acres of good agricultural land receive man-made drainage systems; Indian enrollees do much of that work
- 1,240,000 man-days of emergency work completed during floods of the Ohio and Mississippi valleys
- 7,153,000 enrollee man-days expended on other related conservation activities; including protection of range for the Grazing Service, protecting the natural habitats of wildlife, stream improvement, restocking of fish and building small dams for water conservation
- 800 new state parks developed
- built 13,100 miles of foot trails
- built 318,076 check dams for erosion control
- fought fires totaling more than 8 million man-days
- strung 89,000 miles of telephone wire
- protected 154 million square yards of stream and lake banks
- stocked 972 million fish
- performed mosquito control work on 248,000 acres
- assisted farmer's land by controlling soil erosion and improving 40 million acres of farmland
- provided 814,000 acres of barren & denuded range land with vegetation
- restored 3,980 historic structures
- provided an economic boost to local businesses

Camp Primrose constructed a large pond by damming Sylvy's Brook at the base of Diamond Hill. Visitors used the pond for skating. Enrollees also constructed a ski slope (1936-37) on the hill making it one of the first places to ski in Rhode Island. Podskoch

- enrollee dependents received $662,895,000 nationwide
- physical health of the enrollees improved through vigorous work and good food
- the education program taught approximately 40,000 illiterate enrollees to read[42]

CCC Program in Rhode Island

- constructed over 100 miles of truck trails that were access roads into the forests that helped in fighting fires and later were scenic roads for visitors
- built camping and picnic areas for people to enjoy nature
- built beautiful log pavilion at Burlingame State Park
- built a log building used for meetings and education programs on the shore of Bowdish Reservoir in the George Washington Memorial Forest
- Diamond Hill in Woonsocket converted donated land into a winter sports area when CCC built a ski slope and toboggan run; also constructed a beautiful pond used for skating and an area for concerts
- other winter recreation included cross-country ski and snowshoe trails
- built roadside picnic groves with tables and fireplaces along main roads for travelers to stop on their way to the beaches on the coast (ie: Dawley Memorial Park on Rt. 3/Nooseneck Hill Rd.)
- built fireplaces at state parks and campgrounds with washrooms, lavatories, and septic tank & disposal fields
- worked with WPA in constructing buildings for the Rhode Island Camps Inc., a summer camp for underprivileged children from the inner city (near Beach Pond in Exeter)
- constructed over 200 waterholes, fire lanes, cleared and thinned woods, cleared & marked boundary lines, did fire hazard reduction and trail side burning, constructed telephone lines, built bridges, planted White Spruce and Red Pine trees on burned-over areas, and cleared hundreds of acres of land
- fought tree diseases such as blister rust by destroying gooseberry bushes and doing gypsy moth eradication by searching for & destroying the insect's egg masses

- did forest stand improvement and fire hazard work on state and private properties
- constructed four fire towers
- Camp Arcadia built three fish rearing pools and constructed a new well at the Lafayette Fish Hatchery in North Kingstown
- Camp Escoheag built the popular beach at Beach Pond (near the Connecticut border)
- built hiking trails and shelters (ie: the shelter near the intersection of Plain Rd. and Escoheag Hill Rd., which the Appalachian Mountain Club and volunteers have since rebuilt)
- developed beach areas, park and entrance roads, hiking and bridle trails, Adirondack lean-tos, and overlook shelters
- cleared and restored farm land and burned forest areas and planted thousands of trees as the state acquired more land
- Camp Escoheag/Beach Pond constructed log cabin information/welcome centers at strategic locations on highways for Rhode Island's 300th Anniversary
- built parking areas and swimming areas for parks
- trails were built in the Wickaboxet State Forest
- Camp Arcadia developed a tree nursery that had over 100,000 seedlings
- Camp Putnam's work projects gradually expanded beyond the reservation to Lincoln Woods and Goddard Park
- during the 1938 Hurricane enrollees conducted search and rescue missions, cleared roads and helped restore power line service, recovered salvageable timber from the forest, harvested logs, and built saw mills
- constructed a bathhouse, parking area, and picnic grounds at the Casimir Pulaski State Park that joined with the George Washington Memorial State Forest[43]
- planted approx. 912,000 trees
- did fire hazard reduction on 7,921 acres
- covered 649,244 acres doing disease control of trees and plants
- did tree insect pest control on 639,000 acres
- performed emergency work on 32,181 man-days[44]

This beautiful log pavilion with two native stone fireplaces near the beach on Watchaug Pond in Charlestown was constructed by Camp Westerly/Burlingame enrollees. Podskoch

FDR's CCC program was his most successful New Deal Program. It had overwhelming support from the enrollees, political parties, families, towns, states, and nation. The CCC had a lasting effect on the lives of the enrollees by giving them a sense of worth because they had a job and were helping their families. Enrollees learned self-discipline, developed a lasting love of nature, learned how to get along with many types of people, and in many cases learned a trade they used when they left the CCC. The enrollees' experiences in the CCC benefited the U.S. when it went to war with Japan and Germany because the Army trained them so that they had discipline. Many who were leaders in the CCC went on to become leaders in the military.

The Post War Years

There were a few attempts to revive the CCC concept after WWII. The Student Conservation Program (SCP) proposed by Elizabeth Cushman in her 1955 senior thesis at Vassar College was implemented in 1957 in the Olympic and Grand Teton National Parks. Young people performed jobs such as trail work and collecting entrance fees. In 1964 the Student Conservation Association (SCA) began. Elizabeth Cushman Titus became the president of the organization. It involved high school, college, and graduate students in the 50 states. The volunteers restored habitat, built trails, destroyed invasive plants, and did erosion control work. During the summer over 600 youths (15 and older) worked in crews of 6-8 under the supervision of an adult. Work was on federally controlled lands such as national parks, national monuments, national wildernesses, and those under the Bureau of Land Management. The Departments of Agriculture and Interior and some states operated the conservation projects. Volunteers had to provide their own transportation to the projects. They worked from 21-30 days. At the end they had a 4-5 day recreation trip.[45]

In 1970 the Youth Conservation Corps (YCC) began. The program employed teens (15-18) for 8-10 weeks in the summer doing conservation projects on federally managed lands. This federally funded program involved the youth in projects involving repairing and restoring historic structures, removing exotic plants, marking boundaries, restoring campsites, constructing trails, and doing wildlife research. There were 46,000 enrollees in 1978 in the 50 states, Puerto Rico, Virgin Islands, and Guam. The program ended in 1981 due to federal budget cuts.[46]

In 1993 a Community Service Trust Act passed during the Clinton presidency created AmeriCorps. Each year 75,000 adults covering all ages and backgrounds have the opportunity to work with local and national nonprofit groups doing projects to protect the environment or help individuals. Some of the projects are: helping communities during disasters, fighting illiteracy, cleaning streams and parks, tutoring disadvantaged youths, building homes for the needy, and operating and managing after-school programs.[46]

CHAPTER 2
CAMP ORGANIZATION

The 1934 group photo of the Burlingame/Westerly, Company 141, S-2 located in Charlestown. John MacDonald

Nine CCC Corps Areas

CCC camps were organized into nine regional Army Corps Areas. Rhode Island was in the 1st Corps Area along with the states of Maine, New Hampshire, Vermont, Massachusetts, and Connecticut. An Army general commanded each corps area. The corps area was divided into districts. The general's job was to send messages from the corps area to each district camp, which had an executive officer, an adjutant (an officer who acts as military assistant), a medical officer, and a chaplain.[1]

In 1933 the 1st Corps Area was divided into six districts. Rhode Island was in the Third District with headquarters at Boston Army Base, MA.

Each camp had a company number received when

Nine CCC Corps Area map. Rhode Island was in the First Corps Area. CCC Legacy Archives

organized at an Army post. Example: Burlingame/ Westerly was Company 141. The first number, 1, stood for the 1st Corps Area and the number 41 stood for the 41st company formed. Each camp also had a state letter and number. An S- was a camp in a State Forest, SP- State Park, P- Private Forest, AF- Army. Example: Burlingame's camp was S-2. It worked in state forests. The number 2 stood for the 2nd camp formed in the First Corps Area.

Camp Organization

The Army supervised the men while in camp and provided them with food, clothing, equipment, shelter, and medical care. Each camp had a captain who was in charge of administration, discipline, and welfare of the men. He had one or two lieutenants for assistance. Some camps had an Army doctor/surgeon. If they didn't the Army contracted with a local doctor to do physicals and handle emergencies. In order to help with the supervision of the enrollees, the Army selected enrollees with leadership qualities. They helped supervise the barracks and work assignments. Leaders received $45 and assistant leaders $36 a month. Twenty-six leaders were assigned to each camp. Of these 26 men the Army had eight who worked in the camp and the other 18 were assigned to the superintendent.[2]

The camp was like a little town. At first during the summer of 1933 men lived in surplus army pyramid tents or wooden tent frames. Later the Army hired local

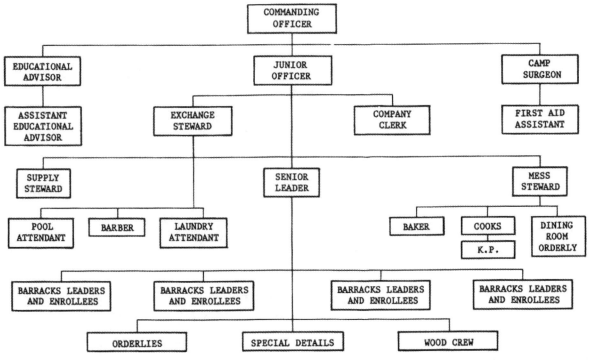

Organization of Civilian Conservation Corps - Lines of Authority. CCC Legacy Archives

carpenters to build wooden buildings that better protected the men. There were approximately 24 buildings in each camp. There was a kitchen/mess hall, recreation hall, barracks, officers' quarters, school/classroom, infirmary, garages for Army and state trucks, vehicle repair shop, blacksmith shop, officers' headquarters, latrine/shower, water and sewage facilities, streets, and sidewalks. The camp had electricity and telephones. The buildings had large stoves that used coal or wood for fuel.[3]

Historian Mathias "Matt" Harpin visited many CCC camps and wrote stories for the Providence Journal. Matt wrote: "Each camp was laid out in the shape of a 'U' around a grassy open space displaying a flag pole with flag unfurled. Buildings were 200 feet long and 20 feet wide. Flower beds were sown around them. There were five barracks with mess hall and kitchen.

"Their kitchens were models of food preparation. They lived on steak, roast beef, poultry, turkey, and plenty of potatoes, every kind of vegetable, gravy and gallons of hot soup and stews of the highest quality.

"Their barracks looked like tar paper shacks on the outside but inside how different. Inside they were all snug and warm and comfortable…The oblong barracks were built of rough pine boards delivered fresh from local sawmills and covered with heavy tarpaper."

A few buildings like the rec hall had "…huge chimneys with fireplaces. Fuel was consumed by the hundreds of cords. [Enrollees] had all kinds of recreational projects to keep them busy. They had pianos, pool tables, plenty of books and magazines. In other buildings there were workshops with tools of all kinds."

Infirmary

Each camp had an infirmary with 4-8 beds. It had a stove and basic first aid materials and medicines. Each infirmary had one or two assigned enrollees who were there 24-7. They had general knowledge in first aid. They cleaned cuts and did bandaging and brought the patients food. If an injury was serious the enrollee called the Army surgeon or the contracted local doctor. If the patient needed to go to a hospital an Army ambulance took him to Fort Adams in Newport or New London, CT and then transferred him by ferry to the Army hospital at Fort Wright on Fishers Island, NY. There were accidents and even deaths of enrollees. About half of the deaths were attributed to vehicles. The enrollees drove the trucks and had frequent accidents due to poor road conditions or lack of experience on the part of the young drivers. Other causes of deaths were drowning, pneumonia, falls, fighting fires, and falling objects.[4]

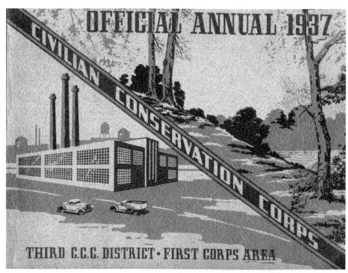

Cover of the 1937 Third District First Corps Area 1937 Yearbook

A view of the Burlingame/Westerly Camp. It had an administration building, four barracks, a mess hall, a recreation hall, and an infirmary. All the buildings surrounded the flag pole and square where the men gathered in the morning and evening. There were also garages and maintenance buildings. Frank Fields

A typical CCC camp kitchen attached to the rec hall. In this camp there were three coal/wood kitchen stoves and prep tables, a large sink and a refrigerator or ice box. Pots hug from the ceiling. There was a counter separating the kitchen from the rec hall picnic tables. Elizabeth Germaine

This is the Burlingame infirmary in Charlestown. An enrollee was responsible for taking care of patients and minor injuries. Most of the camps had an Army surgeon based at the camp while other camps hired local doctors when needed. Webster Pidgeon

If an enrollee required hospital care, the patient was taken by camp ambulance to the Army hospital at Fort Adams in Newport. Infirmary attendant Roland N. Bisaillon is beside the Camp Washington/Putnam ambulance with his friend Al, the driver. Robert Bisaillon

CHAPTER 3
ENROLLEE'S LIFE IN CAMP

Signing Up

At first young, unmarried, unemployed men between 8-25 whose families were on the relief rolls were eligible to sign up. Candidates applied at the nearest public welfare office. In 1933 there were five applicants for each opening. There were four enrollment periods, January, April, July, and October. The number of spots depended on the town's quota and vacancies available. In 1935 the ages were changed to 17-23 to fill the enlarged quota. In 1933 the enrollees could only sign up for six months to allow others a chance to join. This rule changed so that the men could sign up four times for a total of two years. Once selected, the enrollee then had to pass a physical exam and take the oath of enrollment.[1]

An aerial view of Fort Adams in Newport, RI with tents inside the fort where CCC enrollees went through training before being assigned to a camp in Rhode Island or in another state. Albert Klyberg Collection

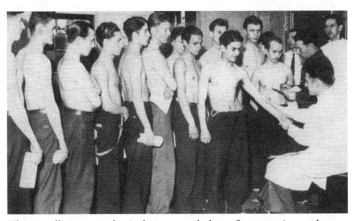

The enrollee got a physical exam and shots from an Army doctor. National Archives

Coming to Camp

In 1933 the Army transported enrollees to an Army base for one or more weeks of conditioning. At the Army base they slept in tents. Groups of 200 men formed a company that was sent to establish a camp.

One can just imagine how many enrollees were homesick as they rode in canvas covered Army trucks or on railroads to their new camp. The young men left their homes in the large cities or small towns and traveled to the backwoods of Rhode Island or to Maine or New Hampshire. It was a real culture shock. Many had roamed aimlessly through city streets or rode the rails. Now their life was regimented and they had to follow orders and a schedule. Some men couldn't take this new life and left after just a day or two. The Army didn't chase after them but they received a dishonorable discharge.

Some men went to various camps in their state while some went across the U.S. on Army trains to National Parks and Forests in Washington, Wyoming, or Oregon, etc. The men did not have a choice of camp location but went willingly to get a job and help their families.

November 1936
Rookies coming in Camp

In November 1936 rookie enrollees arrive by truck from Fort Adams and arrive at the Burlingame camp in Charlestown. They are welcomed by experienced members of the camp and ready for their new home where they will live for the next six months. Webster Pidgeon

Enrollees and their leader taking a rest from setting up their tent camp in Primrose. Lorenzo Harry Frisiello & Kathleen Duxbury Collection

The new enlisted men went to the camp supply office for their clothing and equipment. The clerk gave them work clothes, boots, shoes, underwear, toilet kit, coats, rain gear, and uniforms. National Archives

Enrollees doing exercises before going to work in the forest or park. NYS Archives

Enrollees relaxing in their barracks in the Burlingame Camp in Charlestown. The young men kept their barracks in an orderly fashion because the Army officers had frequent inspections. Webster Pidgeon

CCC boys gathered to raise the flag in the morning and lower it in the evening. Gary Potter

A priest giving mass at a CCC camp. National Archives

Daily Routine

Monday – Friday

6:00 am — Reveille (either a bugle call or a whistle) This is when enrollees did exercises to get the blood flowing; jumping jacks, push ups, etc.

6:30 am — Breakfast

7:00 am — Police (clean) the barracks and camp

7:50 am — General assembly, raise the flag, roll call, and work assigned

12 noon — Lunch

4:00 pm — Work ends and return to camp

5:00 pm — Retreat ceremony involving the lowering of the flag, announcements, and dinner

6-10 pm — Free time to play sports, listen to the radio, write letters, play cards, shoot the bull with friends or attend classes

10:00 pm — Lights out [2]

Rhode Island Historian Mathias "Matt" Harpin described part of an enrollee's day: "By 7:45 am the men had eaten and were on board trucks ready to go…All the way to and from projects they sang songs of the day. There were some true entertainers among them. Some were school teachers, bankers, lawyers, all down on their luck for the moment but given half a break, would come back on top again.

"At 12 noon the lunch wagon arrived bringing sandwiches, pie, and coffee. There was a half hour for lunch. At 3:30 the men climbed into trucks to return to camp.

"Dinner was at 5 o'clock…Food being served in the dining-room every night gave off a pleasant odor. A fire blazed in the huge fireplace, each stocked with three of four, three-foot lengths of cordwood. The atmosphere buzzed with happy talk. Roast beef was common. There was always plenty of cake and ice cream, lots of coffee, plenty of hot soup, and home baked bread. At breakfast, eggs and bacon or ham and pancakes with syrup and milk were served. It was well said: 'No man goes hungry in a CCC Camp.'

"In the evening some men went to school or to the shop to build something or boarded a truck to go into town. All men were back by 9:30."

The camp workweek consisted of 40 hours. The eight-hour day included an hour for lunch and driving to and from a work project. Many projects were 20-30 minutes from camp. A minimum of 6 hours of work a day was required. If it rained during the week, work had to be made up on Saturdays.[3]

The young men worked either in the camp under Army supervision or out on projects under the state's supervision. Eighty-four percent worked on projects, 12% were employed in camp, and 4% were sick or absent.[4]

Saturday

The enrollees had free time unless they had to make up time due to poor weather or emergencies like fires or flood damage to towns or roads. Some men had a pass to go home. In the evening some went to a nearby town to go to the movies, a restaurant, or a bar, or maybe dancing or bowling.

Sunday

There were free time-religious services in camp or trucks took enrollees to local churches.

Camp Activities

"The recreation hall at night had the air of a classroom," wrote Mathias Harpin in his book, In the Shadow of the Trees. "Men sat reading or studying subjects that interested them. Most were preparing for the day when their period of service in the CCC would come to an end. Their work during the day was with ax, shovel, pick, and rake."

Enrollees had opportunities for recreation in the evenings and on weekends. Most camps provided a building for a library or a space in the education building or recreation hall for reading books and newspapers. The rec hall often had tables for pool and ping pong and for card and board games. It also had a beautiful stone fireplace that provided warmth on cold days. Some enrollees brought their guitars and other musical instruments. Enrollees formed bands that performed for the camp.

The Burlingame rec hall with a pool table and chairs for relaxing or watching a movie. During the winter a wood stove and a fireplace kept the room warm. Here, it is decorated for Christmas. Frank Fields

West Cornwall camp enrollees entertaining friends with country music in the rec hall. Connecticut First Corps 1937 Yearbook

Each camp had a Canteen or PX where enrollees could buy candy, cigarettes, tobacco, soda, toilet articles, etc. The enrollee who managed it had the job of selling and ordering supplies and he had the rank of assistant leader. National Archives

Camp Putnam/Washington "Timber Wolves" baseball team played other CCC camps and nearby town teams. Robert Bisaillon

In the rec hall was a PX or Canteen where enrollees could purchase, soda, candy, cigarettes, pipe tobacco, and toiletries. A leader or assistant leader supervised the store and was paid $36 per month. Profits from the sales went to purchase items for the camp such as a pool table, team uniforms, sports equipment, paint, lighting fixtures, etc.

There were opportunities for hunting, fishing, and trapping in the nearby forests, rivers, and lakes. In many of the camps baseball, basketball, and football teams were formed. Boxing and wrestling matches were also popular. Some camps built their own ring for matches. Some camps even had a tennis and volleyball courts. The camps had intramural competition with other barracks or the team competed against nearby CCC camps or local town teams. During the summer boys enjoyed swimming in the nearby streams, ponds, lakes or rivers.

Field Days

"CCC Field Days" were held almost every year. Each district or sub district chose a town and enrollees from all of the camps came to test their skills in various sports. They participated in a parade and then competed in track & field events, boxing and wrestling matches, and baseball games.

Other Activities

Plays and musical performances were held in the rec hall. Enrollees formed bands and performed for the camp. Federal Emergency Relief Act (FERA) sponsored traveling groups of actors who performed plays at the camps.

A wood sawing and chopping contest was held across the border in Connecticut's Camp Fernow in Eastford that involved other camps. CT CCC Museum

The CCC mess hall was a busy place at breakfast and supper where the enrollees could have as much as they wanted to eat. Many of them gained a lot of weight and muscle working in the forests and parks. Gary Potter

Sometimes the camp had dances and invited locals to attend. Many romances developed between enrollees and girls they met in the nearby towns. Sometimes they married and settled in the country towns.

The Army provided religious service at least once a month in camp. If camp was close to a town, the Army provided trucks for transporting the enrollees to religious services on Sundays. There were also Catholic, Protestant, and Jewish Army Reserve chaplains who traveled to camps and held services. There were a few volunteer clergymen who held services in the camp without remuneration, but received board, transportation and lodging.[5]

Enrollees' Cars & Characters

Rules prohibited the ownership of automobiles at camp, but at many camps the officers looked the other way as long as the cars were kept elsewhere. Many enrollees hid their cars in the woods near camp. In those days one could purchase a jalopy for $20 to $60.

There were many unusual characters with nicknames like: "Loan Shark," "Gold Bricker," "Camp Bully," "Camp Comedian," "Shorty," "Slim," "Junior," "Muscles," "Chow Hound," "Stooge," "Apple Polisher," "Brown Noser," and "Stool Pigeon." The "Gold Bricker" was adverse to labor. The 'Loan Shark' was the camp entrepreneur. He would gladly buy a $1 canteen book for 50 or 75 cents and then resell it at face value, $1. He would also lend out money and discount it at 50 or 75 per cent, but would seek his money on payday.

Thieves were punished not by Army officers but by the camp's "kangaroo court," which doled out punishment unbeknownst to the Army officers. The punishment was severe enough that the thief had second thoughts about stealing from his so-called friends again. Generally, penalties involved some kind of duty performed for members of the court, such as doing their laundry or pressing their shirts and pants, military style of course.

"Chow Hounds" had no table manners. They would first grab a platter of food and gulp it down and hopefully wait for the cook's call for seconds. Food was served either cafeteria or family style. In the latter, a "Chow Hound" was the first to grab the platters of meat, potatoes, and vegetables. Then load his plate and even his pockets with anything that was portable.

Nearby Connecticut Chief State Forester, Austin Hawes, stated that there was waste and poor cooking at many of the camps because the cooks lacked experience. He felt the army should have hired trained cooks and it would have paid off in the long run.[6]

An enrollee who had a car hid it near his camp in the woods or at a nearby farm because it was illegal to bring a car to camp. John Cinq-Mars & Larry DePetrillo

Education

There was no mention of education in the ECW Act but towards the end of 1933 Fechner appointed Clarence S. Marsh as Director of Education. An education advisor assisted each corps area commander. The Office of Education who administered the program in their area selected him.[7]

In 1934 the education program began operating in June. Criticism was leveled at the methodology used for teaching and even Fechner had doubts that it might impede the work program. His doubts never materialized. The enrollees' skills and education varied from men with little schooling to those who were university graduates. By 1937 the program taught more than 35,000 illiterate enrollees to read and over a thousand received a high school diploma and 39 men received a college diploma.[8]

If the enrollee satisfied all class requirements, he was given a certificate like the one above. John Cinq-Mars & Larry DePetrillo

Typing was a very popular class at many of the CCC camps. Here is a class at the Escoheag/Beach Pond camp. Annual 1937 Civilian Conservation Corps, Third District, First Corps Area Yearbook

A group of CCC boys leaving camp after serving their six months. The Army provided the boys with transportation home either by bus or train. Gary Potter

CHAPTER 4
WORK PROJECTS

The CCC earned a nickname of 'Tree Army' because of the millions of trees they planted, but this was only one of the many tasks they performed. Camp projects concentrated on forest improvement and forest protection.

In Rhode Island the CCC camps had two classifications: Forest and Park camps. Forestry camps were under the direction of the United States Forest Service (USFS). Forestry camps focused on planting trees, reducing fire hazards, building truck trails, doing forest stand improvement in woodlots, and fighting tree diseases.

The CCC boys not only fought forest fires but also worked to prevent them. The young men built truck trails, fire lines, foot trails, bridges, fire towers, fire tower observer's cabins, and telephone lines to the fire towers and cabins.

Enrollees built truck trails throughout their domain enabling rapid deployment of equipment in case of forest fires. These 'in-roads' had numerous convenient roadside waterholes created along their courses. The roads were 10' wide with 2' shoulders. Roads were built to federal specifications. The subbase was 8"-10" of broken rock that was covered with 4" of fine gravel or shale.[1]

CCC boys worked on land that was abandoned or on depleted farmland purchased by the state or federal government. Here they planted trees and did forest stand improvement projects or silviculture. This involved improving the growth of good trees by thinning the ones that were in the way. They cleared out deadfalls and did reforesting of burned out areas.

Enrollees also did forest pest control and worked

Enrollees are planting seedlings in a field in the Adirondacks. This group used mattocks to make holes while the boys with pails of seedlings followed and planted the seedlings. Jim Corl

A CCC crew is clearing the roadside of hazardous material because many fires were started by careless smokers who threw lit cigarettes and cigars from their cars. NYS Archives

CCC boys fighting a forest fire. Gilbert Lake CCC Museum

The Putnam/Washington camp building a truck trail in the George Washington Memorial Forest. *Seventh Annual Report of State Department of Agriculture* 1933

Pine seedlings were planted by the CCC on abandoned farmland where the soil was poor. NYS Archives

A CCC crew with ribes (black currant) bushes they removed near a white pine forest. Howard White

This is one of the many picnic areas the Escoheag/Beach/Pond and Burlingame/Westerly camps built that had picnic tables and fireplaces. Albert Klyberg Collection

Another project (c. 1936) by the Escoheag/Beach Pond camp was at the Dawley Memorial Park shelter and picnic area on Rt. 3/ Nooseneck Hill Rd. John Cinq-Mars

This shelter was constructed by the Escoheag/Beach Pond Camp in the Arcadia Management Area. Albert Klyberg Collection

Hope Valley/Arcadia Camp officials: (Back Row, L–R) Superintendent Errol E. Tarbox, Technical staff: C. Searle, John Daffey, L. Denning (Front Row, L–R) E.J. Hoxsie, T.J. Knox, C.H. Ladd, J. Rossi. Annual 1937 Civilian Conservation Corps, Third District, First Corps Area Yearbook

on both state and private lands to protect the forests from blister rust, gypsy moths, other insects, and tree diseases. Blister rust is a fungus that damaged millions of white pine trees. In order for the blister rust to spread it needed a host (ribes bushes such as currants and gooseberries) to complete the cycle. During the spring enrollees scouted state and private forests for ribes plants within 900' of white pine trees. They pulled the plants out and let them dry. Once dead they were no longer a threat to the white pines. The CCC fought the gypsy moths by searching and destroying the egg masses in the fall and winter. They painted the egg masses with creosote.

The second type of camps was the park camps. They came under the domain of the Dept. of Interior, National Park Service. They worked to improve existing state parks and developing new campsites. Most of the work was developing picnic areas, roads, fireplaces, shelters, tables, beach facilities, parking areas, hiking and bridle trails, and when needed, fighting forest fires. At campground and picnic areas they constructed latrines and septic tanks with sewage disposal systems. Enrollees established temporary overnight campgrounds with toilet and water facilities, and Adirondack lean-tos. Workers constructed large log shelters with one or two fireplaces for picnics. Enrollees also constructed ski trails.

Camp Superintendent

The camp superintendent was in charge of the work projects. His salary was $200 a month. Eight to ten foremen assisted him. In Rhode Island once the men left camp to work on projects they were under the Department of Agriculture & Conservation (DAC). The Superintendent drew up projects or received projects formulated by the DAC. Projects included order of preference, maps, estimated man-days, and schedules for each project. Copies of the plans were sent for approval to the U.S. Forest Service, the camp superintendent, and the DAC Office in Providence. The superintendent assigned work to his foremen and organized the enrollees into small work crews.[2]

The foremen were paid $70 a month. The camp also hired a blacksmith, a tractor operator, and mechanics. Several enrollees worked in the office doing clerical work. Most of this money went to local men thus boosting the economy of the local towns. All of the financing of the CCC came from the federal government and was distributed by the Army Finance Officer.[3]

The superintendent had to send monthly detailed reports to Providence showing work accomplished, man-days spent on the projects, and work that was contemplated. They also showed fuel and oil consumption, tools needing replacement, and the type of work done by heavy equipment and trucks.[4]

Historian Mathias Harpin wrote: "On the staff were technicians in forestry, soil conservation, bridge building, cooking, first aid, and other subjects in endless variety… The camp took on local experienced men (LEMs) who were physically fit woodsmen."

Enrollee Leaders & Their Jobs

The following is a description of the various camp leaders and workers of a CCC camp by Frank Leonbruno, a former CCC enrollee and leader of the Bolton Landing camp near Lake George, NY: "The CCC camps were composed of maintenance men, mechanics, equipment operators, truck drivers, and clerical workers. This group never left the camp area to engage in fieldwork. The forestry personnel who were called 'Leaders' supervised them. Leaders were paid $45 a month and assistant leaders received $36 a month.

"Truck drivers were important to the company. They had to pass a very strict test administered by an Army officer who traveled from camp to camp just to test these drivers. Drivers also assisted in driving to larger towns for supplies for the kitchen. All trucks were equipped with governors, a mechanical device for automatically capping

These camp Escoheag/Beach Pond boys are dumping and spreading gravel for a road. Each camp had five or more dump trucks to transport gravel, sand, logs or building materials. Enrollees were trained to drive the vehicles and were responsible for their maintenance. John Cinq-Mars & Larry DePetrillo

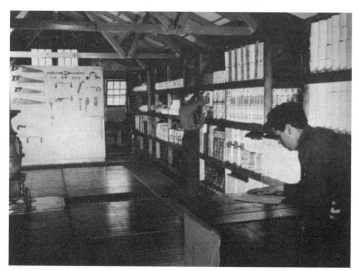

The company supply clerk kept an inventory of supplies used in camp and also did ordering when needed. The Tree Army, Stan Cohen

The captain (L) and lieutenant of the Washington/Putnam camp in their office. The Army was responsible for providing food, shelter, clothing and medical care. Roland N. Bisaillon & Robert Bisaillon

the speed at 35 mph. Although ordered to obey all traffic ordinances, Army truck drivers were not subject to arrest by local police. Only a U.S. Marshall could arrest an Army truck driver.

"About 25 men worked under the commanding Army officer in managing each CCC camp. The first sergeant was the 'top kick' who generally had some prior military service. He also blew the whistle for reveille at 7 am. This man did not win any popularity contests.

"The supply sergeant issued enrollees their long johns, blankets, socks, fatigues, shoes, rubber shoe packs,

a woolen olive drab uniform, a jacket, towels, a few toilet articles, a sewing kit, hats, gloves, mess kit, and cup.

"The mess sergeant had the responsibility of ordering food, preparing menus, supervising cooks, and keeping a daily inventory of the amount of food consumed. He assisted the cooks when necessary.

"Another important position was company clerk. He was an aide to the company commander and had to know how to type, keep records of enrollee attendance, and 'leave slips' for weekend passes. He was notified when an enrollee on a weekend pass did not answer roll call on Monday morning. Missing roll call meant the loss of a day's pay for being A.W.O.L.

"Night guards/watchmen played an important role of checking all stoves in the barracks, mess hall, infirmary, officer headquarters, and other buildings. Some camps burned coal which needed constant watch. He'd poke a small hole in the stove clear to the bottom of the grate. This gave the stove a draft not only to retain heat but also to safeguard against a buildup of gas fumes which could explode and cause serious injury to enrollees. He also had to get the ranges in the mess hall red hot prior to the arrival of the cooks at 4 am. Night guards often assisted the cooks in breaking eggs and making coffee for breakfast. In fact, some of the guards became cooks.

"The officer's orderly delivered meals to the brass. He was known as 'Dog Robber' because he got the choice leftovers that the dog might otherwise have enjoyed. Since he had frequent contact with the brass, he had the opportunity for promotion to a better line of work."

The Army was always happy to find an enrollee who was a good typist, such as the company clerk, who worked in the Administration building. Roger Aubrey

Cooks Bouchard and Broc worked from morning till night at the Burlingame camp preparing food for approx. 200 enrollees, officers, foresters, LEMs, etc. with rest periods between each meal. Frank Fields

The cooks (Front Row) and the servers (Back Row) along with the camp's Captain at the Eastford, CT camp. Gary Potter

The Hurricane of 1938 destroyed many homes in Rhode Island. The CCC helped retrieve and remove bodies along the coastal beaches and clean up downed trees on roads and in the forests. www.newenglandhistoricalsociety.com

Disasters

The CCC camps also helped communities during natural disasters such as floods and fires. Enrollees left their camps to remove debris from roads, distributed pure water, and helped clean flooded homes. The men then worked on cleaning and widening streams.

On September 11, 1938 a devastating hurricane brought torrential rains and winds that swept through southern New York and New England. Winds in excess of 120 mph caused a storm surge of 12 to 15 feet in Narragansett Bay, destroying coastal homes and entire fleets of boats at yacht clubs and marinas. The waters

of the bay surged into Providence harbor around 5 pm, rapidly submerging the downtown area of Rhode Island's capital under more than 13 feet of water. Many people were swept away. Approximately 600 people died in New England with Rhode Island losing 262 lives and nearly 2,000 homes were swept off their foundations. Extensive areas of downed trees littered the forests and roads. CCC enrollees were sent to clear the roads and remove downed trees in the forests, which were a fire hazard.[5]

CHAPTER 5
ESCOHEAG / BEACH POND

HISTORY

- 1935 -

The Escoheag camp was one of four new CCC locations in Rhode Island opened in 1935. The camp was different from the first three camps established in 1933 in that this camp was a 'park' camp rather than a 'forest' camp. It was administered by the National Park Service with the task of improving the state's parks. It devoted most of its work to developing picnic areas, fireplaces, shelters, tables, beach facilities, hiking trails, and when needed, fighting forest fires.

Gary Boden and Sheila M. Reynolds-Boothroyd wrote in The Civilian Conservation Corps in Exeter, Rhode Island, that on June 18th, 1935 Lt. Robert Lloyd arrived with a cadre of 23 men at their camp site on Escoheag Hill in the town of Exeter in the western part of the state near the Connecticut border. His men began clearing the camp area and they pitched four tents and a kitchen fly. The camp site was on a 54-acre parcel that the state purchased in 1935 for a CCC camp. The site was located in the towns of Exeter and West Greenwich.[2]

The March 1936 issue of the camp newspaper, the Escoheagan, reported that final layout of the camp was approved. Lt. Lloyd stated: "Several carloads of lumber and other building materials were dumped in the officer's lap along with lumber and orders to go ahead. The first man was hired on the job on July 22, and a large force of

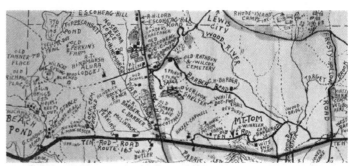

Camp Escoheag is located in the upper center of the map on Escoheag Hill Rd. The actual Beach Pond is in the lower left on Rt. 165. Lewis City and Rhode Island Camps Inc. is in the upper right. The latter was developed by the CCC & WPA in the Beach Pond Area.[1]

carpenters and laborers was rapidly built up."

The Army called the camp "Escoheag" because it was located on Escoheag Hill Road and they received their mail at the nearby post office in the hamlet of Escoheag in the town of West Greenwich. The word Escoheag is an Indian word that is believed to mean "origin of three rivers." The camp was also called by many the "Beach Pond Camp" because of its work at the pond and surrounding area located approx. 3 mi. southwest of the camp on Rt. 165 on the CT/RI border.[3]

Sheila M. Reynolds-Boothroyd, President of the Exeter Historical Association, suggested another reason for calling it the Beach Pond Camp: "The parks areas that were developed by the CCC all came under the 'blanket' of Beach Pond Park not just the pond. They were all managed out of the park's office off Escoheag Hill Rd. All the picnic areas, the camps, Beach Pond Camps/RI Camps, Tefft Hill Campground, two beaches, Beach Pond and Browning Mill Pond/'Arcadia Beach' were interwoven throughout the Management Area. That may be why the camp was called 'Beach Pond Camp.'"

[Author Note: I will refer to the camp as "Beach Pond" since most of the people in the area and the CCC boys called it by that name.]

On July 18th, one-hundred and sixty-five men from Co. 1186 arrived from Fort Adams in Newport where they had undergone training.

On July 25th Capt. Albert Holburn arrived and took command. Construction proceeded rapidly and

After a few months of construction these buildings were completed: four Barracks, Administration Office, Mess Hall, Infirmary, Rec Hall, Garage, Washroom, and Blacksmith Shop. John Cinq-Mars & Larry DePetrillo

Two enrollees sit on the floor of a barracks that is half built. John Cinq-Mars & Larry DePetrillo

These boys are working on roof rafters, a carpentry skill taught by their LEM adviser. John Cinq-Mars & Larry DePetrillo

by the last week of August all the men were quartered in barracks and eating meals in the mess hall. The next spring company commander Capt. Forsythe said: "Everything was in the midst of confusion. No beds, no water, what a night many of you remember. Here was created a company spirit which has been preserved ever since."[4]

During the enrollees second week, the men started digging and constructing an "artificial" well (pumpless hand-dug well).[5] Later a 220-foot deep well was drilled and water was pumped at 10 gallons a minute into a tank, and then distributed to various points in the camp.

Captain Edward C. Forsythe arrived on Aug. 9, 1935 and took command. He supervised the construction and installation of the electric system that consisted of three Le Roi 5 kilowatt generators that were enough to supply the whole camp. This was the first time the village of Escoheag saw electric lights.[6] Lt. Lloyd reported: "The complete cost [was] slightly over $6,400 for labor and almost twice that amount for materials."[7]

An aerial view of the Escoheag camp. The long road on the right is Escoheag Hill Rd. In front of the camp buildings was an orchard that is today the LeGrand Reynolds Horsemen's Area show ring.[9]

Capt. Forsythe stated in an article in the March 1936 issue of the Escoheagan: "For the rest of the long summer months the members of Co.1186 fought against time to complete their camp, get water, and establish their home for the winter."

Workers finished construction of the barracks on September 4, 1935. Four days later the mess hall and kitchen were completed and in use. On September 15th, the camp had their own physician, Lt. Samuel Nathans.[8]

Finally, on the last day in September all of the

History of Arcadia Management Area

The following is an excerpt from "The Civilian Conservation Corps in Exeter, Rhode Island" written by Gary Boden and Sheila M. Reynolds-Boothroyd of the Exeter Historical Association:

"Most of the land that now comprises the former Beach Pond State Park and the History of the Arcadia Management Area had been held privately for two centuries. Soon after the General Assembly of the Rhode Island colony sold the so-called "vacant lands" to speculators in 1710, early settlers arrived to farm the land. They built houses, barns, and stone walls; grew crops and raised livestock; bought and sold lots and passed on their properties to successive generations. After most of the farms were abandoned in the mid-1800s, the forests grew back, but in poor condition.

"The General Assembly became concerned with the situation in 1932 and called for a plan for taking forest lands into state ownership. The plan proposed three distinct properties in western Rhode Island in northern, middle, and southern sections of up to ten thousand acres each. Payment of no more than five dollars per acre would be made and the towns reimbursed four cents per acre for loss of tax revenue.

"By the summer of 1935 the plan had expanded into a proposal to take 80,000 acres from towns along the CT border into cooperating State and Federal forest programs and a state park. Opposition swiftly arose from the towns based on fears of losing tax revenue and the direction of patronage jobs to workers from the cities rather than the affected towns.

"When put to a statewide vote, the proposal failed but the Federal Resettlement Administration continued its pursuit of submarginal lands for conservation purposes and the development of a sustained supply of wood products. At the same time, the National Park Service was optioning private land in western Exeter and West Greenwich. Some landowners agreed to sell, but others refused to abandon their homes.

"As the idea of a national park faded, the State moved to take 1,350 acres for its own purposes by right of eminent domain in 1936. One resident of Escoheag Hill, John S. Tanner, vowed not to give up his 125 acres and the house built by his grandfather without a court fight. His neighbor, dairy farmer Edward J. Gardiner, lost 50 acres to the State seizure. He was left with some land, but it lacked water so his only alternatives were to dispose of his animals or find other pasturage.

"Governor Theodore Francis Green claimed: '...the pressing reason for action now is to provide additional work for the boys of the CCC camp nearby.' Because the Federal government had acquired only a patchwork of tracts, the Governor said it was "necessary for the State to acquire (the other tracts) if the whole area is to be developed as a unit and the greatest good is to be received from it. The purposes of this area are varied. We want to conserve the flow of water so as to prevent damage by flood. We want to develop forests on lands which are practically valueless for any agricultural purpose. We want to provide recreational facilities for the people of the State.'

"Ultimately the State prevailed and the condemned acreage was consolidated with the purchased tracts that the Federal government turned over to the State. Even if generally unrecognized as such, these forests are the enduring legacy of the Civilian Conservation Corps."[10]

buildings were completed, the pumps were operating, and flowing water to the buildings. The enrollees now began working to beautify the camp grounds and other camp projects. This was reported in the Third CCC District First Corps Area 1937 Yearbook.

Throughout the Arcadia Area Management Area there are many remains of projects of the CCC, most of them the work of the Beach Pond Camp, Co. 1186 SP-1.

This is largely because the Beach Pond Camp was a park camp that was under the U.S. National Park Service and assigned with making hiking trails, camping sites, and picnic areas, whereas the Arcadia/Hope Valley CCC camp (to the south) made fire trails, truck trails, water holes and spent most of its time addressing issues pertaining to forest management.[11]

Projects

The forestry foremen, charged with directing the work, arrived on the first of August. Work on the woods commenced on August 5th. A trail to Voluntown in Connecticut was one of the first projects. Another task was controlling white pine blister rust. Water holes were dug throughout the area to provide assistance in forest fire fighting.

Other tasks tackled by the enrollees were cutting trails to Rockville, Grassy Pond, Tefft Hill, and the Sessions Hopkins Trail. They strung five miles of telephone lines and thinned out and cleared deadfalls on 165 acres. Gypsy moth control covered 75,000 acres while white pine blister rust control work destroyed ribes (gooseberry and currant) bushes on 10,000 acres.

During the winter they concentrated on sports projects such as constructing overland cross-country ski

and snowshoe trails.[12]

The CCC made many other enhancements to the Arcadia Wildlife Management Area and beyond including improvement of Camp Yawgoog Road leading to the Boy Scout camp in Rockville northwest of Hope Valley and near the Connecticut border.

– 1936 –

Staff

Commander: Capt. Edward C. Forsythe FA-RES

Mess Officer: 1st Lt. Robert J. Lloyd CA-RES

Camp Surgeon: Samuel Nathans MED-RES

Superintendent: Franklin A. Peirce

Education Advisor: Raymond A. Larkin[13]

On March 7, 1936, a memorandum arrived from the 4th District stating Co. 1186 was the best of the 17 companies in the District for the past six months. They

A few enrollees worked in the truck garage with the head mechanic servicing the vehicles. There were both Army and RI Division trucks in each camp. There were approx. 15 trucks of two different types. Stake box trucks were used to transport boys to their work projects and dump trucks transported materials such as gravel used for roads. John Cinq-Mars & Larry DePetrillo

A line up of the various trucks at the Beach Pond camp garage that ranged from pickup, dump and rack trucks. John Cinq-Mars & Larry DePetrillo

An Army officer, possibly Captain Edward C. Forsythe, and an enrollee are at the camp in winter. Forsythe was commander when John Cinq-Mars was an enrollee. John had a photo album that provided many of these pictures. John Cinq-Mars & Larry DePetrillo

THE EVENING BULLETIN, PROVIDENCE, SATURDAY, MAY 2, 1936

A story in Providence's The Evening Bulletin featuring the Beach Pond camp's log cabins. They were to be used as information booths to celebrate Rhode Island's 300th anniversary. The Evening Bulletin, May 1936

Beach Pond enrollees built these log information booths that were placed at strategic locations to help Rhode Islanders find out what to see and how to find it. The Second Annual Report of the Department of Agriculture and Conservation, 1936

Enrollees are moving an information booth that they built at the Beach Pond camp. The booths were distributed throughout the state to promote tourism. John Cinq-Mars & Larry DePetrillo

won the coveted banner as the "Best CCC Camp in District 4." Then the camp was notified that Co. 1186 was in the running with six other camps for the prize as "Best CCC Camp the 1st Corps Area" that covered all of New England.[14] In that contest Camp Beach Pond came in second best of the six New England states.

In March the leaders and assistant leaders of Co. 1186 formed "The 81 Club." The name of the group was derived by combining rated men's salaries. The leaders got $45 and the assistants leaders got $36.[15]

Projects

Rhode Island historian Al Klyberg who researched the history of the CCC camps in Rhode Island for a State project stated: "In the middle of 1936, as Rhode Island rolled out its Tercentenary Celebration, three hundred years from the settlement of Roger Williams at the convergence of the Moshassuck and Woonasquatucket Rivers, one of the tasks of the Beach Pond construction teams was the creation of small log structures to be posted at the boundary portals of the state and serve as visitor information booths to the events of the Tercentenary. These booths were later relocated to state parks and served as support structures to various park programs.

Klyberg said: "The specific temporary locations of these tourism promotion booths, designated as 'state portals,' were at the East Providence/Seekonk boundary on Route 6 (Fall River Road), at the junction of Routes 3 and 84 in Hopkinton, Route 146 and Park Avenue in Woonsocket, the Junction of Route 6 and Foster Center Road in Foster, and Route 1A at the state line in Pawtucket."

Co. 1186 improved the land around the Stepstone Falls near the West Greenwich and Exeter border. They developed the area as picnic grounds along the Wood River and preserved it for wildlife. Some projects involved clearing lots and building shelters for the public to use.

Another project was in the Hendrick Area of the Beach Pond Park reservation where the enrollees constructed 18 fireplaces, benches, and rustic tables. They built a system of trails near Breakheart Brook and two small picnic areas that were part of the Resettlement program.[17]

Dawley Memorial Park

Dawley Memorial Park was another major work of Co. 1186. It is a 200-acre tract that was given to the State in 1933 by Mrs. Mary W. Dawley of the village of Wyoming. She wanted it to be a memorial to her husband, Amos J. Dawley, a descendant of an early Colonial family. The land is located on State Rt. 3 (Nooseneck Hill Rd.) in the town of Richmond at the Exeter/Richmond town line. In 1930 forest fires ravaged the area east of Nooseneck Hill Rd. It was not until 1936 that members of the Beach Pond CCC camp cleared the burned area and planted approx. 70,000 seedling trees. The young men also planted a demonstration road screen of 7-10 yr. old trees on the boundary of the land and Rt. 3 to block the unsightly section. They constructed truck trails and water holes to aid the control of forest fires.

In 1936 The Second Annual Report of the Department of Agriculture and Conservation reported that enrollees constructed a Picnic Grove on the west side of Rt. 3 that covered 59 acres and was one of the largest in the state. Co. 1186 constructed 32 fireplace sites, a water supply, tables, benches, foot trails, a parking area, and supplied firewood. Enrollees also built a large shelter with flush toilets. During the Tercentenary celebration, an information booth was set up. The picnic grove became very popular with traveling tourists.

In 1937 there was a formal opening of the park facilities at the beginning of summer. A full-time caretaker supervised the scheduling of picnic parties and over-night camping, and he was housed at the park.[16]

(L – R) A rear view of the log shelter at Dawley Park. Postcard, Albert Klyberg | The collapsed shelter at Dawley Park in 2014. Albert Klyberg | After years of use by picnickers and campers, the park lost its popularity when more travelers used the nearby I-95. The large building fell in disrepair and in approx. 2017 the DEM removed the building and just the large fireplace remains. Podskoch

Recreation

The November 1936 Escoheagan reported that during the fall the boys were involved in these sports: pool, ping-pong, soccer, boxing, and inter-barracks soccer with the four barracks. In the opening soccer game of the season, the Escoheagans defeated the Mt. Vernon team 2-0. The basketball team was beginning to practice for the winter season.[18]

The actual State land on Beach Pond on Rt. 165, near the Rhode Island and Connecticut border, was acquired by the state in 1937. Co. 1186 cleared the adjacent woodland for trails and constructed picnic sites, bath houses, and bathing facilities for the swimming area. John Cinq-Mars & Larry DePetrillo

43

The Escoheag/Beach Pond camp newspaper was called "The Escoheagan." The Education Adviser of the camp supervised enrollees who wrote stories and drew illustrations about camp. The Escoheagan, March 1939

1186th Company at Escoheag, Rhode Island

A collage of activities at Beach Pond camp from the 1937 Third CCC District First Corps Area Yearbook.

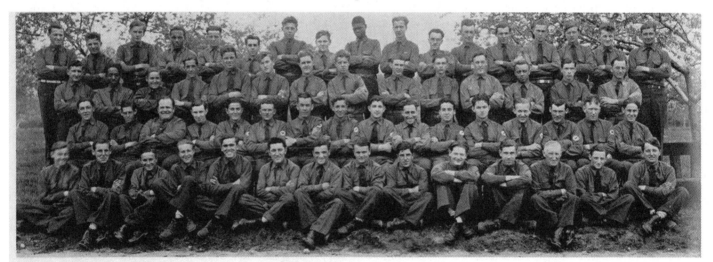

CAPT. EDWARD C. FORSYTHE, *FA.-Res.*, COMMANDING

FIRST LT. HENRY R. LEFFINGWELL, *QM.-Res.*, EXCHANGE OFFICER

Roster

FIRST LT. SAMUEL NATHANS, *Med.-Res.*, SURGEON

ARTHUR J. SPRING, *CEA*

TECHNICAL PERSONNEL Stephen M. Quinn, Supt.; Albert Faubert, Foreman; Edward Lohr, Mechanic; Alva North, Foreman; Bruce Hawkins, Engineer; Sydney Markoff, Jr. Foreman; Rodney Sherer, Sr. Foreman; Jeremiah O'Leary, Foreman.

LEADERS Albert Bisordi, Pawtucket, Rhode Island; Thomas Gaito, East Providence, Rhode Island; Thomas H. Hogan, Providence, Rhode Island; Perley T. Howard, Providence, Rhode Island; Roy H. Patterson, Providence, Rhode Island; John B. Pierre, Woonsocket, Rhode Island; William J. Randall, Providence, Rhode Island; Kenneth J. Shea, Providence, Rhode Island; Edward J. Sullivan, Cranston, Rhode Island.

ASSISTANT LEADERS E. J. Black, Pascoag, R. I.; F. DiRaimo, Thornton, R. I.; J. A. Francis, Providence, R. I.; A. L. McCoombs, Providence, R. I.; W. J. McWeeney, Providence, R. I.; J. F. Moan, Providence, R. I.; F. A. Pagliarini, Cranston, R. I.; V. A. Pettine, Providence, R. I.; F. V. Reilly, Pawtucket, R. I.; A. J. Roberts, Providence, R. I.; P. J. Salcone, Bristol, R. I.; J. Shewchuk, Manville, R. I.; H. G. Vierra, Providence, R. I.; F. F. Wolowicz, Central Falls, R. I.

MEMBERS

Allen, R. J., Providence, R. I.
Ambrosini, L. M., P'vidence, R. I.
Anderson, C. L., E. P'vid'ce, R. I.
Angell, F. S., Providence, R. I.
Antonelli, R., Providence, R. I.
Audette, R. W., Pawtucket, R. I.
Barney, V., Auburn, R. I.
Bellini, O. G., Providence, R. I.
Berard, B. A., Providence, R. I.
Bourgoin, P. E., Providence, R. I.
Boyer, O. J., C'tral Falls, R. I.
Brown, W. J., Providence, R. I.
Bucci, J., Providence, R. I.
Burke, T. E., Providence, R. I.
Burlingham, R., Providence, R. I.
Burton, R. H., Providence, R. I.
Cabral, W., Bristol, R. I.

Caldarone, R., Providence, R. I.
Callave, J., Providence, R. I.
Campbell, J., Providence, R. I.
Campopiano, L. G., P'vid'ce, R. I.
Cappucci, M. J., Bristol, R. I.
Caramello, M., Providence, R. I.
Carreiro, L. J., Providence, R. I.
Carson, H. T., E. P'vidence, R. I.
Cassella, L. B., Providence, R. I.
Cedar, W., Providence, R. I.
Cerbo, F., Providence, R. I.
Clavin, W., Pawtucket, R. I.
Collins, J., Providence, R. I.
Conneely, J. L., Cranston, R. I.
Corradini, H., Providence, R. I.
Crump, S. N., Providence, R. I.
D'Ambrosia, P., Providence, R. I.
Davis, W., Point Judith, R. I.
Dawson, W., Providence, R. I.

DeNoncour, E. J., P'vidence, R. I.
DeVito, P. J., Providence, R. I.
Dillon, L. A., Providence, R. I.
DiPrete, S., Providence, R. I.
Dovidio, H. A., Providence, R. I.
Drabik, J., Providence, R. I.
Dutra, J. M., Providence, R. I.
Dygd, F. E., E. Cranston, R. I.
Eaton, B. E., Jr., W'nsocket, R. I.
Fiske, L. H., E. Greenwich, R. I.
Flynn, F. E., Pawtucket, R. I.
Foran, R., Providence, R. I.
Fredett, E., W'nsocket, R. I.
Geremia, R., Providence, R. I.
Gistedt, R., Warren, R. I.
Gosselin, E., Woonsocket, R. I.
Grieco, A., Providence, R. I.
Hart, D. S., Woonsocket, R. I.
Jennings, J., Providence, R. I.

Kane, J. F., Providence, R. I.
Kelly, A. E., Providence, R. I.
Kendzierski, H., W'nsocket, R. I.
Laird, R., Lonsdale, R. I.
Lutynski, L., Providence, R. I.
Manchester, R. T., Bristol, R. I.
Marion, O. F., Woonsocket, R. I.
McDermott, R. L., P'vidence, R. I.
Miller, E. J., Pawtucket, R. I.
Miozza, P. A., Cranston, R. I.
Morgan, D. W., Wickford, R. I.
Murphy, F. T., Providence, R. I.
Myette, R. T., Pawtucket, R. I.
Nawrocki, J. B., Providence, R. I.
Nicholson, R. S., Providence, R. I.
Niemczvk, T. F., W'nsocket, R. I.
Noonan, J. H., Oakl'd B'ch, R. I.
Norcini, J. V., Providence, R. I.

Olbrys, E., Providence, R. I.
Paiva, R., Bristol, R. I.
Pannone, V., Providence, R. I.
Papineau, O. R., C'tral Falls, R. I.
Pascone, L., Providence, R. I.
Pearcey, G., Central Falls, R. I.
Peloquin, J., Woonsocket, R. I.
Perry, G. A., Pawtucket, R. I.
Pitrowski, S. F., W'nsocket, R. I.
Pollitt, H. L., Central Falls, R. I.
Przybylo, A. W., W'nsocket, R. I.
Raiche, A., Woonsocket, R. I.
Rawlins, F. J., Pascoag, R. I.
Rec, B. J., Pawtucket, R. I.
Roach, T. F., Pawtucket, R. I.
Robillard, J. A., C'tral Falls, R. I.
Robillard, L. E., C'tral Falls, R. I.
Rouillier, L. A., Jr., C'l Falls, R. I.
Rouseau, E., Providence, R. I.

Rousseau, W. F., Providence, R. I.
Russell, R., Providence, R. I.
Ryder, J. A., Providence, R. I.
Salisbury, E. F., Cranston, R. I.
Santos, R. I., Providence, R. I.
Santos, T., Providence, R. I.
Sappa, C. J., Central Falls, R. I.
Savicki, F. J., Pawtucket, R. I.
Scorpio, B., Cranston, R. I.
Sheridan, W. A., Providence, R. I.
Soucy, E. J., Warren, R. I.
Spinella, S., Providence, R. I.
Stanlewicz, W. P., Pawt'cket, R. I.
St. Clair, R. E., Howard, R. I.
Stell, W. E., E. P'vid'ce, R. I.
Stevens, E. F., C'tral Falls, R. I.
Stott, C., Providence, R. I.
(See back page for additional names)

The roster of the 1937 Beach Pond Camp. Supervisors, and group photo of approx. half of the enrollees.[19]

– 1937 –

Staff

There were some changes in administration by March 1937:

Commander: Capt. Edward C. Forsythe FA-RES

Quartermaster: 1st Lt. Henry R. Leffingwell Quartermaster-RES

Camp Surgeon: Samuel Nathans MED-RES

Education Adviser: Arthur J. Spring

Instructors: Angelo P. Morrone & Dominic Caprio

Superintendent: Stephen M. Quinn

Forestry Foremen: Brooks Hawkins, Alfred Faubert, Sydney Markoff, Jerremiah O'Leary, Alvin North, Paul Curtis, Edward Lohr, and Rodney Sherer [20]

In 1937 the Division of Forest, Park and Parkways acquired 1,608.27 acres in the Beach Pond Park Area by purchase and condemnation. This gave the CCC boys more land to develop. [21]

Projects

During the early part of 1937, Co. 1186 completed work on Dawley Memorial Park. This was one of the first parks completed by CCC workers in the State of RI. Many picnickers visited the new park and the number increased every year. [22]

Albert Klyberg in his research on the Beach Pond camp wrote: "The year 1937 saw the continuation and expansion of Beach Pond [camp] assignments state-wide to provide 'furnishings' for parks: tables, benches, small buildings, as well as hiking trail clearing, and 'rustic' signage. The year also saw the physical growth in woodland designated as Beach Pond by some 1,600 acres. Trailer camps were added to park amenities. Following a survey of the most efficient distribution of fire towers, the one previously built at the Washington Memorial State Forest was relocated to Escoheag Hill, the original base of the Beach Pond camp."

The Third Annual Report of the Department of Agriculture and Conservation, 1937 stated that enrollees from the Escoheag camp, built log structures, fireplaces, trailer camps, and hiking and riding trails in the Arcadia Area.

The Escoheag camp also traveled to Goddard Park in East Greenwich where they constructed fireplaces.

At Dawley Park Mr. Sherer's crew began landscape work around the shelter that was completed in the fall of 1937. Sherer had a lot of practice landscaping shelters from when his crews worked during the RI Tercentenary in 1936. [24]

Recreation

Almost every month Camp Escoheag had their monthly Company Dance. The March dance was held on the 31st at the Anthony Patrons of Husbandry Grange at 585 Washington St. Anthony is a village in the town of Coventry. The dance was to honor the enrollees who were leaving the camp. [25]

The November 1937 issue of the Escoheagan reported that there would not be a football team because of the high cost of equipment. The company fund would have had to pay approx. $150 for equipment.

There were other sports that kept the boys busy

This Adirondack lean-to was one of the many structures Co. 1186 built along hiking trails. [23]

Enrollees loved having at least one pet dog. These boys had a puppy to love and share their camp food. John Cinq-Mars & Larry DePetrillo

such as soccer and boxing. Four company boxers traveled to the YMCA in Norwich, CT for lessons. As usual the basketball team was in quest of a place to practice and the coach was trying to secure the YMCA courts in Norwich.[26]

Once or twice a month "Stunt Night" was held at the Beach Pond camp. Enrollees and even neighbors in the hamlet of Escoheag sang songs, danced, told jokes, boxed, and competed for the coveted prizes of a carton of cigarettes for the first four winners. The prizes were donated by Capt. Forsythe, Mr. Benoit, the Officers' & Foresters' Club, and the "81 Club." If the winner wasn't a smoker, he received the equivalent in Canteen checks.[27]

1937 Christmas Party Given for Youngsters in Escoheag

The following is an excerpt from the December 1937 *Escoheagan.*

"A gay song festival composed of local talent gave many laughs to the nearby residents invited to this company on Christmas Eve. The camp musicians, among which are our celebrated harmonicists, including Mr. Thomas Wowak, who was successful in running off 'Silent Night' on his mouth organ on the first try. 'Sam' Crump and his long 'choo-choo' train chugged up Escoheag Hill towing 'Santa Claus' in its wake.

"Our Christmas tree was a thing of brilliance with its numerous lights, bulbs, snow, tinsel, etc. Around the base of the tree were strewn presents which were presented to the children. These children are some to whom 'Santa' will not make his annual visit.

"Our only regret was that 'Santa' upon reaching the top of the chimney of the rec hall was unable to descend due to the extreme heat arising from below.

"Through the kindness of the Commanding Officer, Christmas Baskets were distributed on Christmas Day.

Signs of Christmas

"Signs of Christmas with all its cheer were marked throughout the camp. Our rec hall with its tree, presents, lights, and wreathes in the windows; the parade grounds with its numerous lighted fir trees; extensions of lights rising diagonally to the flag pole, the many barracks with their wreathes; the Reading Room with its small tree, its

The enrollees took pride in planting grass, trees and shrubs and building beautiful walkways. The Beach Pond camp received many awards and was chosen the Best Camp in the 4th District. John Cinq-Mars & Larry DePetrillo

snowy decoration, and moss-covered base; song festivals upon the four nights preceding Christmas; finally marked by our Christmas Eve Party in the day itself with one of the biggest and best meals ever served in a CCC camp."[28]

Education

The Fall Education Program got under way at the end of October and the boys had these classes to choose: Carpentry, Photography, Woodworking, Block Printing & Cutting, Masonry, Art, Electricity, Copper Plumbing, English, Arithmetic, Auto Mechanics, and Soccer.[29]

– 1938 –

Camp Escoheag enrollees were saddened with the news that their Company Commander for the past three years, Capt. Edward C. Forsythe, was leaving and going back to civilian life. He led the camp to numerous awards such as after only six months as commander of the Escoheag Camp their camp was chosen as the best camp in the 4th District and second in all of the six New England states. Since then it placed near the top and in the last inspection period in March the camp was ranked number three. Forsythe was also influential in promoting the landscaping of the camp with grass, trees, shrubs, and flowers. Sports also benefited from his administration. He promoted the building of a boxing ring, soccer field, baseball field, two tennis courts, and a volleyball court.[30] Forsythe's replacement was 1st Lt. Albert C. Darcy CARES. He previously worked at the West Cornwall CCC camp in Conn.[31]

The May 1938 issue of the Escoheagan reported: "On May 3, 1938 Superintendent Quinn received a letter of commendation from the RI Division of State Police for their "systematic, thorough covering of the ground…" in the search for John Lessa who was a missing patient at the Exeter School from April 19th to the 21st. Then on Thursday the 21st the CCC enrollees from Escoheag found Lessa. The letter stated: "[the enrollees] Forced to traverse a wide area swamp infested, heavily-wooded ground thick with impenetrable underbrush, the boys exhibited a discipline and well-ordered adherence to the task in hand which spoke volumes for their courage and perseverance and flashed into sharp outline an esprit de corps highly admirable."

Projects

In May, the fire crew from Co. 1186 fought a fire in West Greenwich that destroyed seven miles of woodland. The crews fought the fire for three days and two nights. They had to use many back fires to protect properties.[32]

Also in May 1938, Camp Superintendent Stephen Quinn announced that the Stepping Stone Park in the Wood River area was nearly completed. The construction crew built a well-constructed gravel road to a parking area. Historian Sheila Reynolds stated: "This area was later re-named Wickaboxet Picnic Area and today is called 'The Backpack Area.'" From there visitors could take gravel paths to many sections. They also built several wooden bridges overlooking the river and falls. After this work was completed the crews would move to work at Beach Pond and Hendricks Pond.[33]

The Fourth Annual Report of the Department of Agriculture and Conservation in 1938 reported that improvements were made at the Wickaboxet Picnic Area on Escoheag Hill. The Escoheag/Beach Pond camp had a well driven and built the central control house at the entrance on Escoheag Hill Rd.

In June 1938 Mr. Faubert and Mr. North's crews were building a road from the Control Headquarters in Hendricks Park to the center of the picnic area.[34]

The 8th Annual Indian Pow-Wow was held on July 16-17, 1938 at the Dawley Memorial Park. The admission was free and open to the public.[35]

A junior student at Brown University, Charles J. Carragnan, spent two months at the camp studying how many people visited the nearby parks at Dawley, Hendricks, Beach Pond, and Stepping Stone Falls parks.[36]

In August, a carpentry crew of three enrollees supervised by Assistant Leader Fierlet began constructing an addition to the shelter at the Dawley Memorial Park. When work was completed, the crew was to build another shelter at Wickaboxet.[37]

Another project of Co. 1186 in August 1938 was extending the telephone line to the fire tower in the Wickaboxet State Forest.[38] A work order was approved to develop the Wickaboxet Picnic Area along Wood River and Stepstone Falls to build 30 fireplaces and 25 tables and benches.

On September 21 the terrible "38 Hurricane" caused a lot of damage and deaths in Rhode Island. The Beach Pond camp was called out to help in the search for approx. 30 missing people along the South Shore. They joined forces with the Burlingame Camp in the search. After working that night and the next day, enrollees recovered 25 corpses.[39]

The Beach Pond camp was pretty classy having their own tennis and volley ball courts. John Cinq-Mars & Larry DePetrillo

Enrollees loading the dump trucks with gravel that was used in road construction. John Cinq-Mars & Larry DePetrillo

Lewis City - Rhode Island Camps Inc.

In the spring of 1938, a large construction project began to build a children's summer camp in what was called Lewis City in the town of Exeter. Some work was done by the Beach Pond camp but the majority was done by the WPA. Two hundred WPA workers from Warwick, West Warwick, West Greenwich, and Exeter helped build the children's camp. This was a cooperative project with the National Park Service consisting of an organization camp. (An organization camp is one that is available to rent to schools, non-profit organizations, economically disadvantaged groups, and organizations for persons with disabilities.) The project was completed in the spring of 1938.

Albert Klyberg in his research on the CCC wrote: "The Beach Pond area around Lewis City grew to some 53 buildings to be known as the Rhode Island Camps Inc. The goal of the Rhode Island Camps, Inc. was to serve as a destination for disadvantaged,

mostly urban, youths in 'Fresh Air'-type programs administered by various philanthropic organizations, aiming to mitigate many of the health and social problems of the Depression-era. Among the buildings, principally constructed by the Beach Pond (CCC) company were lodges for both leaders and campers, an administration building, a dining hall, quarters for the camp help, service buildings like a garage, pump house, and latrines. Rhode Island Camps was on a hill overlooking the Flat River, which had been dammed by the CCC to create a swimming pool.

"The consortium of charitable organizations, under the umbrella of Rhode Island Camps Inc., was led by Walter Adler, President, C. P. Sisson, Vice President, Mrs. Winthrop B. Field, Secretary, Ernest L. Anderson, Treasurer, and F.E. Traficante, Assistant Treasurer. The camp was filled all summer by underprivileged children selected by various organizations, like the Community Chest forerunner of the United Way of America). The season (prior to the Hurricane) was considered a success, both programmatically and financially. Some two hundred and eighty children were served.

"The next season, 1939, at Rhode Island Camps Inc., despite the disruption of the September storm of '38, more than 600 children were served in an eight-week season."

BEACH POND CAMP

operated by
RHODE ISLAND CAMPS, INC.
a non-profit, tax exempt organization

LEASED FROM THE STATE OF RHODE ISLAND,
DIVISION OF PARKS AND RECREATION

TWENTY-SIXTH SEASON – 1963

● CAMP PERIODS ●

June 30 to July 13   July 28 to August 10
July 14 to July 27   August 11 to August 24

REGISTRATION HEADQUARTERS:
Post Office Box 2263, Edgewood Sta., Edgewood 5, R. I., HOpkins 7-8518

Boys 7-14 years inclusive — Girls 7-12 years inclusive

TELL ME ABOUT BEACH POND CAMP

It is located deep in the woods in a beautiful rustic setting and accommodates 160 children in six divisions. All are housed in log cabins, which are reminiscent of pioneer days but are fully screened and weather protected. Each division is staffed by trained counselors. A lodge for recreation, camp cooking and meetings, a lavatory and a wash-house with running water are provided for each division. Boys and girls occupy separate divisions and are grouped according to age.

Just Where Is Beach Pond Camp?

"From Providence take Route 2 to Route 95. Turn right upon reaching Route 165 toward Voluntown, Conn. At a distance of 2.9 miles from this intersection turn right onto gravelled road near the white church. From this point directional signs will indicate balance of the way, 1.8 miles to the camp.

A few pages from a 1963 Beach Pond Camp Inc. brochure with some photos of children's activities. Albert Klyberg Collection

Here is one of the deteriorating cabins at the Beach Pond Camp Inc. that has been closed for many decades. Albert Klyberg

(L – R) CCC boys also learned how to drive trucks. Here is a Beach Pond camp driver by his truck with three information booths in the back. John Cinq-Mars & Larry DePetrillo | This Beach Pond road crew learned how to use a grader in building roads under the direction of the LEM in the light-colored shirt on the right. John Cinq-Mars & Larry DePetrillo | CCC boys learned how to operate heavy equipment like driving a bulldozer to build roads in the Beach Pond Park. John Cinq-Mars & Larry DePetrillo

These CCC boys look like they are all dressed to go to one of the camp dances. John Cinq-Mars & Larry DePetrillo

CCC enrollees received the sacrament of Confirmation at the Burlingame camp from the Bishop of Providence. Frank Fields

By October the Escoheagan reported that nearly all the damage to the camp caused by the devastating 1938 Hurricane was cleaned up and the camp was getting back to normal. Coal stoves in the camp were replaced with wood stoves because of the abundance of fallen trees. New 2' x 4' wood boxes were installed in the buildings. Two civilian carpenters were hired to repair the Forestry Garage. Company Commander Darcy instituted competition each week to see what barracks was the best. The reward was Friday night passes.

Many of the CCC camps were called out to help clear roads of fallen trees and do salvage work from destroyed trees in the state forest. "One of the impacts of the great storm for Beach Pond and Hope Valley/Arcadia camps was the rescue of many ornamental shrubs and trees from the state park nursery which had been set up in Cranston, along the Pawtuxet River. This low-lying site experienced great damage from the rise of the adjacent river. So as not to lose its entire benefits to the park and parkway system, many plantings were removed to safer spaces in West Greenwich," stated Albert Klyberg in his CCC research.

Recreation

In May plans were underway to build a grandstand for the new stadium adjacent to the boxing ring. The seating would rise nearly to the side of barracks #4 and provide a good view of the matches.[40]

Each of the Rhode Island CCC camps had to arrange their sports schedules with nearby CCC camps or local town teams. The teams that were scheduled to play in the summer were: baseball, softball, tennis, horseshoes, and volleyball.

On June 18th, the Edward C. Forsythe Athletic Field was dedicated to honor the camp's captain. The Copper Class engraved a plate that was installed on the flat side of a large rock. The plate was engraved with these words: "Edward C. Forsythe Athletic Field. Play Fair." [41]

Education

In May workers were nearing the completion of the new schoolhouse that was surrounded by an apple orchard. The building would have an education office, a reading room, and two classrooms. The first classroom was for academic subjects such as math, geography, English, typing, etc. The second room would have vocational classes: electricity, plumbing, etc. There were also two small rooms for photography.[42]

The Summer Education Program emphasized job training classes. Courses were drawn up by the Camp Superintendent and classes were taught by the technical staff. Each crew met with their foreman in the Apple Orchard one night each week to go over what they were doing in the field. The foremen discussed the methods used, costs of materials, labor, commercial bids, etc. The goal was to prepare enrollees for when they were searching for jobs when they left the camp.[43]

There were quite a few vocational classes. One night each week Forester Rodney Sherer taught a class on raising trees. He operated a large nursery in Lewis City (town of Exeter) that had approx. 9,000 trees and shrubs. Another vocational class was Blacksmithing taught by Mr. McComb who was the camp blacksmith. Mr. Dietz taught the Gardening Class and students had nine plots adjacent to the school building where they raised their own crops. Some of the vegetables they planted were: peas, radishes, beans, tomatoes, lettuce, squash, cucumbers, peppers, string beans, and beans. There were other vocational classes: Typing, Bookkeeping, Auto Mechanics, Masonry, and Woodworking.[44, 45]

The Photography Class was very active and they had two 14' x 6' dark rooms that had 2 enlargers, 3 contact printers, 2 complete Kodak safe lights, print timers, and studio scales. Classes were held nightly from 6-9 pm. Each month a member wrote a full-page photography article for the camp newspaper.[46]

For the past two weeks in June, enrollees at camp signed up for religious instruction for First Communion and Confirmation. On the 29th 10 enrollees traveled to the Charlestown camp in a bus to receive the sacrament of Confirmation from the Catholic Bishop of Rhode Island. It was the first time this sacrament was administered in a CCC camp in the state.[47]

– 1939 –

In 1939 Co. 1186 was working on the Beach Pond Area that contained 1,483 acres of wild woodlands, a large lake, streams, and rocky hills. The cost of the land was $9,619.43 but it was not the total cost since some of the condemned land was not paid for due to pending court claims. Enrollees continued to work in conjunction with the National Park Service in developing organized camping and picnicking for the general public.[48]

North of the Beach Pond Area was the 288-acre Wickaboxet State Forest that the CCC used for experimentation and preservation of wildlife. Their projects were to improve the timber stand, maintain the trails & roads, and repair recreational buildings.[49] "The Wickaboxet State (Forest) Management Area is in the town of West Greenwich off Plain Meeting House Rd.," said Sheila Reynolds.

Enrollees on a road construction project in the Beach Pond Park. John Cinq-Mars & Larry DePetrillo

The truck is dumping gravel for the boys to level out on a new road in the Beach Pond Park. John Cinq-Mars & Larry DePetrillo

(L – R) A June 2020 side view of the men's and women's toilet the Beach Pond camp constructed at Ledges Park. Podskoch | The Escoheag/Beach Pond camp began constructing the caretaker's home with wavy board siding on Austin Farm Road, but they never completed it. Later the state finished the home. It is located near the Beach Pond Park Headquarters that the CCC constructed. Sheila Reynolds said she and her husband LeGrand lived there when he was the caretaker for the Horsemen's Area. Today the house is abandoned and going back to nature. Sheila Reynolds | The LeGrand G. Reynolds Horsemen's Area sign & show ring in the background. This area was originally an orchard and behind it was the Beach Pond CCC camp site. Podskoch

This enrollee was one of many young men who learned how to survey land, and build roads or buildings. John Cinq-Mars & Larry DePetrillo

These enrollees are taking a break and showing their saws Notice their warm Army clothing. The New England CCC camps, were integrated. Some have suggested the reason was because there weren't enough black enrollees for a separate camp in RI. John Cinq-Mars & Larry DePetrillo

– 1940 –

In a part of the Beach Pond Area called Lewis City, the Rhode Island Camps Inc. ran a summer camp of 372 children for an eight-week period. It was under the National Park Service. It was hoped that a new unit would be built that would accommodate a larger number of children in 1941.[50]

Projects

Both the Beach Pond CCC Camp and WPA worked on the following projects in the Beach Pond Area:

- Recovered lumber from felled trees during the "38 Hurricane" and salvaged 100,000 board feet of sawed wood

- Constructed a shelter at the Wickaboxet picnic area that had two inside fireplaces
- At Beach Pond men completed the construction of a fire trail south of the Ten Rod Road
- Planted 75,000 tree seedlings
- On 75 acres men did fire hazard reduction work
- Installed a chemical latrine at the large picnic grounds
- Constructed a parking area for service buildings at the central administration point
- Completed a sewer system for buildings at the central administration
- Placed guard rails at several culverts
- Improved the nursery so that there was a large

51

number of shrubs and trees ready for planting

- Some other work projects were: repaired roads and buildings, and removed debris from the forest to reduce fire hazards[51]

The following structures were built at the camping area (Lewis City): Office and infirmary, help quarters, dining hall, unit lodge, councilors' cabins, play fields, council circle, council camps, pioneer camp, and a rubbish burner.[52]

The Beach Pond camp also extended trails at Dawley Memorial State Park, built forty new fireplaces, 4 new drinking fountains, and a new sewerage disposal plant.

Wickaboxet Projects

The Sixth Annual Report of the Department of Agriculture and Conservation, 1940 stated the CCC enrollees worked on two projects in the Wickaboxet Forest: they removed the debris from the forests and a cabin was repaired.

– 1941 –

At the "Ledges" picnic area, Co. 1186 built a toilet building and disposal system. They also built a garage and workshop at the camp control center on Austin Farm Rd. and began work on a house for the superintendent but it was not completed.

The Seventh Annual Report of the Department of Agriculture and Conservation, 1941, reported the Beach Pond camp closed in 1941 and left many incomplete projects.

LEGACY

Today the site of the Beach Pond camp is the LeGrand G. Reynolds Horsemen's Area on Escoheag Hill Road in Exeter. It is not far from the Tippecansett Trail. The CCC made many enhancements to the Arcadia Management Area and beyond, including improvement of Camp Yawgoog Road near the Connecticut border.

Most of Beach Pond Co. 1186 camp projects were in a large part of the over 14,000 mostly forested acres of the Arcadia Management Area. It is the state's largest recreational area, offering users a great variety of opportunities to enjoy the outdoors. It is co-managed by DEM's Divisions of Forest Environment and Fish & Wildlife. Many people enjoy hunting, fishing, boating, hiking, mountain biking, and horseback riding and they owe thanks to the hard work of the CCC who started developing the roads, trails, camping area, shelters, and reforested submarginal land.

Fishing and boating is allowed in Breakheart Pond, but not swimming, cooking, or fires. The Wood River, which flows through the heart of the Management Area, is also stocked with trout and offers anglers one of the best freshwater fishing experiences available in Rhode Island.

Canoeists and kayakers can enjoy the Wood River's Class I and Class II stream rafting for an unforgettable outdoor experience for both novice and experienced alike. Horseback riders can enjoy camping at the LeGrand G. Reynolds Horsemen Area. "Walk in" camping is also available, by permit, at the "Backpack Area", and a shelter is available for overnight rental at the Frosty Hollow Pond Recreation area.[53]

Wickaboxet CCC Shelter Restored

Leader Dominic Zachorne led an effort to restore a circa 1936-1938 CCC picnic pavilion in the Arcadia Management Area in the Wickaboxet picnic areas. The project was partially funded by a Trails Advisory Committee (TAC) grant. The restoration took six on-site work days and was carried out by groups of 25-30 volunteers.

The following is a description of how volunteers and the Appalachian Mountain Club (AMC) restored the Wickaboxet Shelter. Here is the dedication speech

The Wickaboxet shelter about 2015 was deteriorating after years of a rotting roof. Albert Klyberg

The pavilion, picnic area, and an old chimney from the Beach Pond CCC camp are now part of the LeGrand G. Reynolds Horsemen's Area. There are also water hand pumps, fireplaces, picnic tables, and riding trails. Podskoch

A second CCC chimney still stands at the Reynolds Horsemen's Area. It might have been from the Beach Pond camp's mess hall or rec hall. Today they are used by campers & picnickers. Camping is only for horseback riders. Podskoch

Historian Sheila Reynolds leaving the Escoheag Hill Road Central Control cabin that is now used by the RI Trials Bikes Club (RITC). The RITC, under a temporary agreement with the RI DEM, provides motorcycle trials & bike riders access to about 900 acres within the Arcadia Management Area. Podskoch

Just off Escoheag Hill Rd. are the "Ledges" where hikers and motorcyclist enjoy climbing the rocky terrain. Podskoch

The CCC constructed the stone lined ditch along the road to the "Ledges Trail." It is still in perfect shape after over 80 years of use. Podskoch

"Beach Pond beach, at the western end of Rt. 165 and the border with Connecticut, is still owned by the State. It is only available for boating and fishing. The bath house facilities have been removed and the beach strewn with jagged rocks to prevent its use by bathers. The entire Beach Pond area is now under the Arcadia Reservation administration," stated historian Podskoch

of Kerry Robinson, a member of AMC and volunteer worker, on July 20, 2017.

Ribbon-Cutting Ceremony, Remarks on Pavillion Project
Kerry Robinson

"Some of you may know the history of this area—others may not—so I'd like to just briefly share with you the story of how there came to be this great big building in the middle of the woods. In the late 1930s, the boys of the Civilian Conservation Corps, 1186th company, of Escoheag/Beach Pond Camp, were tasked with carving out a great park in the wilderness, where folks could drive out in their cars to see what nature had in store for them. The great granite slabs of Step Stone Falls being the focal point, this hillside around us was turned into what was first called Stepping Stone Park, then, later, Wickaboxet Picnic Area. Trees were cleared, to enjoy the view of the falls all along the river; fireplaces were built, using native stones to shape them; picnic tables were scattered throughout the hillside and parked cars lined the newly-graded roadway. They crafted stone water fountains, gravity-fed by a water tank, uphill from the pump house, built massive stone steps leading up and down, to make the going easier for the visitors, put in Men's and Women's latrines…and they built a great pavilion as the centerpiece for all!

"Eight decades later, their vision is still holding on…

"It was a little over four years ago, on a rather snowy, February day-hike, when the old picnic pavilion—then, still standing (albeit a bit worse for wear)—sparked a fire in the hearts of a few Appalachian Mountain Club (AMC) members. Five tons of custom-milled native timber, 85 feet of ¾" iron rod, 100 hours of post and beam carpentry work, 1,200-plus hours of volunteer labor and a few shingles later…we stood the building back up, anew, from the pile of rubble it had become, over the following winter. And we did it in 6 days. Yes…6 days—from August 'til October of last year, 25-30 volunteers at a time—both AMC members and non-members, alike—came out to show their passion and dedication to preserving the memory of this special place, honoring the CCC boys who built it and paying it forward to the next several generations, through their tireless efforts. We truly couldn't have done this without all of you…

Two of the organizers and workers of the shelter restoration project at the July 20, 2017 dedication ceremony were Project Leader, Dominic Zachorne and Kerry Robinson. Podskoch

From the Trails Advisory Committee, who believed in and valued our vision enough to grant us the funds, to the crew of the Forestry Division who milled all these timbers and clapboards you see in front of you, the Division of Natural Resources for your support and enthusiasm, the Trails Committee for putting their faith in two "newbie" members, and each and every volunteer, from all walks of life—and age!—this is your legacy…your mark on history!

"Without further ado…I'd like to pass the baton to our trusty Project Leader, Dominic Zachorne, who will have the honor of cutting the ribbon."

Directions

The old Beach Pond camp site is now the LeGrand G. Reynolds Horsemen's Area (200 Escoheag Hill Rd., Exeter, RI).

From Voluntown, CT: Go E on Rt. 165 (Ten Rod Rd.) As you come into RI you will pass Beach Pond. From here travel approx. 2 miles. Turn left on Escoheag Rd. and go N about 1.1 miles. On your left will be the LeGrand Reynolds Horsemen's Area.

From Providence: Go S on I-95 and travel approx. 22 miles. Take Exit 5A (Victory Hwy., 102 S) and turn right toward Exeter. Go 1.1 miles on Rt. 102 and turn

(L – R) Wickaboxet Picnic Area water fountain built by CCC boys. Podskoch | Water pump house is near the restored shelter in Wickaboxet Picnic Area. Podskoch | Huge stone steps from parking area to restored picnic shelter. Podskoch

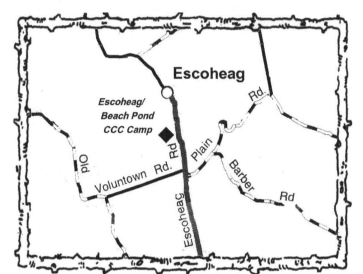

Escoheag/Beach Pond Map by Paul Hartmann

This Escohegan camp boy might have been anxious for quitting time and a great supper in the mess hall or thinking about his girlfriend he left back home. Webster Pidgeon

right onto Nooseneck Hill Rd./Rt. 3. Go 1.3 mi and turn right onto Ten Rod Rd./Rt. 165. Travel approx. 5 miles and turn right on Escoheag Hill Rd. Then go approx. 1.1 miles and old CCC Beach Pond camp is on the left.

MEMORIES

Thanksgiving Dinner Menu, Nov. 1937

Roasted Vermont Turkey & Giblet Gravy
Creamed pea soup
Hearts of celery
Creamed mashed potatoes
Mashed turnips
Buttered carrots
Lettuce & tomato salad
Cranberry sauce
Pumpkin pie
Fresh fruits / Nuts
Coffee / Cider[54]

Armistice Day

"And Yet"
by J. Noonan

Each year that passes,
Sees the masses,
Still remembering them;
Who sailed across;
Fought a cause;
Never returned again.

Days, months, and years roll on,
Memories begin to fade,
Of the November Armistice morn,
Yet here at our side;
With the troops still alive;
We drink a toast to the dead.[55]

"Hitchhiking"
by Henry Vashey

Have you ever been on the road,
When the stars were shining bright,
And the wind came whistling through the trees
Chilling up the night.

Have you been atop a hill
In dear old Escoheag,
Thumbing each car which came up
To have it turn you down?

You have waited for hours and hours
In discouragement and despair
Your thoughts traveled homeward
But you remained right there.

The wind seems to blow right through you
As you stand on top of Old Tom
You ask yourself, "Will I come home again?"
And your answer? "I never will."

And then your luck, it changes,
A car stops to give you a ride
He says he's going to Providence
The city where you abide.

You enter the car in happiness,
Is it all a dream?
At last you are really homeward bound
In joyness supreme.

You forget all those chilly hours
You spent on old Mt. Tom.
You forget all those selfish fellows
Who kept turning you down.

You forget all the promises you made
When you said it didn't pay,
All you care to remember is
At last I am on my way.

And when the weekends roll around
You're on your way again
To have some experiences

That you had the time before.[56]

With Apologies to Fall Leaves
Tom, Tom, the camper's son
Dropped a match and off he run.
The fire with ease
Burned up the trees
Now Tom is out of the CCC.[57]

The March 1939 the Escoheagan newspaper had a special section called "After March, So Long Pals!" It had short descriptions of all the boys who were leaving the Escoheag/Beach Pond camp. Here is the description of John B. Cinq-Mars whose photos are sprinkled throughout this chapter:

John B. Cinq-Mars – 82 Toronto Ave. Providence, RI. Transferred from Mt. Vernon camp. Truck driver and finally promoted to assistant to Mr. Lehr, Technical Service Mechanic. Very popular with the fairer sex in Compton and vicinity. Active in social affairs of camp. Ass't Leader Photography Leadership Auto Maintenance Dance Committee

[Author Note: Special thanks to Rhode Island Historian Larry DePetrillo of Cranston, RI who shared his collection of photos taken by enrollee John B. Cinq-Mars.]

Historian Larry DePetrillo in his library of Rhode Island books and memorabilia at his home in Cranston, RI. Nancy DePetrillo

CHAPTER 6
GREENE / MOUNT VERNON

A wide view of Camp Greene/Mount Vernon in the Town of Foster. In the middle left are four barracks and in the center is the water tower. Foster Historical Society

HISTORY

Camp Greene, Co. 1187 was established on June 1, 1935 in the Town of Foster in the southwest section of Rhode Island. Lt. Leo Guibault led a cadre of 23 men to a blueberry pasture that was part of the Betsy Hollis farm. Enrollees began clearing the land and erecting tents. The farm was on one of the highest elevations in the state. After clearing the brush, they leveled the land and hauled gravel. On July 15th, the main group of enrollees arrived under the command of Capt. Stanley H. Franklin. They worked on constructing roads and camp buildings.[1]

The Mt. Vernon Camp in Foster bore the name Camp Greene because the post office in Greene, a part of the Town of Coventry, was the nearest to the site. The camp was located at 16 Howard Hill in Foster. It was on an 8.37-acre piece of land purchased by the Director of Agriculture and Conservation for the purpose of establishing a CCC camp.[2]

Camp Greene P-55 was a forestry camp under the direction of the United States Forest Service. The 'P-' meant it was a camp on Private Land. Forestry camps focused on building truck trails throughout their domain enabling rapid deployment of equipment in the case of forest fires. These 'in-roads' had numerous convenient roadside waterholes installed along the way.

Other work of the forest camps was divided between clearing out deadfalls, reforesting burned out areas, and treating tree diseases like gypsy moth infestation, Dutch

Elm, and pine blister rust disease. Not all work took place at the camps and state lands. There were parallel Federal programs of buying up marginal woodlands to discourage private owner's attempts at producing unproductive wood products. Many of these properties also received the attention of the CCC by establishing demonstration forest where enrollees cleared the land of poor varieties and planted productive trees that later could be sold for a profit.

In 1935 the state acquired 14,486 acres of sub-marginal land for general conservation purposes. One section of parcels had 7,607 acres in the Arcadia Area in nearby Exeter and Richmond. This gave Camp Greene areas to work on forestry projects.[3]

– 1935 –

Projects

Camp Foster's projects were planned and supervised by Superintendent Milton Willard. Here are some of the projects they worked on in 1935 to January 1936:

In July 1935 enrollees constructed a 0.3 mi. approach road to camp. They also did blister rust eradication.

Then in August the young men began building waterholes. They also constructed the West Meadowbrook Trail and 1.5 mi. Old Trail Rd.

In October they constructed a 0.4 mi. Dynamite Trail.

Mount Vernon & CCC Camp

Foster Town Historian, Stanley Hopkins, gave this description of Mount Vernon when asked why the CCC camp was called Mount Vernon?

"The CCC camp sat in the village of Mount Vernon. There is a home there that has been called Mt. Vernon since the Revolutionary War. It's not far from where the camp was. It's on Plainfield Pike (Rt. 14). It once housed, in an ell that was added later, the Mount Vernon Post Office and also a bank. It was also a tavern, general store, and a stagecoach stop. Houses were built around this central meeting place and it became the hamlet or village of Mount Vernon.

"During the Revolutionary War, Rochambeau marched his fifteen hundred troops by there on the way to join Washington at Yorktown. It has also been said that Washington slept there which is entirely possible on his 1790 visit to Rhode Island. I would guess that it probably started to be called Mount Vernon at that time.

"Mount Vernon Tavern as it stands today is a two and one-half gable roofed main house with a one and one-half gable roof addition all built by Pardon Holden who was not the original owner of the property. The original home was built around 1740 by a member of the Clark family. It was probably an end chimney home because it had a walk-in fireplace which would be unusual for a center chimney home.

"It later became an ell to the original Holden home but was torn down in the late eighteen hundreds.

Two Clark brothers settled there in the 1730s as original proprietors of the Westconnaug Purchasers. In 1731 the Westconnaug Purchase became part of Scituate.

"In 1781 Foster was set aside from Scituate. The original Westconnaug land now comprises about half of Foster. Holden built the current main part in 1814 and added the addition a little later. The post office operated from 1828-1864. The bank opened in 1823. A couple of years later it was moved to another building in the area.

"Nearby is the newly restored Mt. Vernon Church which started as a Friend's meeting house. Perhaps this is a little too much information but it gives you some of the background on the name. I think most of the locals called the camp Mt. Vernon Camp."

Mount Vernon Tavern. Wikipedia

The next month the boys constructed a dynamite and cap magazine (storage unit) and they did blister rust eradication in the area.

In December Co. 1187 did gypsy moth control work and mapping.

During the winter of January 1936, the camp constructed the 2.3 mi. Central Trail in the central part of the Arcadia Management Area.[5]

Co. 1186 did fire suppression and sanitation work in the Wickaboxet Forest area.[6]

Staff

The Commanding Officer was Lt. Francis G. Lee who was assisted by Ensign Lawrence Lord. Education Adviser was Edmund B. Barton and his WPA instructors were: Henry C. McSoley and William Foley. The camp physician was Dr. Benedict Kudish.[7]

These were the men who were the original Camp Foster's technical staff: foremen, Edward A. Hart & Benjamin Hoxie (truck trails); John Ayers & John Kaylor (blister rust); David Robbins, Russell Littlefield, and Henry Fallon (state mechanics).[8]

A June 17th, 1936 group photo of the Greene/Mount Vernon CCC camp in the town of Foster. Glenn Dusablon and Veterans Memorial Museum in Woonsocket, RI

Enrollees were assigned as drivers to one of the approx. 15 Army or Division camp trucks. Their duty was to keep the truck maintained, transport workers and materials to projects or on weekends transport enrollees to towns, movies or dances.[4]

– 1936 –

Education

During the summer a group interested in gardening was busy selecting plots of land and seeds to grow. The project was very successful and profitable and was a good learning experience.[9]

In the Fall of 1936, evening classes began and the most popular were: Motor Mechanics, Electricity & Radio, Forestry, and Typing. Mr. Fallon taught the motor class to a group of 40 interested students who enjoyed his talks incorporating the use of various engine parts and how they worked. The other popular class was led by Mr. Pentz who was able to gather approx. 20 radios for his students to learn on.[10]

Each week there was a radio broadcast featuring members of the camp performing: impersonations, singing, jokes, harmonica solos, and the camp's musical group.[11]

Sports

Swimming was very popular in the summer. One of the big events was the District Swimming Meet that was held at Bliffin's Beach on North Main St. in Fall River. A few of the Mount Vernon members took home prizes.[12]

Two boys spent a week at Fort Adams learning life saving techniques to help share their acquired knowledge with the other members of the camp. These skills were very important during the swimming season.[13] In the fall the camp had a travelling soccer team.

In the summer of 1936, Camp Greene provided the enrollees these sports: horseshoes, volleyball, swimming, archery, and baseball.[14]

During July 1936 three guest speakers came to camp. On July 8th Joseph Broderick spoke on the early history of Rhode Island. Chaplin Capt. Nuzum came on July 12th for his regular monthly visit and gave a sermon. Then on the next day, Capt. Nuzum showed a movie. On the 28th Rev. Herbert Whitelock, the "The Gospel Ranger," gave an evening sermon under the stars.[15]

In the Fall of 1936, "Tree Planting Day" was held at the Mt. Vernon camp. Enrollees from Co. 1161 in Primrose and Co. 1141 from George Washington joined together and planted 600 trees. Officials from the state Forestry Dept. and town officials from Coventry, Foster, Scituate, Cranston, Warwick, West Warwick, and West Greenwich attended. They were joined by local children of Foster. Many speeches were made and music was provided by the Sockanosset School Band in Cranston. After the festivities, the guests were given a tour of the camp.[16]

By October the company reached a total of 157 men for the winter. The crews that were busy building waterholes and fighting blister rust turned their attention to searching for gypsy moths, roadside fire-prevention, road and truck-trail construction. There was one crew

"Tent Life at Camp Mt. Vernon [1935]"
by Old Timer

The following story was written by an enrollee who helped set up the Greene / Mount Vernon camp. It was published in the March 1937 Wayfarer, the camp monthly newspaper.

"It takes some imagination to picture our present [camp] as a blueberry patch, but that is exactly what it was when the twenty-three men of the cadre arrived on the scene June 1, 1935, under the command of Lt. Gibon (sic). Before we even got onto the camping ground, we had to break down part of a stone wall, and build a rough ramp in order to get the trucks in. Then the next job was to pitch the tents: one for the bunks, one for a supply room, a headquarters tent, a canteen, and even one for the recreation. A rough shack was built for the mess and the first meal. I might want to tell you, it was cooked in the rain by Phil Powers: beans and franfurts (sic). And did it taste good. The cadre worked hard for six weeks, cutting out brush, tearing down stone walls, and carting gravel. It was rough and ready work and we worked hard, but we got a lot of fun out of it. That first Fourth of July we had a weenie roast, to which some of the young ladies of the neighborhood were invited, and we had just as good a time as we have now at a Company Dance, only of course, it was different.

"Now, tent life, which we still continued after the arrival of the main body of 175, is quite another thing from living in the barracks. There were twenty men to a tent, no floors, and no lights except lanterns. It was so rainy the first month that you often woke up to find a brook running under you bunk. If you wanted a shower you had to find some nearby stream, or do as Top Sergeant Card did. He got a man to climb a tree and pour a bucket of water over him. The mosquitoes were so thick that we had to use mosquito netting.

"In spite of these difficulties we had a good time and got healthy and strong. The work was mostly reclaiming the land and getting it into shape for a camp site. This meant clearing away brush, hauling gravel, and building roads. It was hard work, but the fellows soon began to get hardened and learned to take it cheerfully. There are only a very few of the old original cadre left in the company now, but to them those early days are a happy memory."

Company 1187 first lived in Army tents before the wooden buildings were constructed. Podskoch Collection

doing forest survey work.[17]

Five members of the camp were accepted to take college classes that would be held on Tuesday and Thursday evenings at Central High School in Providence.

Dr. Morris from the RI State Dept. of Health spoke at the camp on Tuesday, November 10 on the topic of "Sex Hygiene." He also showed an informative sound motion picture to the men.[18]

During the 1936 Thanksgiving Holiday, most of the boys had gone home except for a few boys and members of the fire detail. Mess Officer, Lt. Schreiber served a delicious meal consisting of: celery, mint jelly, roast stuffed turkey, baked sweet potatoes, cranberry sauce, succotash, lettuce & tomato salad, bread & butter, squash pie, cheese, ice cream, candy, cider, and coffee.

– 1936 –

Staff & Roster

During the 1936-37 winter, Camp Greene experienced a lot of sickness due to an influenza epidemic.

(L – R) After a hard day working in the forests, the boys loved going to the Mess Hall where they could have delicious meals and even go for seconds.[19] | Here are three servers and three cooks who worked in the mess hall to feed approx. 200 enrollees and camp supervisors three meals a day.[20] | The Infirmary/Dispensary was staffed 24/7 by an attendant (standing in front of the infirmary). He took care of the sick and aided the camp doctor.[21]

187th COMPANY   P-55   GREENE,

FIRST LT. FRANCIS G. LEE, *13th Inf.-Res.*, COMMANDING   *Roster*   FIRST LT. GORDON E. MENZIES, *Med.-Res.*, SURGEON

FIRST LT. ALFRED R. WOOD, *FA.-Res.*, MESS OFFICER   EDMUND B. BARTON, *CEA*

TECHNICAL PERSONNEL Milton Willard, Supt.; Frank R. Hinkley, Edwin A. Hart, John H. Ayers, Benjamin R. Hoxsie, John D. Kaylor, David Robbins, Arthur Deslandes, Gualtiero Aurecchia.

LEADERS Raymond F. Heinig, Providence, Rhode Island; Charles Holden, Pawtucket, Rhode Island; Frederick S. Kelso, Providence, Rhode Island; Frank E. Nichols, Foster Center, Rhode Island; Frank O'Donnell, Providence, Rhode Island; William H. Pentz, Providence, Rhode Island; Phillip Powers, Providence, Rhode Island; Chester S. Wujciski, Providence, Rhode Island.

ASSISTANT LEADERS L. J. Benson, Lakewood, R. I.; J. J. Bertoncini, Pawtucket, R. I.; M. M. Correira, Bristol, R. I.; M. DaPonte, Newport, R. I.; G. E. Finnerty, Providence, R. I.; J. A. Happeny, Central Falls, R. I.; A. G. Hart, Hope, R. I.; H. J. Hebert, Central Falls, R. I.; R. A. Keefe, Providence, R. I.; R. Lacroix, Woonsocket, R. I.; O. Pinto, Natick, R. I.; J. Sylvia, Barrington, R. I.; E. Wargal, Providence, R. I.

The roster of the 1937 Greene/Mount Vernon Camp supervisors and enrollees from the Third CCC District First Corps Area Yearbook

A 1937 Third CCC District First Corps Area Yearbook photo of the Greene/Mount Vernon camp in Foster, RI

Twenty-seven men were transported to the Fort Adams hospital for care, but the majority of the young men continued working.

Activities

In January 1937, the basketball team had to travel across the border into Connecticut to practice and play their games in the Plainfield Community Gym. Their first game was on January 13th against Sterling, but they lost a close game, 32-30. In their second league game, they beat Jewitt City 41-19. In their third game, they crushed Plainfield 23-10.[22]

On January 22, 1937 forty Camp Greene enrollees were invited by Miss Mildred E. Lister of the N.Y.A, to attend their dance at the West Warwick Lodge. A few days later, Co. 1187 had their dance at the Anthony Grange Hall in West Warwick on Monday Jan. 25th.[23]

The Mount Vernon boys enjoyed bi-weekly movies through a subscription to an organization called Films Incorporated. The camp also had Amateur Nights that were very popular. To get more participation Lt. Lee offered the winning barracks a $5 prize.[24]

Education

The winter education program continued for three months and ended on March 31. There were many interesting courses: Game Management, Modeling, Auto Mechanics, Forestry, Electricity & Radio, and Dynamiting. At the end of each class, boys who completed the work satisfactorily were given certificates that were helpful when they searched for a job. In December 1936, 24 certificates were presented to enrollees.[25]

Camp Greene was fortunate to be close to the campus of the University of RI and had frequent professors give talks at the camp. In February Dr. Christopher gave a talk on small fruit culture. The boys enjoyed the talk especially the Garden Club.[26]

The Mount Vernon Camp celebrated the Fourth Anniversary of the founding of the CCC during the week of April 4th,1937. On Tuesday, local town officials were invited to dinner in the mess hall and enjoyed a movie in the recreation hall. On Wednesday, an Open House was held from 5-7:30 pm. There were displays of crafts made by enrollees, educational materials, and posters. Then on Thursday a movie was shown and followed with a

The March 1937 issue of the Wayfarer, the camp newspaper, stated there were some new education classes for the spring: General Science, Salesmanship, Music, Forestry, and Nature Study. New recreation classes included Fencing and Archery.

company dance. N.Y.A. girls were invited from the camp at Chepachet in the town of Glocester.

The Education Adviser was always looking for speakers and activities for the enrollees. He was fortunate to get the Debate Team from RI College to visit the camp on March 3rd and debate an interesting topic on government regulation of wages.[27]

On April 8, 1937, the Company Dance was held in the recreation hall. The girls arrived at 8 pm. The music began with many popular tunes and a few danced while some stood and watched. At 9 pm refreshments of cake and punch were served. The dance ended at 10 much to the regret of everyone. Later that month the N.Y.A. girls in Providence invited fifty Camp Greene enrollees to their dance. The N.Y.A. Orchestra provided the music.[28]

There were frequent changes in the camp personnel.

In May 1937, this was the camp personnel: 1st Lt. Francis G. Lee, Commanding Officer; 1st Lt. Alfred Roger Woon, Second in Command; 1st Lt. Dr. Gordon E. Menzies, Camp Surgeon; Edmund B. Barton, Education Advisor; Wilfred Laliberte & Rudolph Hebert, WPA teachers; and Charles Holden, Senior Leader.[29]

During the spring and summer, Forestry Foreman Edwin A. Hart and his landscaping crew did a great job of transforming the camp into a park-like setting with lawns, stone walkways, shrubs, and trees.[30]

There were a few additions to Superintendent Willard's staff: Frank R. Hinkley was Assistant to the Superintendent; Gualtiero Aurecchia, forestry foreman; and Arthur Deslandes, state mechanic.

Sports

The baseball team began practicing in April in Foster and Sterling, CT. In the summer these additional sports and activities were operating: volleyball, archery, hand (wood) carving, photography, nature study, and stamp collecting.[32] By the end of August, the camp baseball team won the Southern International League series. They then traveled to Roosevelt Field in Blackstone, Mass. to play the East Douglas team. In the end the Mount Vernon team lost 4-1.[33]

Enrollees loved swimming especially after working in the hot sun. At the beginning of July, trucks regularly took the boys to Moosup Lake where shallow water was helpful in teaching swimming and life-saving. There were also inter-barracks softball games and a horseshoe tournament.[34]

On June 10, 1937, The Federal Theater Players visited the camp and performed a new play, "Murder in the CCC." The traveling group selected 30 enrollees to have parts in the play. The play was both humorous and entertaining and enjoyed by the enrollees and an audience that included a number of friends and neighbors of the camp.[35]

Education

In the summer of 1937 these were the classes offered to the enrollees: Surveying, Forestry, Gardening, Nature Study, Landscaping, Auto Mechanics, Typewriting, and Wood Carving.

Awards

Forestry foreman Edwin A. Hart was praised for his outstanding work in supervising the landscape gardening of Camp Greene.[37]

Company Leader William Pentz of Providence was named the outstanding enrollee of Co. 1187 and listed on the Company Roll of Honor because of his outstanding cooperation and work for the welfare of the company.[38]

Also, like the Primrose and Nooseneck camps, the camp in Foster had a brief existence. It was put into service in 1935 but by the Fall of 1937 it was closed in September.[39]

Sports were very popular with the Mount Vernon camp. Teams played other CCC camps or local town teams. Here is the 1937 baseball team.[31]

Typing was one of the popular classes at camp. Getting a certificate for taking classes was an advantage in getting a job when they left camp.[36]

A 1939 aerial view of the former site of Camp Greene in the upper part of the map. The camp was on Howard Hill Rd. that runs southeast to Rt. 14 at the bottom. It looks like there are only about four buildings at the camp site. The camp was closed in 1937 and some of the buildings have been removed. It shows the roads and pathways used by the enrollees. The camp was also not near the main road but set back.[40]

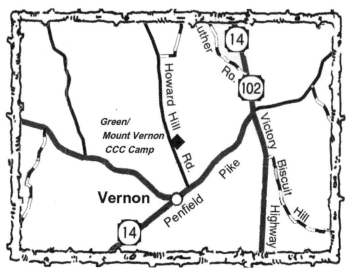

Greene/Mount Vernon Map by Paul Hartmann

LEGACY

Today, the old Camp Greene camp grounds are now the Woody Lowden Recreation Center, that are the playing fields for the town of Foster. There are no remnants of the former CCC camp. The only photos of the camp have been preserved by the Foster Historical Society.

The two years of work by Camp Greene/Mount Vernon have had a lasting effect on the forests that comprise The Arcadia Management Area in western Rhode Island. Their forestry work of cleaning the forest, fighting insects and tree diseases, planting thousands of trees, building roads, fire trails, waterholes and fighting fires helped to invigorate damaged forests destroyed by fires. They also improved marginal farmland by planting thousands of trees. They constructed trails and roads that enabled fire fighters to get to the source of the fires. Some of the trails and roads were: West Meadowbrook Trail, Old Trail Rd., Dynamite Trail, and the 2.3 mi. Central Trail in the central part of the Arcadia Management Area. Their fire suppression and sanitation work in the 678-acre Wickaboxet Forest helped to make the forest flourish. Today people can enjoy the serenity and natural beauty of the state forest that are the fruits of the CCC labor.

Directions

The camp was located at Woody Lowden Recreation Center, 16 Howard Hill Rd, Foster.

From Providence: Take I-295 to Exit 6 (Rt. 14/Plainfield Pike). Go West on Rt. 14 for 13.4 miles. Turn right onto Howard Hill Rd. and go approx. ½ mile to Woody Lowden Recreation Center on the right.

From Westerly: Take I-95 N and go 16.9 miles to Exit 5B West Greenwich. Turn left onto Rt. 102 Victory Hwy. and travel N for 10.5 mi. Then turn left onto Plainfield Pike Rt. 14. Go W for 1.14 miles and turn right onto Howard Hill Rd. and go N for approx. ½ mile to Woody Lowden Recreation Center on the right.

MEMORIES

"Journey to Mount Vernon" by Russell Allen

"You have received your notice and the time for your departure has arrived so with some reluctance and mixed with curiosity you leave for the appointed place. You find however, on arriving that you are not alone but preceded by four or five others equally as curious and anxious as are you. In due time a truck arrives to take you to Providence where herded together in groups of ten you are allowed to ascend four flights of stairs. In view of the fact that there are two elevators to the building, it is quite clear that this is the first step in 'getting in shape.' When your group is finally examined, you are given the O.K. or words to that effect, and as you descend the stairs your mind perhaps wanders back to the kid who's seventeen 'goin' on eighteen and weighs only 102 pounds and because of this discrepancy in weight has been promised, by a considerate officer, two dinners instead of one, and you notice that he seems to have a look of superiority in his eye, as if he had just outwitted the War Dept.

"On arriving at Newport and Fort Adams you again disrobe for further examination, and then you redress, disrobe, redress, disrobe, redress etc. until you eventually begin to feel like a chorus girl. You merge into the sunlight with open shirt tucked into unbuttoned trousers, your feet encased in a pair of high-topped shoes in which you can walk with all the pleasure that is found in a Chinese boot. With a faintly aching arm you carry a blue duffle bag, into which with all the fiendish glee of perhaps 12-months service, some over enthusiastic supply sergeant has thrown your civilian clothes, and then with a maniacal leer jumped upon, once-twice-three times, until your hats, coats, ties, etc. are hardly noticeable at the bottom of the bag.

"And as you emerge puffing, blowing, sweating and as you mop your perspiring forehead, on that cold, grey, April afternoon, you set down on the stairs, try to catch your breath, and wonder if it would not have been wiser had you consulted a psychologist before enrolling in the President's pet project."[41]

A Year in Mount Vernon

"The day we arrived in Camp was one of the most thrilling I ever spent. We were transferred from Fort Adams to our destination in New England by bus

Local carpenters and enrollees helped build the camp buildings like these barracks. John Cinq-Mars & Larry DePetrillo

A barracks at the Greene/Mt. Vernon camp. The two coal stoves kept the enrollees warm in the winter. The young men learned Army discipline, the beds were made and room was spotless. Foster Historical Society

and upon emerging from our vehicles I observed the picturesque surroundings of the campsite, our future home. There were two rows of canvas tents pitched in a fairly large field which was adjacent to the barracks' site. We were assigned to our tents immediately after leaving the buses and a meal was served to us from a field kitchen and eaten in the open.

"The next day and following three weeks we were busily engaged in the construction of the camp and the clearing of the camp area. The work we were doing could easily be compared with that of a fearless pioneer opening up a new frontier for civilization.

"In the evening after supper we sang songs and indulged in sports of various kinds. Frequently some of the fellows would take a walk in the vicinity of the camp to become better acquainted with our surroundings. We soon realized that our environment would be a great deal healthier and that our time would not be spent in vain.

"Meanwhile, the barracks were being hastily constructed by civilian carpenters aided by some of the men. The day we moved into the barracks was an eventful and exciting one. Some of the boys were so anxious to get their bunks into quarters that they nearly caused a riot. If a visitor could have seen us at that particular moment he would have been deeply impressed by our enthusiasm. The reason for our excitement could easily be determined. It not only meant electric lights, cleaner living quarters, and better shelter from the elements but it also showed the marked improvement we had made in our camp. It was a milestone of great importance. After we had settled in our new homes, educational and sporting activities began in earnest. Also, we had more entertainment and time for leisure.

"Daily the camp improved in its appearance and morale and eventually we all had a different outlook on life. We all seemed brimming over with health. Likewise, our desire to obtain an education and indulge in sports became more apparent. We were part of the camp: we had built it!

"All of these events have elapsed within the period of a year. Men have left the camp at the end of their enlistment to seek employment in private industry, others have been transferred to the West Coast companies, others have reenlistment for another term at Mount Vernon. I know that I can say for these men as I say for myself that I am better physically, mentally, morally, and spiritually for having joined the Civilian Conservation Corps."

- The Wayfarer, July 1936

"Mount Vernon Poem"
by Robert Templeton

M is for man-days, whatever that means
O is for the onions we peel
U is for united, that's what we are here
N for "No Automobile"
T is for tidy, as barracks must be
V is for valiant men
E's extra duty or eats, take your choice
R is for rookies, and N, well,
N is for nickels we spend at the canteen
O is for wild oats, now and then
N is for the name of our camp which I've spelled:
    so now I will lay down my pen[42]

"A Vet Soliloquizes"
by Robert Templeton

Once I was only a rookie
And sorry that I had signed on
They pushed me about and razzed me,
But now that is over and gone.

Each day I would think of my dollar
In gravel pit, trail, or K.P.
And that first weekend pass seemed like heaven
When I was a budding C.C.C.

Meanwhile I was learning to take it,
And to steer clear of the gold-bricking guys,
But the first job I got as a straw-boss,
Was swatting a roomful of flies!

However, I stuck to it steady
Until I was husky and strong,
And then I re-enrolled for another six months
And that didn't seem very long.

So now I'm a regular veteran
And counted as one of the "gang."
You'll find me the first, when I used to be last
Whenever the chow bell rang.[43]

Advice Editorial
by Charles Holden

"A word to the new men. The CCC must be considered not only a place to work until a better job can be found but it must be thought of as a place where

New recruits and old veterans learned to get along and work together. John Cinq-Mars & Larry DePetrillo

The entrance to Camp Greene also called Mount Vernon. Foster Historical Society

(L – R) The June 1937 cover of the Wayfarer newspaper. The February 1937 cover of the Wayfarer newspaper.

Get them while they last!
2 cans Hi-Plane tobacco & pipe for **25¢**

Keep out of the Dispensary!
Use Vicks Cough Drops - **10¢**

A Bright Idea! Noxon - **8¢**

Keep Your Nose Clean! Handkerchief - **5¢**

Smoke your troubles away!
Free Book of Matches with every package
of Cigarettes - **10¢** and **14¢**

FREE! • FREE! • FREE!

$1.50 Pipe for ten coupons from
Edgeworth Tobacco - **15¢**

Remember the profits from the Canteen
Go Towards Recreation, Welfare, and
Happiness of you men in camp.

Ad [not original design] for the Camp Canteen in the Feb. 1937 issue of the Wayfarer.

you can obtain invaluable information and experience which you will never forget. In the CCC certain subjects are frankly discussed by our Supervisory Personnel which otherwise you might not have ever known for a number of years. Subjects which lay the foundation for a number of trades are taught by experienced teachers. I have often thought that a man who is ambitious enough can learn as much by taking the subjects taught here for a year as he could in two years of high school.

"With regard to the work in this organization, so many times I have heard members who are about to be punished for some misdemeanor say: 'Oh, this is only the CCC; it won't mean a thing later.' That is where they are wrong, it will mean a great deal in later life. Everywhere you work, you will encounter the same obstacles. The habits formed now will without doubt be the basis of your future life. The men in the CCC should work now and endeavor to attain a respected position in the camp. It will bring self-satisfaction and it is highly possible that it will lead to a better position."
- The Wayfarer, January 1937

"Advice to Swimmers"
by Dr. Gordon B. Menzies

"First of all, you are required to get a special pass from the office to go swimming: secondly, the buddy system should be strictly adhered to. By the buddy system we mean that you must have at least one other fellow with you. This is for your own protection.

"Here are a few things that will help keep you from the undertaker. Don't go swimming for at least two hours after a full meal. Don't dive into unfamiliar places without first assuring yourself of their depth." [44]

The last issue of the Wayfarer announced the farewell of the enrollees due to the closing of their Mount Vernon Camp.

A Farewell to Mount Vernon

"In view of the recent order which has come through to close our camp, we have delayed the publication of the Wayfarer long enough to include the signatures of the Company, and a brief farewell. The good old 1187th will soon be nothing but a memory. The spirit, companionship, and good will, however, and the work and play which we have shared will not be forgotten. We have built up one of the finest camps in New England; we have been commended by distinguished guests and visiting officials for our superb road construction; we have turned out a winning baseball team, and gained the reputation for good sportsmanship. These are achievements of which we may be justly proud when we look back and live over again Mount Vernon days. The Wayfarer is making its final bow and extends to everyone its heartfelt wish for a happy and successful future." [45]

CHAPTER 7
HOPE VALLEY / ARCADIA

A model of the Hope Valley/Arcadia CCC Camp constructed by some enrollees of Company 1188. The two long truck garages are on the far left. To the right of the garages are two barracks labeled A & B and behind them is the Clinic/Dispensary with a Cross on the roof. Then there are four buildings. The first one nearest the road looks like the Administration Building. The furthest building of this group has MH which might be the Mess Hall. The building on the far right is the 3rd Barracks and not seen is the 4th Barracks that can be seen in the aerial photo.[1]

HISTORY

CCC Camp Hope Valley/Arcadia P-54, Co. 1188, was located on a 55-acre site on the Wood River in the village of Arcadia in the town of Richmond. The CCC camp site was where the present Arcadia Management Area Headquarters is at 260 Arcadia Rd., Arcadia. In 1935 this land was purchased by the State Director of Agriculture for the establishment and maintenance of the CCC. Although the camp was in Arcadia the Army called it Hope Valley (in the Town of Hopkinton) because

A 1939 aerial photo of the Arcadia camp. In the lower part is the tree nursery.[2]

that was the nearest post office. Today the Arcadia Management Area Headquarter's mailing address is still 260 Arcadia Road, Hope Valley, RI 02823.

In 1935 there were now six CCC camps in RI after four new camps were added at Primrose, Beach Pond, Mt. Vernon/Greene and Arcadia/Hope Valley.[3]

On May 30, 1935 a detachment of 23 men from the Charlestown/Burlingame Camp, Co. 141, arrived at the future camp site. Lt. Teed led these men in clearing the site and setting up their tents.[4]

The next task was hauling shipments of lumber from the Hope Valley Railroad Station to the camp site. The men then surveyed the site for the location of buildings. Lt. Labbee, the construction officer, arrived and replaced Lt. Teed. The men first constructed the mess hall and then barracks "B" allowing the men to move out of their tents to a more comfortable shelter.[5]

On July 22, 1935, a large contingent of men from Co. 1188 from Fort Adams arrived at Arcadia Village under the command of Capt. Cobb. All of the buildings had been constructed except the rec hall and part of the officer's building.

Projects

The Arcadia Camp was a forestry camp under the direction of the United States Forest Service. Their work

Enrollees were trained to operate heavy equipment such as the tractor on the left and the bulldozer. An LEM (Local Experienced Man) or a mechanic is giving instruction on the right. This experience sometimes had a positive effect in securing a job after enrollees left the CCC.[6]

focused on building truck trails throughout their area enabling rapid deployment of equipment in the case of forest fires. These 'in-roads' had numerous convenient roadside waterholes installed along their way.

The Dec. 19, 1935 issue of the camp newspaper called Check reported that on Nov. 27th the Commanding General of the 1st Corps Area granted the camp 1,500 man-days to construct the interior roads of the camp. Crews were to fill in and level the camp quadrangle with gravel. Camp Superintendent Errol Tarbox was to supervise the work.

In December, the Olson Artesian Well Co. hit water at approx. 580' and installed a pump. This finally provided running water to the camp.[7]

– 1935 –

The camp's main work was fire protection. Two of the most important projects were the construction of water holes and truck trails. Camp Arcadia built nine water holes along roads in the forests in the towns of Hopkinton, Exeter, and Richmond. The holes had stone walls, guard rails, and contained from 15,000 to 30,000 gallons of water. They usually had a space for trucks to park while crews filled their tanks.[9]

The forestry foremen charged with directing the work arrived on the first of August. Work in the woods commenced on August 5th. A trail to Voluntown in Connecticut was one of the first projects. Another task was controlling white pine blister rust. Among the other tasks tackled were cutting trails to Rockville, Grassy Pond, Tefft Hill, and Sessions Hopkins Trail.

Camp Arcadia men cleared 45 acres of cut-over land next to their camp of slash, undesirable trees, and debris. Five miles of telephone lines were also installed.[10]

During the summer, crews scouted 13,000 acres of land in northern Hopkinton searching for gooseberry and currant bushes that were the hosts of blister rust that destroyed white pine trees. Over 11,000 bushes were destroyed.[11]

Gypsy moth control occurred on 75,000 acres while white pine blister rust control was directed at 10,000 acres. A total of 30,000 acres were in Richmond and Hopkinton. The boys destroyed the egg clusters by painting them with creosote. The most clusters were found in Richmond in the area between the two small villages of Usquepaug and Kenyon along the South County Trail. The crews also traveled to Goddard Park (Warwick) and scouted the forests where several thousand egg clusters were destroyed.[12]

During the evenings and on Saturday and Sundays, boys volunteered their free time to beautify the camp site by planting and gardening. They were supervised by members of the forestry department.[13]

Sports

For recreation, the boys swam in the nearby Arcadia

Every month the Arcadia Camp newspaper was illustrated and written by the enrollees. It was filled with camp projects, sports, events and jokes, cartoons, and gossip. The first paper was called Check and was followed by Ye Arcadia Scroll in the March issue 1936.

It is 8 am and the boys are gathering at their assigned trucks and ready to work on projects in the Arcadia Forest. One of the LEM or Foresters is also ready to go with his truck and supervise the work of his crew.[8]

Pond. On July 15, 1935 tragedy was averted when a group of boys who were swimming noticed their friend, Albert Plamondon, was drowning. Enrollee Lawrence Gadrow swam to Albert and saved his life.[14]

In the Fall of 1935, the Arcadia soccer team won the Western League Championship. They then traveled to Fort Adams for the Championship of New England but lost 2-0.[15]

As winter approached enrollees participated in basketball, ping-pong, and boxing.

During the Christmas' and New Years' holidays, enrollees had the choice of either getting leave from Dec. 21, to midnight Dec. 26th 1935 or to take leave for the New Year Holiday from Sat. Dec. 28-midnight to Jan. 2, 1936.[16]

Before the boys got their leaves for the holiday, there was a Christmas Party on Dec. 19, 1935. After a delicious meal, the enrollees enjoyed music provided by the five-piece camp orchestra composed of a drummer, pianist, saxophone player, violinist, and guitarist. This was then followed by a seven-piece harmonica band, comedy skits, a singer, and tap dancer. At the end was an acrobat and tumbling act.[17]

– 1936 –

Projects

Work began on the construction of two truck trails. The first trail ran from the Boy Scout Camp at Yawgoog (Rockville) westward to the Connecticut border. The other trail ran from Rockville to Canonchet. These trails are both in the town of Hopkinton. This area was very rough and rocky and the location of many fires that destroyed most of the forest. These truck trails were a great benefit to the local government which did not have the funds to build a good gravel road.

During the winter Mr. Woolley's crew was busy surveying the Grassy Pond Trail. "When Woolley and his assistant came to a field where a bull was quietly grazing, they figured it would be safe to cross. When they got halfway they heard a farmer yell: 'I wouldn't trust that bull!' They quickly turned around and saw a puffing, snorting bull charging after them. You never in your life saw Mr. Woolley do the 50-yard dash to the fence in world record time."[19]

In January the camp had a 580' drilled well but the water was not suitable for drinking. The Arcadia boys could only use the water for washing. The water was chlorinated in a Lyster bag for drinking. Samples of the well water were sent for testing at the State Board of Health until the water was suitable for drinking.[20]

The January 19th issue of the Check camp

The enrollees built up their muscles and appetite digging and breaking rocks with sledge hammers while they built truck trails that were a plus in getting to forest fires at their beginning stages.[18]

newspaper reported 40 Arcadia Camp boys responded to a nearby fire that destroyed a garage owned by Mr. Pials. Damage was estimated at $2,000.

A terrible snow storm on a January weekend prevented 19 enrollees from getting back to camp due to closed roads. When they called the camp and told the commanding officer of their plight, he gave them Absence Without Pay Leave.[21]

The March 1936 Ye Arcadia Scroll newspaper reported that a radio station was established in the camp boiler room. A two-way radio was installed so that the Arcadia Camp was in contact with the Beach Pond Camp. Definite hours were established so that both camps had someone manning the radio.

Education

Weekly Evening Schedule of Classes

Monday, 6:30 - 7:30 - 8:30

Chemistry Algebra Business English
Current Events Leather Craft Public Speaking
Navigation Typewriting - B Short Hand

Tuesday, 6:00 - 6:30 - 7:30 - 8:30

First Aid Hygiene Elem. Arith. Business Arith.
Slide Rule Typewriting - G Elem. English
Communications Woodworking Music
Typewriting

Wednesday, 6:00 - 6:30 - 7:30 - 8:30

Chemistry Algebra American History
Civics Leather Craft Business English
Communications Camera Club
Typewriting - A Short Hand

Thursday, 6:30 - 7:30 - 8:30

Spelling Elem. Arith. Elem. English
Surveying Typewriting Business Arith.
Typewriting - C Woodworking

Friday, 6:30 - 7:30 - 8:30

Current Events Current Events Auto Mechanics[22]

Boxing was very popular at the Arcadia Camp. They had an outside boxing ring but during the winter set up a ring in the Rec Hall. Many disagreements were settled with boxing gloves.[23]

Sports

In the winter the Education Adviser scheduled different sporting activities at the Arcadia Camp. There was basketball, boxing, skating, ping-pong, and skiing. Bill Foley, who was on the Maine Ski Team, was teaching Telemark and Christiana ski techniques to the enrollees.[24]

In January, the basketball team traveled to Glocester to play the George Washington Camp at the Forester's Hall. The Arcadians lost 23-17.[25]

In March the Arcadian basketball team defeated the Charlestown team 49-8. The team came in second place for the season in the Western CCC League.[26]

Boxing matches with other CCC camps were postponed in January because the three opposing CCC camp teams refused to box at the Arcadia camp unless it had a regulation ring in the rec hall. Finally, ring ropes were ordered and matches were held.[27]

In the next couple of years beginning in 1936 Arcadia/Hope Valley, CCC Co. 1188 established itself as a premier forest fire fighting organization.

– 1937 –

Staff

Commanding Officer: Capt. Herbert Radcliffe
Adjutant: Lt. William. V. Lalli
Surgeon: Dr. Jachyn Davis
Education Adviser: John H. Crowell
Project Superintendent: Errol M. Tarbox
Foremen: Colgate Searle, James Woolley, Thomas Knox, Clarence Morancey, John Duffy, & Henry Hoxie

1188th COMPANY   P-54   HOPE VALLEY,

A group photo of some of the members of the Arcadia/Hope Valley CCC camp. Third CCC District First Corps Area Yearbook, 1937

Roster

CAPT. HERBERT E. RADCLIFFE, *Inf.-Res.*, COMMANDING   FIRST LT. JACHIN B. DAVIS, *Med.-Res.*, SURGEON
SECOND LT. WILLIAM V. LALLI, *Inf.-Res.*, EXCHANGE OFFICER   JOHN H. CROWELL, *CEA*
DR. RICHARD WOLSIEWICK, FRANK RACCA AND IRVING E. PODRAT, *WPA Instructors*

TECHNICAL PERSONNEL Errol E. Tarbox, Supt.; Thomas J. Knox, John E. Woolley, L. J. Denning, Charles H. Ladd, Clarence E. Morancy, James V. Rossi, Colgate M. Searle, John E. Duffy, Edwin J. Hoxsie.

LEADERS Joseph DeBartolo, Westerly, Rhode Island; Leo Debeau, Woonsocket, Rhode Island; Anthony Fellela, Jr., Providence, Rhode Island; William E. Fillo, Providence, Rhode Island John F. Power (L.E.M.), Providence, Rhode Island; Marcus Russo, Newport, Rhode Island; Russel A. White, Providence, Rhode Island.

ASSISTANT LEADERS J. Alves, Bristol, R. I.; E. Costa, Lonsdale, R. I.; G. Donnell, Pawtucket, R. I.; T. J. Foley, Providence, R. I.; A. Gentes, Providence, R. I.; H. S. Goodson (L.E.M.), Washington, R. I.; J. J. Hudson, Tiverton, R. I.; T. A. Kohut, Pawtucket, R. I.; T. F. Maher, East Providence, R. I.; F. Malone, Woonsocket, R. I.; A. H. Murray, Bristol, R. I.; T. P. Piwowarczyk, Holyoke, Mass.; C. F. Riley, Woonsocket, R. I.; G. J. Ventriglia, Providence, R. I.

MEMBERS

	Carbonetta, A., Providence, R. I.	Farland, J. E., Pawtucket, R. I.	Larkin, W. S., Westerly, R. I.	Miranda, A., Portsmouth, R. I.	Sheridan, E. J., Providence, R. I.
	Carley, F. B., Providence, R. I.	Ficket, E. F., E. Greenwich, R. I.	Lasch, N. A., Providence, R. I.	Moretti, C., Cranston, R. I.	Shread, C. H., Lakewood, R. I.
Andrade, A., Pawtucket, R. I.	Carter, R., Providence, R. I.	Gareau, A. J., W. Warwick, R. I.	Lavoie, G. J., Pawtucket, R. I.	Natalia, A., Cranston, R. I.	Silva, J. R., Apponaug, R. I.
Andrews, H. R., Jr., L'wood, R. I.	Caryoski, J., Providence, R. I.	Gent, R. D., Westerly, R. I.	LeHoullier, A. A., Pawt'cket, R. I.	Nugent, W. D., Westerly, R. I.	Silvia, F. A., Providence, R. I.
Appolonia, J. A., W. W'ck, R. I.	Cherenzia, N. D., Westerly, R. I.	Gingerella, S. A., Westerly, R. I.	Littlefield, E. G., Jr., James'n, R. I	Oskirko, L., Providence, R. I.	Simon, E. V., Hope Valley, R. I.
Autieri, J., Providence, R. I.	Chrupcala, M., C'tral Falls, R. I.	Goff, G., Pawtucket, R. I.	Lopes, I., East Providence, R. I.	Osofsky, J., Bristol, R. I.	Sisson, J. E., E. Greenwich, R. I.
Baluch, L., Central Falls, R. I.	Cimino, F., Providence, R. I.	Grace, T. L., Oakl'd Beach, R. I.	McCall, J. A., Hopkinton, R. I.	Palmer, F., Pawtucket, R. I.	Souza, J. J., Warwick, R. I.
Bates, E. C., Greenwood, R. I.	Cochran, E. M., Rockville, R. I.	Grandidge, J., Pawtucket, R. I.	McGannon, J. G., Pawt'cket, R. I.	Paola, J., Jr., Providence, R. I.	Spinney, A. M., W'k Downs, R. I.
Bator, E., Pawtucket, R. I.	Corcoran, M. M., N. P'v'ce, R. I	Grenier, P., Woonsocket, R. I.	Manchester, D. S., N. King'n, R. I	Perrone, J. J., Westerly, R. I.	Stamp, G. H., Providence, R. I.
Belliotti, M. E., Providence, R. I.	DeConto, J., Providence, R. I.	Gressak, A., Pascoag, R. I.	Mancini, F., Providence, R. I.	Perry, J. G., Newport, R. I.	Stephenson, A. J., P'vidence, R. I.
Blanchette, D. J., P'vidence, R. I.	DeLuca, J. J., Westerly, R. I.	Grogan, T., Pawtucket, R. I.	Mangiacapro, L., Providence, R. I	Pierce, W., Providence, R. I.	Stevens, J. W., E. P'vidence, R. I.
Blanchette, H. W., C'l Falls, R. I.	Dimsey, H. M., Lakewood, R. I.	Herbert, R. J., Oakl'd Beach, R. I.	Marino, D., Providence, R. I.	Pisaruk, G., Woonsocket, R. I.	Strzeak, E., Pawtucket, R. I.
Boisvert, M. P., C'tral Falls, R. I.	DiPippo, V. J., Cranston, R. I.	Johanson, O. F., Newport, R. I.	Masterson, G. F., Pawtucket, R. I.	Prete, A., Providence, R. I.	St. Saveur, A., W'nsocket, R. I.
Boucher, L., Central Falls, R. I.	Donelly, R. C., W. Kingston, R. I.	Johnson, W., Hillsgrove, R. I.	Mayo, J. B., Lakewood, R. I.	Radloff, P. W., Providence, R. I.	Sunday, J. S., Providence, R. I.
Bowen, S., Providence, R. I.	Dortch, G. M., Jr., Westerly, R. I.	Jordan, A. D., Hope Valley, R. I.	Medeiros, E., Providence, R. I.	Ricci, E. E., Johnston, R. I.	Sweet, F. E., Providence, R. I.
Brennan, E. J., Providence, R. I.	Dziedzic, W., Pawtucket, R. I.	Keenzel, J. E., Apponaug, R. I.	Meehan, J. J., Pawtucket, R. I.	Ripa, V. S., Newport, R. I.	Sylvia, H. J., Warwick, R. I.
Brown, H. J., Cranston, R. I.	Fagundes, M., Providence, R. I.	LaFleur, N. J., Pawtucket, R. I.	Meldren, E. J., Providence, R. I.	Rocchio, R. H. P., P'vidence, R. I.	(See back page for additional
Cabral, T., Pawtucket, R. I.	Fargnoli, F., Providence, R. I.	Lamka, J. W., Central Falls, R. I.	Miller, J. H., Newport, R. I.	Sanschagrin, N. G., Slocum, R. I.	names)

The Roster of the 1937 supervisors and enrollees at the Arcadia/Hope Valley Camp. The Technical Personnel are the LEM men. The Leaders are the enrollees that were chosen by the Army because of their leadership qualities and who received $45 a month. The Assistant Leaders were also enrollees and received $36 a month.[28]

A group of camp Arcadia/Hope Valley enrollees with possibly an LEM and an Army officer in the front row. The bugler seated far right had the job of waking up the camp at 6 am and also playing for the raising and lowering of the flag each day.[31]

Junior Foreman: Lester Denning

Teacher: Dr. Richard Wolsiewick, Frank Racca, Irving Podrat[29]

In March, Capt. Radcliffe assumed command of Co. 1188 and inaugurated a contest to spark competition among the barracks by giving a weekly prize to the cleanest and neatest. A banner was awarded to the winning barracks and weekend passes, too. This sparked other improvements to the barracks' "Spring cleaning" that included installing screens, painting, unsightly trees removed, grass planting, and other beautification projects.[30]

In September there were some Army changes. 1st Lt. Philip Haas: Company Commander; 1st Lt. J.E. Condron, Junior Officer; Lt. J.E. Menzies, Surgeon.[32]

Then in December Capt. F.D. Lindahl arrived and became the new commander and Lt. Haas became the junior officer.

Education

Camp Arcadia celebrated the 4th Anniversary of the CCC in March with an Open House that included tours of the camp for visiting parents, friends, and neighbors. There were refreshments in the mess hall and educational exhibits. Judge Stephen Casey spoke on the merits of the CCC, and Education Adviser, John Crowell, presented educational certificates for those students who had successfully completed courses during the past three months.[33]

The Vocational Interest Blank Test was given to most of the rookies to help determine what occupation the boys would be best suited for. Later other tests were administered, such as the Minnesota Clerical Test and the Minnesota Form Board Test, to see if the men were suited for clerical or mechanical work.[34]

In June a section of the rec hall was fenced off and made into a Reading Room. A writing table, chairs, reading lamps, books, and textbooks were received from Co. 1190 in Fall River, Mass. when it closed.[35]

By October the 20' x 30' Reading Room had comfortable chairs, two library tables, and three writing desks. The shelves were filled with over 2,000 fiction and non-fiction books and current periodicals. Enrollees enjoyed this quiet place to read and write.[36]

An enrollee is working in the wood & metal shop repairing a chain while two teachers are watching.[37]

Education Adviser Crowell and teacher Ladd prepared teaching materials to be used by the foremen who taught vocational classes in the summer of 1937. Classes were held on Monday evenings from 6-7 pm.[38]

WPA teachers Frank Racca and Dr. Richard Wolsiewick attended a summer school session on the 28th of June at Rhode Island College. The afternoon sessions were devoted entirely to adult education.[39]

The Summer Education Program began in June included these activities: varsity baseball, tennis, team rowing, life-saving, track, inter-barracks baseball & volleyball, softball, and horseshoe tournaments.[40]

The Education Dept. was happy to get a new film strip projector that was very helpful in the General Science class.[41]

Recreation

In March 1937 Mrs. Van Aken, State Director of Girls Activities for the N.Y.A., and several of her instructors volunteered to teach dance classes in the mess hall. These classes were in preparation for the next camp dance. Girls from several N.Y.A. chapters in Providence were to attend.[42]

Also in March, a crew began working on a new tennis court near the athletic field. Mr. Woolley was supervising the project. The boys were digging a foundation with the hope of securing enough cement for the court.[43]

Some members of the camp began collecting wildlife for observation and study in the Schoolhouse building. A small aquarium had pollywogs and goldfish. Other animals such as wood mice and turtles were collected.[44]

On June 10, 1937 forty girls from the N.Y.A. Camp in Quonochontaug (a beach community in Charlestown) were invited to the Arcadia Camp. They were first served supper in the mess hall. This was followed by a movie. At 8 pm there was dancing in the mess hall. Then favors were passed out to everyone. Dancing ended at 10:30 pm and the boys were sad because the N.Y.A. camp was closing for the season. The reporter from the camp newspaper wrote: "There were many close friendships formed between the boys and girls. But the best of friends must part sometime, so don't grieve too much boys, providing you have the addresses." [45]

In October, the rec hall was painted ivory and green and had a new glass bulletin board at its entrance. There was also a new ping-pong table, over-stuffed chairs, and divans for relaxing. "With a bright blaze in the fireplace, the rec hall is a popular spot. Bingo, ping-pong, pool, cards, checkers, music, and good-natured conversation make the evening pass all too quickly." [46]

On Oct. 20, 1937, the first dance of the fall was held at the Anthony Grange Hall. The N.Y.A. Orchestra from Providence provided the music. The Arcadians were happy that some of the local girls attended the dance. [47]

A Leaders' Club was established at Camp Arcadia on October 25th through the efforts of the new Company Commander, Lt. Haas. They had their first banquet in October at the Dial Restaurant. [48]

Also during October, Superintendent Tarbox and his crew moved a 20' x 30' building from the closed Nooseneck Camp in West Greenwich. They placed it on the camp trailer and moved it eight miles to the Arcadia Camp. The building was placed on a foundation and was used as a supply house. [49]

During the Fall sports teams were active again. The camp basketball team began practicing on the outside court, boxers traveled to Randolph, Mass. for matches, and the soccer team traveled to Beach Pond where they won 5-1. Other winter sports were touch football, hockey when the ponds froze, and pool in the rec hall. [50]

On Dec. 9th, Co. 1188 held a dance at the Anthony Grange Hall which 250 enrollees and their guests attended. During the intermission, Miss Ethel Holmes, daughter of WPA instructor Guy Holmes, performed a military tap dance and a waltz clog rhythm. [51]

A few weeks later the annual company Christmas Party was held on December 20th in the rec hall. A festively lighted Christmas tree adorned one corner of the room and Mr. Crowell presented the boys with gifts.

Ethel Holmes, her sister Helen, and Bernice Johnson provided tap dancing. Enrollees also provided tap dancing, harmonica solos, and carol singing. [52]

On December 20th, a convoy of 18 trucks under the supervision of forester Colgate Searles traveled to the CCC camp in Alps, NY to drop off 15 Army trucks. The trip to NY took two days and on the way the boys stayed overnight at CCC Co. 113 Camp in Chester, Mass. After sleeping and a big breakfast at the Alps camp, the boys drove straight home to their Arcadia camp. [53]

Projects

Here are some of the projects completed by enrollees during 1937:

- Construction of the 2-mile James Trail in the Town of Richmond
- Built three fish rearing pools in the Lafayette Fish Hatchery in North Kingstown. Camp Arcadia men were responsible for constructing a new well that had a flow of 70 gallons a minute. They also made improvements to the pond layout [54]
- Performed forestry improvement demonstration plots of 24 acres for three different owners in Hopkinton and Richmond
- Covered 4,000 acres doing gypsy moth control work in the town of North Kingstown and state lands owned by the Exeter School; also covered tracts of forests in South Kingstown and West Greenwich
- Blister rust control on approx. 4,000 acres in the west central portion of the Town of Exeter

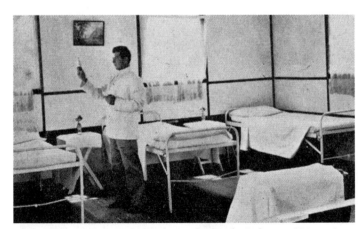

This is the attendant/orderly who worked in the Infirmary/Dispensary. He was trained by the camp doctor to help with minor injuries. He worked there day and night and had a separate bedroom. [56]

- Forest improvement work on 75 acres in the Wickaboxet State Forest in West Greenwich
- Fought and extinguished several fires in the surrounding towns [55]

– 1938 –

In January Dr. T.E.J. Carroll spent a few days at the Arcadia camp cleaning, pulling, and filling enrollees' teeth. This was one of the bonuses of joining the CCC, free dental care. [57]

Recreation

The monthly camp dance was held on Jan. 27 at the Anthony Grange Hall in Coventry. Young ladies from Arctic (in the center of West Warwick) and surrounding towns attended. Music was provided by the Hathaway Swingsters. The night before the dance, lessons were given in the rec hall by Mr. Holmes and Mr. Crowell. They were assisted by Ethel Holmes, Ilona Delancy, Helen Holmes, and Bernice Johnson. [58]

Each week the basketball team traveled to the Westerly Armory and played against National Guard members. At the rec hall, enrollees were competing in pool tournaments with the winner receiving a prize of five packs of cigarettes! [59]

Education

The Education Advisor, J.H. Crowell, continued to emphasize the importance of attending evening classes to achieve either elementary or high school equivalency certificates. In a February article in the camp newspaper Crowell said that only 2 out of every 100 young men in New England have a chance of securing a job if they do not have a grammar school certificate. He cited a survey of 500 New England employers who hired 15,547 men each year, and stated that 97% of the employers required a grade school diploma and 35% wanted a high school diploma. [60]

Crowell stated that by joining the CCC, enrollees were not only earning money to help their families but by attending evening classes they earned certificates. These certificates would help them when they went searching for employment.

In the spring members of the woodworking class, supervised by Mr. Becker, began a school building. This was a great learning experience for the young men and would benefit them when they searched for a job. The new building would have a reading room, education office, classroom, crafts shop, dark room, and a large workshop. [62]

The Spring Education Program included these classes: Agriculture, Landscaping, Woodworking, Typing, Photography, Leather Craft, Journalism, Literature (Book of the Month Club), Current Affairs, High School Equivalency, and Grammar School Equivalency. [63]

There were 50 members of the Book of the Month Club. The librarian of the Westerly Public Library, Miss Sally M. Cole, was very generous in lending enrollees books and the library also made frequent donation of books to the camp library. [64]

During the spring the Arcadians were busy with sports. The boxing team traveled to Quincy, Mass. for a tournament on March 24th. The ping-pong and pool

A proud group of young men at the Arcadia/Hope Valley wood shop where their works were displayed. [61]

Typing classes were very popular at the Arcadia/Hope Valley CCC camp in the town of Richmond. Third CCC District First Corps Area Yearbook, 1937

teams competed at the Beach Pond Camp.[65]

On April 4, Co. 1188 celebrated the 5th Anniversary of the CCC. An Open House was held for friends and family and tours were given of the 53-acre site. Track events were held in the afternoon. A dinner was held and Charles H. Cushman, Manager of the Westerly Branch of the State Employment Service, spoke on the achievements of the CCC. After dinner movies were shown and all had a great time.[66]

The monthly dance was held on Apr. 21st and was again held at the Anthony Grange Hall. A prize was given to the best waltz dancers: Norman Lavalee, the second cook, and his partner Miss Lena Gauthier. Refreshments were served at the intermission.[67]

In April Miss Sally M. Coy, the librarian at the Westerly Library, donated 75 books to the camp reading room. Reading was very popular at camp and during the month of March, 131 enrollees read an average of two books each.[68]

The woodworking shop received new equipment: a grinding machine, lathe, drill press, band saw, and two motors. The camp also purchased new hand tools and measuring instruments.[69]

In September, the Radio Class was going to obtain and assemble a shortwave receiver and sender. The boys would have to learn International Morse Code. The class had its own room in the School building next to the Educator's Office.[70]

Projects

In April enrollees began working on a tree nursery in back of the camp garage. Seven acres were plowed up and later 100,000 seedlings were received from a nursery and heeled into beds (firmly fixed with a back kick) and later to be transplanted. The Landscaping Class began working to improve the grounds of the camp. The Agriculture Class began planting radishes and lettuce. The Poultry Class began planning the purchase of chicks and hoped to make a profit selling the eggs and later market the meat. They also planned to visit farms in the area to learn about raising the chicks and possibly go into the business when they left camp.[71]

On August 23, the camp maintenance crew spent almost 11 hours pulling the 3½" pipe from the 573' well in order to replace the damaged foot valve. The reason

it took so long is that it was a heavy metal pipe. Today plumbers use lightweight plastic PVC pipe. After they finished the well work, the next project was installing a new water sterilizing system.[72]

The Hurricane, 1938

All of Rhode Island CCC camps were called into action following the devastation wrought by the September 21st "Hurricane of 1938." The hurricane hit on a Wednesday and on Friday the Governor of RI called the Washington/Putnam and Arcadia/Hope Valley camps and asked them to help the public utilities in removing the wires in the North Providence and Westerly areas that would help in restoring the telephone, light, and power. This was very important in helping the dairy farmers throughout the state who were dependent upon electricity in running their farms.[73]

Most of the work in the remaining weeks of 1938 and well into 1939 was devoted to rescuing salvageable timber for the lumber industry as well as getting all the public areas of the forests and parks back to order.

At the end of 1938, the Arcadia/Hope Valley Camp Co. 1188 left and the responsibility for their work went to Co. 1116-V. This company originated in Fort Belvoir, Virginia in 1933 as Co. 392. The 'V' indicated it was one of the 'Veterans' units. While most Americans applauded the concept of putting unemployed young men to work in the nation's woods and prairies, one of the remaining high unemployment groups was veterans of WWI and the 1898 Spanish American War.

The cooks, top row, were trained by the Army to serve approx. 200 meals three times a day. Their kitchen was a separate section of the Mess Hall. Their day started around 5 am when they began preparing for breakfast. The servers, bottom row, had the job of serving the enrollees and officers.[74]

"A Year Ago"
by A.E. Holburn, C.E.A.

[Author Note: This is an eyewitness description of what happened to the Hope Valley CCC Camp on September 21st, 1938. It was in the October 1939 issue of the camp newspaper, The Arcadia Veteran, a year after the hurricane.]

September 21, 1939 marks the first anniversary of the hurricane which resulted in the loss of many lives and the loss of millions of dollars worth of property to the citizens of RI. At that time, 1188 Company, a junior outfit under the command of Capt. Frank A. Lindhal, occupied this camp.

By the time the storm reached hurricane proportions, approx. 3:30 pm, all of the enrollees except the one small crew had returned to camp safely. It rained early in the afternoon of that fateful day but the company reported for the afternoon work call and were working on the several projects "when the hurricane "hit" this section of the state. It was shortly after three in the afternoon when the wind reached gale force. At this time the foremen assembled their crews and most of them returned to Camp. One or two crews experienced a little difficulty on this trip and were forced to make frequent stops to remove fallen trees and other debris from the road before being able to reach camp, and another crew of two enrollees with junior foreman Morancy were unable to reach camp until about 10 pm.

By the time the storm reached hurricane proportions, approximately 3:30 pm, all of the enrollees (except the one small crew) had returned to camp safely. The storm continued to increase in intensity. Trees about the camp were being blown down, telephone poles were being snapped off at the base, all power and the lines of communication were out and the roofing paper was being blown from the buildings.

At about 4 pm, Capt. Lindhal decided that it was no longer safe to allow anyone to remain in the buildings. He accordingly issued orders to kill all fires, evacuate all buildings, and assemble in the vicinity of the motor pool. All buildings were at once evacuated with the exception of the mess hall, where the mess steward and cooks remained as guards, and the dispensary, where the hospital orderly who remained to administer first aid to those who might require their services.

As the company was evacuating the barracks, the wind picked up the latrine and carried it to parts still unknown. Shortly after this incident it was decided to remove all Army and private vehicles from the Army garage (which showed signs of weakening). The enrollees worked like mad men clearing this building and just as the last car was being removed, the garage fell victim to the storm and was demolished. At this point it was actually raining saltwater. After seeing the Army garage destroyed, the forestry personnel held a "council of war" and it was decided to remove all of the forestry trucks from their garage to the nursery. This movement was accomplished with the minimum of confusion. Upon the completion of this task, all precautions had been taken for the protection of life and government property. The only thing that remained was to stand by and "weather the storm" as best we could. We watched the hurricane damage property in and about the camp. Hundreds of trees were uprooted or snapped off several feet above the ground and the telephone and power lines were completely demolished.

At about 7 pm, the force of the storm had diminished somewhat and Capt. Lindhal inspected the mess hall and ordered the cooks to prepare sandwiches and coffee. Since the power had been cut off, it was necessary to use kerosene lanterns and candles for light. "It was about 8 o'clock when 'chow' was served. No one was allowed to enter any of the buildings or eat in the mess hall. During the serving of the meal, a thorough inspection was made of all the barracks, by the C.C."[75]

The 1938 Veterans of WWI and Spanish American War Co. 1116 who lived in Barracks 2 in Vermont building a dam were called the "Concrete Company." In 1939 they were transferred to Arcadia where they did forestry projects at the Arcadia CCC camp.[76]

– 1939 –

After being organized at Fort Belvoir, the company became the 1116-V and went to Vermont to work on a number of river and reservoir projects designed to tame the rambunctious Winooski River. One of their big assignments was working on the construction of the Wrightsville Dam where they picked up the nickname the "Concrete Company."

The full year of 1939 was spent by 1116-V at Arcadia. In 1939 the Veterans in the Arcadia Camp traveled to the Goddard Memorial Park and planted several thousand white pine trees in an area that was destroyed by the hurricane.[77]

In the Arcadia Area, the Hope Valley Veterans planted 285,00 red pine, white pine, Scotch pine, and white spruce trees. These new forested areas were considered demonstration forests to show the public what can be done on this type of land.

The CCC Veterans of Co. 1116-V did work at the Arcadia Pond where the public was using the bathing facilities, picnic areas, bathhouse, fireplaces, and parking area. Workers were building roads and trails. The bathing facilities were to be opened in 1941.[78]

At the end of 1940 the Hope Valley camp closed. The Co. 1116-V was on the move again. It moved north to the George Washington Memorial Forest in Glocester.

By the early 1940s CCC camps all over the country were beginning to close as the war in Europe and diplomacy with Japan caused the bulking up of the United States Army and many CCC men exchanged

The Veterans produced a more professional newspaper than the 17-28 year-old boys. The cover was silk screened and the number of the pages were almost doubled in size and had quality written stories and illustrations. Rhode Island State Archives

one uniform for another. Since most of the 'V' company veterans were too old for combat, their companies were the last of the CCC units to disband.

LEGACY

Today, with more than 14,000 acres of the Arcadia Management Area is a significant presence in the towns of Richmond, Hopkinton, Exeter, and West Greenwich. More than 5,000 acres of its current holdings were marginal woodlands taken out of production by the United States Soil Conservation Service in the 1930s as a way to discourage their use in lumbering. Much of the CCC work of the Arcadia/Hope Valley CCC Camp, contributed to the improvement of the forest land in the Arcadia Management Area.

The Hope Valley/Arcadia CCC camp built many roads and trails that enabled fire fighters to get to fires that in the past were inaccessible. Enrollees built the 2-mile James Trail in the Town of Richmond; also trails to Rockville, Voluntown, Grassy Pond, Tefft Hill, and the Sessions Hopkins Trail. They constructed two truck trails: from the Boy Scout Camp at Yawgoog (Rockville) westward to the Connecticut border and from Rockville to Canonchet trail. They planted thousands of trees and helped fight the spread of blister rust and gypsy moths. They did forestry improvement work on 75 acres in the Wickaboxet State Forest. All of the Arcadia/Hope Valley CCC camp work created thousands of acres for people to enjoy hiking, hunting, fishing, camping, horseback riding, mountain biking, motor cycling, picnicking, swimming, and nature observation.

Directions

Use your GPS or map to locate the site of the Arcadia/Hope Valley Camp: Arcadia Management Area Headquarters at 260 Arcadia Rd., Hope Valley.

From Westerly: Take I-95 N and drive 10.37 mi. to Exit 3B toward Wyoming. Turn right and go W onto Main St. & Rt. 138. and go approx. .5 mi. Then turn right on Bridge St. just past Nooseneck Hill Rd. Go .24 mi. and turn right on Bank St. that becomes Arcadia Rd. Travel 2.2 miles. The DEM Office is on the left.

From Providence: Take I-95 S for approx. 20 miles to Exit 5A Exeter. Go E on Rt. 102 for 1.16 miles and turn right on Rt. 3/Nooseneck Rd. Travel 1.30 miles and turn right on Ten Rod. Rd/Rt. 165 W. Then go 1.46 miles and turn left on Arcadia Rd. that becomes KG Ranch Rd.

One of the many trails in the Arcadia Management area that travels through beautiful terrain are enjoyed by thousands of people each year. DEM

Go approx. .5 mi. and turn a slight right onto Arcadia Rd. The road will turn left and continue on Arcadia Rd. for approx. .3 mi. The DEM Office is on the right, the former site of Camp Arcadia.

MEMORIES

Colgate Searle, LEM

On August 15, 2017 I visited Colgate Searle Jr. at his landscape architect's office in Pawtucket. He told me about his father who had worked in the Civilian Conservation Corps as a supervisor in the 1930s.

"My father was born in Exeter, RI on June 19, 1905. His father was Andrew and his mother was Cora. They had two children: my brother Andrew and me.

"My grandfather had a few jobs. He was the

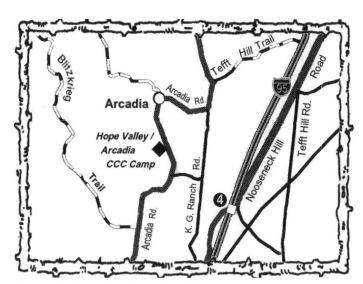

Hope Valley/Arcadia Map by Paul Hartmann

Colgate Searle worked as a LEM supervising CCC boys at the Hope Valley camp in Arcadia. Third CCC District First Corps Area Yearbook, 1937

caretaker of an estate and he was also a farmer and sold milk.

"My father only went as far as the eighth grade. For his last two years of elementary school he stayed with his aunts in Killingly, Conn. and went to school there because there wasn't a 7th and 8th grade in his town.

"After 8th grade he worked for his father on their dairy farm.

"He saved his money and in the 1930s bought a 100-acre farm on Rt. 3 in Exeter. Twenty acres of the farm were cleared and he raised chickens and vegetables. He also worked as a carpenter. He learned his carpentry skills when he was in about 8th grade and worked with a carpenter who built homes and additions.

"My father made a subsistence living. He also worked at the Weehoose Estate as a caretaker. It was at the same time that he built a house on his own farm.

"During the Depression he took a job as a supervisor in the Hope Valley CCC camp in Arcadia State Forest. He built an open-air pavilion [Dawley Memorial Park Shelter] off old Nooseneck Hill Rd. and did other projects by Browning Point and Mill Pond. He may have also worked on the Tefft Hill Trail.

"One day while driving with my dad, he showed me the stone foundation that was the base of the CCC camp. The CCC boys that he was working with were about 19 to 21 years old and they had never used a shovel or axe in their lives. He had to keep teaching them new skills all the time as they worked.

"After working for the CCC he was an inspector of trees that were damaged during the 1938 hurricane. He measured the wood that was damaged. It was during this work that he skinned his shins very bad and had to take 10 days off from work.

"In 1939 he got a job with the railroad. He ran a bulldozer for a New Hampshire contractor and did work on the railroad to Quonset Point. He laid ballast (crushed rocks) for the railroad tracks.

"In 1941 or 42' my father joined the Army Sea Bees. He built bases in the Pacific.

"When he came back from the war in 1945, he married Yvonne Rondeau. I have two siblings, Lucille and John. My father built another house on his farm for the people who worked for him. He also did part-time contracting and farm chores that included haying, raising six sows and beef cattle.

"In 1990 my father died at the age of 92."

William "Bill" Doran
Worked in Three CCC Camps

I attended a Christmas party at a writer's group in Salem, Conn. Where I met Elizabeth Yeznach, of Gales Ferry, Conn. She told me that her brother-in-law, Bill Doran of Norwich, was in the CCC in Rhode Island and he probably had some good stories to tell.

I contacted Doran at Ahepa Senior Housing on Hamilton Ave., in Norwich. Bill told me:

"I was at the Arcadia Company 1188 near Hope Valley on Rt. 3 on Beach Pond Rd. in 1937. I worked there for 1 year.

"We built roads through the woods and shoveled gravel into dump trucks. We built waterholes near springs to help fire fighters.

"On weekends we just sat around. There was one building with a pool table. Everyone got to learn how to play it well.

Colgate Searle supervised the Arcadia/Hope Valley CCC boys in constructing the Dawley Memorial Park log shelter. Walter Pidgeon

Gravel was an important product in building the roads in the Arcadia Area. These enrollees are busy with their picks and shovels in loading the dump trucks while the truck drivers watched from inside the cab. One is on top of the box watching. Sometimes they'd have contests to see what crew could load their truck the fastest.[79]

"The food was average. You worked in the woods all day and you had a good appetite. You took a mess kit with you to work and at lunch a truck brought you a hot meal.

"For recreation they had boxing smokers about once a month. Guys went from camp to camp to box. They gave the boxers 6-7 dollars for 'gas money.' They were amateurs and couldn't get paid.

"Some of the guys got injured in the woods because they used axes and saws. They took the seriously injured guys to the Fort Wright Hospital.

"If there was a forest fire, we carried Indian tanks and fought fires. You smelled of smoke when you were finished.

"On some Friday nights, we walked to the nearby town of Hope Valley.

"After the September Hurricane of 1938, we went to the Westerly Beach to help clean up. There was nothing left standing. You'd find a body and motion to state police. They'd get a door and carried the body off.

"Then veterans took over our Arcadia camp and our whole company was moved to East Jaffrey in the southwestern part of New Hampshire. It was near the Massachusetts border and two miles out of town. We were there in the winter and did the same jobs as we did in RI. We built roads and cut trees. We even used some trees for fill and put gravel over it for roads. It wasn't the best thing to do.

"For recreation we went to the high school for pickup basketball games.

"Then I dropped out of the CCCs for about six months. I rejoined again in 1939 and went to Charleston, RI and our camp was at Burlingame State Park.

"There was just a mud hole and we made a nice pond. We used to walk to Westerly on weekends for a grinder. There was nothing else to do.

"I was there for six months and I signed up again even though I had been in for two years which was the limit for enrollees."

I asked Bill to tell me about his early life and what he did after he left the CCC.

"I was born on September 22, 1919 in Bristol, RI. My father Joseph was a carpenter and my mother was Kathryn Taylor Doran. I attended local schools and graduated from Bristol High School.

"After I left the CCC I worked as a laborer for

The September 1939 cover of the Arcadia Veteran.

Union Local #547. Then I joined the Navy and was in WWII.

"Then after the war I married Alice (Jeznach) Doran. We had two sons, Frank Busch and William P. Doran, and two daughters, Joan and Nancy.

"The CCC really helped me and my family survive the Great Depression because I was able to earn money for my family."

Bill Doran died on October 4, 2012.

Ruby Wilcox

Hopkinton resident Ruby Wilcox said she can still remember when the CCC had a camp in the area.

"I was about 6 years-old and my father sold gravel to the state, The men would shovel and haul gravel away from my family's farm."

Camp newspapers consisted of practical information such as activity schedules, inspirational essays, as well as stories, jokes, and other news about camp life. A typical issue of The Arcadia Veteran contained about 30 pages of mimeographed copy with a screened color cover displaying art work depicting a theme appropriate to the month for example, Mother's Day for the May issue and Veteran's Day for November. Circulation of these publications generally was scaled for the size of the camp, although copies found their way home and out into the local community. Here are some excerpts from the Camp

Arcadia newspapers and some of the advertisement of local businesses that helped sponsor the paper.

"The Pioneer"
by Anonymous Enrollee

It was quite simple. Yes, indeed. The local relief administrator did want a lot of information, though. Lucky, I told him I had been unemployed for nine full months. The physical examination in the Providence Post Office, I thought was tough until later. The meal they gave us in the Providence restaurant was good, even though I did anticipate it to be the last good one. And the bus trip. I never knew so many "wise cracks" existed.

Having never seen a fort before, Fort Adams, was a treat. The soldiers on guard duty were, to me, outstanding. I'll never forget that "mill" I went through. I have been through the house of horrors, but that was tame. I would never attempt to list every channel in the mill of the fort. First, I passed a row of young clerks. One would swear to God they were Philadelphia lawyers. Inquisitive and morose.

The most joyful of my "rookie" daze, went the first few nights. "Short-sheet," "cornflake bed," and "latrine guard," I got all of them.

But now I'm a "veteran," a "pioneer." I can distinguish an LEM from a "politician." I know nine-tenths of the answers and one-tenth of the questions. I am on my fifth dead relative. I know that sick call is a habit and one degree above normal is a day off. I know that an inspector is an officer in distress, and that a forester is a man out of work.

I am a full-fledged member of the Civilian Conservation Corps.[80]

"K.P. Dirge"
by H.H.

Poor little me,
I'm a K.P.
I scrub the mess hall
On bended knee.
I wash the dishes,
Against my wishes,
To make these wild, wild woods
Safe for the C.C.C.[81]

"Not So Happy"
by Henry Sylva

Wandering through the woods one day,
I felt very jolly, happy, and gay.
I gazed and I stared at the silvery gleam,
I sang and whistled to the rippling stream.

I walked till I came to the top of a hill,
There I stopped and stood very still,
For a faint sound I did hear,
Turning I saw a wounded deer.

The poor thing lay there so
Helpless and still,
That doing away with his misery
Was against my will.

I had to do it
For it was nearly dead,
So I took a club
And struck its head.

One clout and he was done,
But doing it was no fun.
As his end came so shall mine,
But the end of this poem is all YOU will find.[82]

"Such Bashful Boys"
by Anonymous

"Oh, you're tough huh?"
"I'll paint your eyes black!"
"Oh yeah! I'll bash your face
"So that it will look like a squash pie."
"You think so, eh?"
Bang! "Take that!"
"All right let's get the gloves."

That's the way Sousa and Goff were going at it.
The fight was announced over the P.A.
Before you could say apple bottom,
Seventy-five men were gathered to see the great event.
But where were the boys and the gloves?
The boys I'm sorry to say were a bit bashful
To put on an exhibition in front of such a crowd of spectators.

So they shook hands and invited each other to a bottle of soda.

It just goes to show you,

That the spirit of friendship still marches on.[83]

"The Mess Kit Lifting Episode"

One bright chilly morning last month, a couple whose honey mooning days were a thing of the past, were motoring leisurely along a dirt road where members of the gypsy moth crew were working.

These men eat their dinner on the job. They had brought their mess kit with them and had left them at a convenient spot along the road.

It must have been the glare of the brightly polished G.I. hardware; at any rate the driver of the car suddenly applied his brakes, and engaged in a heated conversation with his wife, probably trying to decide the fate of the mess kits. They undoubtedly reached an agreement and the obliging husband went into action. He jumped out of the car, ran to the row of mess kits, stacked up all his arms could hold, and brought them to the car, and hurried back for the remainder.

It looked for a time as if they would make a clean sweep of the job, but such was not to be the case.

A lone member of the crew, backchecking, heard the excited voice of the wife as she urged her hubby to more speed. It didn't take him long to reach the scene of the attempted theft, and the culprit was unpleasantly surprised.

"I say there my friend:" said our hero. "Where are you going with those mess kits? Has it ever occurred to you that we might want those for dinner time?"

At those words the mess-kit picker dropped what he had in his hands and hastened to explain: "I thought they were just junk. I was going to sell them for aluminum."

His wife proceeded to put him in the bag by saying: "I thought they'd be nice for our children and us to use when we have picnics."

"I knew you would find them to be too good for junk," replied the lad, "but I didn't know you had twenty-five children."[84]

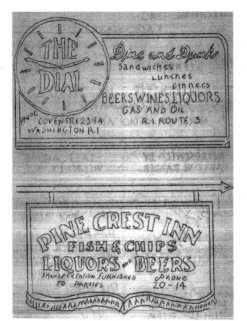
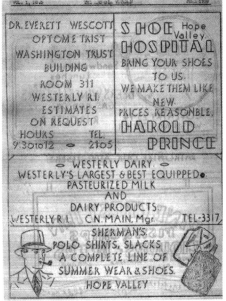
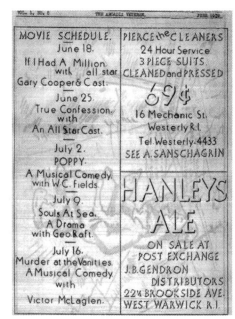

Local business ads in the Arcadia Veteran camp newspaper in 1940.

CHAPTER 8
KENT / NOOSENECK

HISTORY

There is very little information on the Kent/Nooseneck CCC camp but historian Albert Klyberg was able to glean this information:

On the 31st of March, 1933 a jobs bill was passed by Congress in Washington that would take unemployed single men to work in the forests of America. A week later a notice was printed in the Providence Journal newspapers that enlistments were open. Governor Theodore Francis Green (1933-1937) set out to produce a third CCC forestry camp since the first two were so oversubscribed that Rhode Island enrollees were being sent off to Maine and Vermont to work. Two thousand hopeful young men mobbed the facilities at the Providence Federal building filing their applications. Police had to be dispatched to quell the scene.

The third work site following on the coat-tails of Burlingame and George Washington Memorial CCC campsites, was on land in West Greenwich, on Nooseneck Hill Road (Rt. 3), that was leased to the program from the Rhode Island Bureau of Forestry. It was just north of the Richmond Town Line on Nooseneck Hill Road.

A handsewn Camp Kent/Nooseneck Company 195 emblem. Chris Jennings & Ann Perkin

After having basic training at Fort Adams, Company 195 arrived at the camp site on Nooseneck Hill Rd. on June 19, 1933. Enrollees spent most of the summer of 1933 transitioning from a tent town to wooden buildings. Carpenters were hired to do the construction of these buildings: administration building, four barracks, mess hall, recreation hall, infirmary/dispensary, garage, blacksmith shop, washroom, and other equipment facilities. Enrollees wanted to get out of the tents before the snow and winter came.

The Meaning of "Nooseneck"

Nooseneck is an interesting name that has had other meanings. West Greenwich lore suggests it came from the local Narragansett tribe's practice of stampeding deer towards the nearby Big River. The deer ran through a birch forest where the Indians hung nooses from the limbs at strategic heights to snag the deer. This hunt helped supply needed meat for the Indians for the coming winter.

Mathias "Matt" Harpin in his book, In the Shadow of the Tree, co-authored with Waite Albro, wrote that it has been spelled as two words and as one word, Nooseneck. "It has been attributed to an Indian derivation: 'at the place of the beaver.' It has also been associated with the Indian word 'Noozalogue' meaning 'beaver pond.'"

Another explanation can be found in J.R. Cole's History of Washington and Kent Counties (1889). He suggests it was named because of the narrow neck of land that lay between the two branches of Big River which had an elongated shape like a noose.

It seems that those who were in charge of naming the West Greenwich CCC camp refused to call it "Nooseneck" and chose Camp Kent, the name of the county it was in. Locals, however, called it the Nooseneck Camp because of the road it was on.

This postcard shows the Camp Kent Infirmary/Clinic. Clockwise top left: The enrollee attendant at his desk/table with medicines on the shelf; the fireplace that the attendant maintained for heat; the camp ambulance/truck that transported patients to the Army hospital at Fort Adams; and the outside view of the building with two doors. The attendant staffed the clinic 24/7 and had his own bedroom. There were usually 6-7 beds for patients and an Army doctor present. Hopkinton Historical Society

A 1939 aerial view of Camp Kent/Nooseneck in West Greenwich. There are four barracks to the left of the oval and the entrance is on Rt. 3, which is the diagonally running road from top to bottom to the right of the camp. The long garage is at the top of the photo. The other buildings are unknown but the building along Rt. 3 might be the Administration building.[1]

Projects

The Seventh Annual Report of State Department of Agriculture 1933 stated that: "Due to delays in obtaining equipment from the Federal Govt. little field work was accomplished before the middle of July, although the men were given training in camp life and in forestry work and were employed in constructing the camps."

Little is known as to what projects Camp Kent worked on since the state records do not mention the Kent camp specifically. Since it was a forestry camp run by the United States Forest Service these are the types of projects these camps performed: constructed truck trails, fire lanes, and waterholes, cleared and thinned forestry growths, maintained fire lanes, fought fires, and planted trees.[2]

After leasing the site of Camp Nooseneck in 1933, the Director of Agriculture and Conservation purchased a 15.36-acre plot in 1935 in West Greenwich.[3]

Kent's nearest and newest camp in 1935 was Beach Pond. For a while Beach Pond was the only camp run by the National Park Service with programs aimed at park development as opposed to forests and forest fighting. It was Beach Pond that worked on the Dawley Memorial Park just down the road from Camp Kent. The other nearby possible project convenient to Camp Kent was

the new Wickaboxet Forest in West Greenwich, but no record of their work there has surfaced as yet.

Sports

Even though there are very sparse records of Camp Kent, the author was able to find valuable information in the camp newspaper called The Nooseneck Tattler. During the summer the camp baseball team played nearby CCC camps and competed in the Pawtuxet Sunset League. During August, they played four games a week. There was also inter-barracks baseball competition with four of the five barracks competing. The fifth barracks was composed of the "camp overhead" and it was hoped they would enter for the second half of the season. In the fall enrollees had a camp soccer team composed of 25 players who practiced at Duff's Field.[4]

In the Fall of 1935, a "Smoker" was held at the Nooseneck CCC camp that drew approximately 300 spectators. Members of the Beach Pond Camp came and there were boxing and wrestling matches between the two camps. The event was organized by Education Adviser Edmund Howarth who also led the nine-piece camp orchestra between each of the bouts. The judges of the bouts were Colgate Searles of Camp Kent, Lt. Archie Lowe of Beach Pond, and a few referees from both camps. The announcer was the camp surgeon, Dr. Kudish. The event started at 7:30 pm and ended at 10:30 pm.

"Home-made doughnuts and coffee were served at the end of the matches to quench the parched throats and allay the hunger pangs following the strenuous exercise of pounding the fellows in front."[5]

The September 1935 issue of the The Nooseneck Tattler stated the camp was led by Lt. James L. Wiggmore, Superintendent Craig, and the Education Adviser Edmond Howarth.

Also in the September issue of the "Nooseneck Tattler" a Letter to the Editor entitled "Camp Improvement and Project Work" criticized the management of the camp. The writer stated: "Other Emergency Conservation Work Camps located on State Land have better managed and appearing campsites than our own. On these campsites drainage systems have been constructed, land graded and seeded, road improvement work carried on, and other outside and inside work all as regular work projects of the camp. This camp is now a static State reservation, and such work improvement projects could be done.

"It appears to me that Inspectors fail to realize the entirely different aspect 'camp improvement' work takes when done in a camp on private land. An inordinate amount of extra work is required of enrollees to repair damage to roads when washed out by rain. Also, the inordinate amount of work to try to even parallel the appearance of some camps more fortunately situated.

"Further, if the project of camp improvement became an 'Approved ECW Project,' in reality, the camp commanders would be relieved of that worry of constantly nagging the men into extra work. Camps now operate under the old system 'Camp Improvement'

details, might be more reasonably and fairly compete for the title 'Best Camp in the Fourth CCC District' or 'Best Camp in the First Corps Area.'"

During the month of October, Camp Kent had two important visitors. On Oct. 1, 1935 Robert Fechner, ECW Director, made a brief 15-minute visit. He was followed by Maj. Gen. Fox Conner, the commander of the First CCC District. He gave a thorough inspection of the records and camp and seemed to be pleased at what he saw.[6]

Education

Just as the camp was to be closed the Education Adviser announced the opening of the new camp library. Enrollees were busy signing out books for education classes that were about to begin. The classes covered elementary, vocational, and high school subjects. Here is a list of the classes: Electricity, Carpentry, Drafting, Road Building,

The Nooseneck Tattler was the monthly Camp Kent/Nooseneck newspaper that was written & illustrated by the enrollees under the supervision of the Education Adviser.

Enrollee Vin Gormley dressed up in camp uniform and at right by the garage door wearing work clothes. Hopkinton Historical Society

Botany, Forestry, English, Spelling, Mathematics, Arithmetic, Letter Writing, First Aid, History, Civics, Typewriting, Geography, and Americanization.[7]

On Thursday, Oct. 10, 1935 the camp held its last dance at the Anthony Grange Hall.[8]

Camp Kent closed in October of 1935. Formal reports in the RI First Annual Report of the Department of Agriculture and Conservation simply say that with other camps (Arcadia, Beach Pond/Escoheag, Greene/Mount Vernon, and Primrose) coming online, and with the limit in Rhode Island to be six camps, Camp Kent was the easiest to let go in terms of the overall state program of forest work.[9]

The 1939 Rhode Island Department of Agriculture and Conservation Report stated that the former site of the Noose Neck CCC camp the: "…buildings of which are now used as project headquarters of the National Park Service."

LEGACY

The Kent/Nooseneck CCC camp was a forestry camp under the direction of the United States Forest Service. Enrollees worked on these types of projects: constructed truck trails, fire lanes, and waterholes; cleared and thinned forestry growths; maintained fire lanes, fought fires, and planted trees. Without the help of Camp Kent, the forest would not have been improved and protected from forest fires. These camp projects helped in the improvement of both state and private lands.

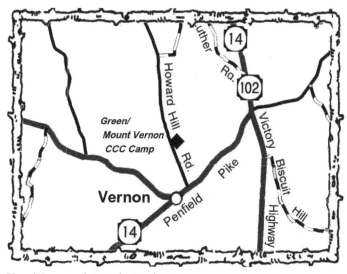

Kent/Nooseneck Map by Paul Hartmann

Directions

Use your GPS to locate the Nooseneck Campsite that is at: Lineham Family Learning School, 859 Nooseneck Hill Rd., West Greenwich, RI.

From Westerly: Take I-95 N and travel 16.5 miles to Exit 5A toward North Kingstown. Turn left on Nooseneck Hill Rd./Rt.3 and go N for 1.3 mi. The Lineham School is on the left side of Rt. 3 and the campsite to the right and in the woods.

From Providence: Take I-95 S for approx. 22 miles. Take Exit 6 toward West Greenwich/Coventry Rt.3. Turn left onto Nooseneck Hill Rd/Rt.3 and travel 3.3 mi to the Lineham School on the left side of Rt. 3.

Just behind the Lineham sign is the entrance to the Kent/Nooseneck CCC camp. The right photo is a cement hatch cover that was found in the woods. The cover might have been for the Mess Hall kitchen grease pit. All of the camp buildings are gone. Podskoch

MEMORIES

West Greenwich Historian Roberta Baker introduced me to an author on the history of her town. Mathias "Matt" Harpin in his book, In the Shadow of the Tree, co-authored with Waite Albro, had firsthand experiences of the CCC camps in West Greenwich and Escoheag. Matt wrote: "I remember those places well. I was just beginning my career as a journalist on the Providence Journal and wrote hundreds of stories about the service [CCC]. I had occasion to spend hours with the men, ...and ride to and from the fields with them, and watch them work. They bridged streams, dug water holes, and opened fire lanes, hence providing accessibility to large areas of isolated woodland. There was a lot of such woodland in West Greenwich and Exeter. CCC work was the salvation of the thousands of acres of submarginal land, cut over forest districts, and abandoned farms rapidly going back into woodland.

"The list of CCC major projects is too long to be given here. Trucks loaded with men in olive green garb and wide-brimmed cloth hats set out each morning with trained technicians and lunch kits and returned late in the afternoon. It was a sight to see the men, their cheeks aglow and hungry as bears. The meals that awaited them were not skimpy either. From red hot kitchen ranges there was delivered delicious food of excellent quality and in wide variety. A youth learned a lot at camp. All kinds of opportunities came to prepare himself for the future.

"Most of the boys arrived in camp without a goal in life and returned home months later filled with renewed faith in the future and body and mind strengthened by months of rugged outdoor life.

"Many young men came to camp illiterate and were taught to read in addition they were taught good manners, American History, motor mechanics, photography, journalism, gardening, masonry, radio, and hundreds more of subjects.

"One of the rules was to develop in each man his power of self-expression, self-entertainment, and self-culture. Books on every conceivable subject were delivered to the camp by the truck load. Ditto for magazines and newspapers.

"Men did not all come from the ghetto. Some were from the upper class. I remember chatting with a man in the recreation room. He was reading a Popular Mechanics magazine and [he] was working on an invention that could make him a millionaire again. Before I left he showed me a cashed check for one million dollars that he had once been given in payment of a debt.

"Discipline was not a problem. A man shaped his own career among the men, and if he fell out of line, spelled his own destiny. Even so the camp director had his particular problems. Crime among so large a corps of men was not the biggest problem. Cocaine was an unknown subject here. For the most part all the men were happy and hated to leave. Life-long friendships were made. In short, the CCC was so good that when it expired it was a great loss to the nation. Most people considered it one of the best things to come out of the dark days of the Depression.

"The town [near the camp] benefited immensely from the projects carried out by the CCC. They built plank bridges, opened trails, cleared streams, created water holes to impound water from which fire trucks could pump water to fill tanks for use against fires.

"Many a family caught with inadequate food in the winter, was supplied by the men of the Triple C.

"People in the western Rhode Island area could look back on work valued at millions of dollars when the CCC program came to a close."

Here is a story about a son, Mike Wilk, who is longing to find out where his father spent his time working in a CCC camp in Rhode Island. Follow his quest.

A Quest for CCC Information on Father

I first met Mike Wilk on April 18th, 2009 at the Sterling Historical Society, Connecticut at one of my CT CCC talks and he asked me if I had any information on CCC camps in Rhode Island because his father worked in one. He wanted to find it and see if he could get more information on the camp. I told him I knew nothing about them and suggested he write to St. Louis where the Army records were kept on CCC enrollees. He should ask for his father's "Discharge" papers. The papers would tell him where his dad was, when he joined, what he did, and when he was discharged. I figured I was so busy doing research on Connecticut camps that I'd never get to doing a book on RI camps.

I then got this email from Mike Wilk on July 21, 2009:

Edward Wilk joined the CCC in 1933 and was assigned to the Kent Camp. He is standing in front of one of the tents where he and other enrollees lived. He is holding a ukulele for entertainment. Mike Wilk

"After these many weeks I have obtained information from the St. Louis records center. I learned that after serving the first three months in the CCC at Fort Adams, RI, my father then served the next six months at CCC Camp Kent in Washington, RI. My goal is to find the location of the former Camp Kent and walk the grounds which my father walked in 1933.

"I find that Washington, RI is not a town but a village in the town of Coventry. I emailed the Coventry, RI librarian and also emailed and phoned the Coventry Historical Society. Today, I received the reply that they have no information on Camp Kent.

"Thank you again for your suggestion of my writing to St. Louis. I learned that my father sent home $12.50 to his mother and $12.50 to his father. I learned the names of his Commanding Officers and that after he was discharged in September 1933, transportation was furnished for him from Washington, RI to Providence, RI. I received a copy of his oath of enrollment containing his signature signed in 1933.

"I have always believed that he attended the RI School of Design after WWII on the GI Bill, but in reading the papers sent from St. Louis, I see that his attendance at that school occurred before he joined the CCC. What a surprise."

On July 31, 2013 Mike Wilk wrote again and sent this email:

"What an adventure in trying to find the location of my father's RI CCC Camp Kent. It took more than a year. Long story short...thanks to a 1930s newspaper article in the Providence Journal, the help of the RI Historical Society, and the help of a kind lady at the West Greenwich Library, the location of Camp Kent is found to have been at the current site of the Lineham Elementary School on Nooseneck Hill Road in West Greenwich, RI. Looking around the site the only artifacts from Camp Kent I found was a small pile of cement slabs. Across the street from the site, and a short distance North up the road, is the Big River Management Area, a public forest. I assume that forest is where the CCC guys from Camp Kent worked.

"The search for Camp Kent resulted in finding artifacts from other RI CCC camps including three and possibly a fourth CCC chimney, a small CCC stone incinerator, an elevated CCC water tank with its external glass tube to indicate the water level in the tank, still intact, not broken by vandals, and the jewel of the finds, the location of a large CCC mess hall with the chimney and cement elevated stove/cooking area still there.

"Visiting the CCC Museum in Stafford Springs, CT a few times, I was disappointed in how little they have on RI CCC camps. They did have a group picture of the CCC guys at Camp Kent but it was taken two years from when my father was there."

Another email came from Mike again on January 15, 2014.

"In reviewing the papers received from St. Louis, I see that my father first served in the CCC at Fort Adams, RI 4/28/33 to 6/16/33 – Disbursing Officer, Captain G.W. Cooke.

Then Camp Kent 6/17/33 to 9/30/33 – Disbursing Officer, Major F.E. Parker.

Discharges 9/30/33, Camp Kent, because of completion of term of enrollment – Captain George F. Davis, 13th Infantry."

Mike's search continued:

"A quote from an email from the Rhode Island Historical Society Library, 121 Hope Street, Providence, RI 02906: 'According to an article in the April 1, 1934 Providence Journal, page E2, there were three CCC camps in Rhode Island. One known as Camp Washington, was in the George Washington Memorial Forest in Glocester, the second was in the Burlingame reserve in Charlestown, and the third was at Nooseneck Hill in West Greenwich. No name is given in the article for the latter two camps, and no numbers are mentioned...my guess is that Camp Kent was the one at Nooseneck Hill, which goes through the Big River State Management Area' - Ms. Lee Teverow 2/23/11.

"After talking to an Andy Marchesseault at your CCC talk in Sterling, CT, I received an email from him days later. He took an interest in my trying to find the location of Camp Kent. He wrote, 'I emailed the RI DEM and they replied with they're not being positive but thinking that there was a CCC camp just outside the Big River Area back in the 30s. A chimney stood in the woods near the Lineham Elementary School until 2006 when it was removed due to safety issues."

Then Mike finally knew where his dad's camp was. He then traveled to the site but there were no buildings just a few pieces of concrete. "I now had a chance to walk the area that my dad lived and worked in 1933." His search was over.

Mike Wilk told me: "My father was born in February 1914 in Central Falls, RI. His parents were Stanley and Mary Wilk. My father was one of 10 children. Dad had one year of high school. He had a few jobs after he dropped out of school probably to help his family. One of his jobs was a jewelry worker, which was pre CCC. The jewelry industry was big in RI back then. It employed many RI residents. As a boy, I've seen various dies to make jewelry which he had and rings which he made. He must have been in a course at the RI School of Design which was more of a 'hands on' course in the design and production of jewelry. I remember his having a sketchbook, which he had at the RI School of Design, which contained his drawings of jewelry.

"After serving in the CCC from April 28, 1933 he was honorably discharged on September 30, 1933. A fact which you found interesting which I told you years ago was that the allotment, which was sent home, was split, $12.50 to his mother, Mary, and $12.50 to his father, Stanley.

"After the CCC he worked as a jewelry worker, truck driver, and at that point in time, an auto mechanic for 3 years.

"Then he served in the U.S. Army during WWII. After the war, he got married to my mom, Alice and they had two children. He continued working as an auto/truck mechanic. He had his own garage until 1960 when he took a job as a trucking fleet mechanic until he retired.

"The greatest gift he gave me was teaching me how to repair cars. I figure I've saved close to $30,000 lifetime in doing my own car repairs and maintenance. My father died in 1982."

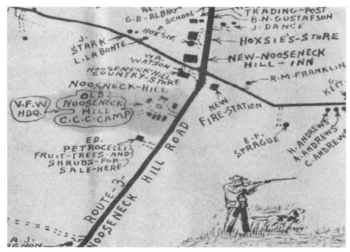

Mike Wilk and I came across a town map in the West Greenwich Library and it showed exactly where the Kent Camp was, on Nooseneck Rd. West Greenwich Library

Edward Wilk during retirement. Mike Wilk

CHAPTER 9
PUTNAM / WASHINGTON

A May 1939 photo of the Washington CCC camp in front of the garage. Glocester Heritage Society

HISTORY

In March 1933 the Emergency Conservation Work program of President Roosevelt passed Congress and three Civilian Conservation Camps were established in Rhode Island in May and June. Camp Washington Company 142 was the second camp. The Army called it the Putnam camp. This was strange because Putnam wasn't in RI but in nearby Connecticut.

Chepachet historian Edna Kent suggests that there are two reasons for the Army designating the camp in the George Washington Memorial Forest in the town of Glocester, RI as the Putnam camp. The first reason is that the Glocester's post office was about 6 miles east of the camp and Glocester's mail route (RFD or Star Route) did not go as far as the CCC camp. The Army decided to use the post office in the hamlet of Hawkins' Village that was closer approx. 2.5 miles west of the camp. Even though Hawkins' Village was in the Town of Glocester, their mail route traveled to the Putnam Post Office. A second reason for designating Putnam as the camp's name was the New York & New England Railroad station was in Putnam and most of the shipping of supplies in those days traveled by rail. Although the Army named it the Putnam camp, the locals and CCC boys all referred to the camp as 'Camp Washington.'"

[Author Note: To avoid confusion I will refer to the camp as 'Camp Washington'.]

Camp Washington S-52 was established on June 1, 1933 when Company 142, under the command of Capt. Prindle, arrived from Fort Adams. The S in the camp number meant that it was located in a state forest. The reservation was located in northwestern Rhode Island on the banks of the Bowdish Reservoir (AKA Bowditch). The land was donated by a women's organization as a memorial to George Washington. The Washington CCC

Capt. Prindle the head of the Washington Camp posing with two enrollees. Roland N. Bisaillon (1933-34) Robert Bisaillon

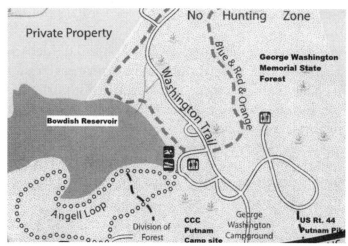

The site of the Washington CCC camp was located between the present-day Rhode Island Department of Environmental Management (RI DEM) Division of Forest Environment Office (2185 Putnam Pike, Chepachet) and the entrance road to the George Washington Campground both on Rt. 44.[2]

The Edgewood Women's Club

RI Historian Albert Klyberg received this information from the Rhode Island Historical Society Archives: "The Edgewood Women's Club was founded in Rhode Island in 1903 for the purpose of 'mental and social culture, and the promoting of educational, literary, and benevolent objects.' The club adopted the motto: 'Nothing great is ever achieved without enthusiasm' (Ralph Waldo Emerson). Upon its inception, the club's membership was limited to one hundred members, with an annual 'tax' of $1.00. In later years, membership was extended, as were the annual dues. At several times during its existence, the Edgewood Women's Club was a member of the State Federation of Women's Clubs, the Rhode Island Council of Women, and participated as a section of the Needlework Guild of America. Each year, the club made donations to numerous local and national charitable organizations, and in later years, provided an annual scholarship to be granted to a young woman enrolled at the Rhode Island State College, which was later renamed the University of Rhode Island. During the two World Wars, the club participated in Red Cross activities, sold 'war stamps', and supported military and Veterans' functions. Other general club activities included dramatic, comedic, and musical performances, educational lectures and programs, as well as regular outings and dinners. The club was dissolved in 1993, in its ninetieth year, after a period of decreased participation. In honor of the club's ninetieth anniversary, a formal luncheon was held as the Edgewood Women's Club's final function."

The Edgewood Women's Club donated money to establish the Rhode Island's first state forest as a memorial to George Washington in 1932. The Putnam CCC camp was established in part of the forest and today the George Washington Memorial Forest has a state campground and hiking trails. RI DEM

camp was located at the site of the George Washington Memorial Forest on Bowdish Reservoir off Rt. 44 in the Town of Glocester.[1]

Company 142 lived in tents while Lt. Merrick supervised the construction of permanent camp buildings: barracks, mess hall, infirmary/dispensary, rec hall, garages, etc. Later, Lt. N.A. Peavy was in charge of the improvement of grounds and buildings.[3] The camp was set amid a dense grove of oaks making it cool in the summer. There was an attempt not to carelessly remove trees. Although the Army called the camp Washington the enrollees called it Camp Washington.

Projects

Camp Washington was a forestry camp under the direction of the United States Forest Service and its work concentrated on various reforestation projects.

Superintendent Arthur C. Cole was in charge of projects for the camp. Work projects began on June 1st and were confined to the reservation. Camp Washington supplied manpower for the RI Department of Agriculture's efforts to eradicate gypsy moths and control the spread of white pine blister rust. They also began cutting fire trails needed in fighting forest fires, building waterholes, scoping out a site for a fire tower, the start of a telephone line, surveying boundary lines, and general cleaning and thinning forest growth.[4]

Work projects gradually expanded beyond the reservation and covered all of northern RI. Enrollees also traveled approx. 35 miles to Goddard Park, in East Greenwich where they built fireplaces.[5] The George Washington CCC crew also pruned limbs and removed deadwood from a 1912 pine plantation. They also traveled to East Greenwich Bay in the south and worked.[6]

The newly constructed Administration Building. Roland N. Bisaillon (1933-34) Robert Bisaillon

The Infirmary/Dispensary was near the headquarters building with the water tower in the rear. Glocester Heritage Society

Education

Rhode Island camps realized the importance of providing education for the boys since most of the enrollees only had an eighth-grade education. In the fall of 1933, the Army had officers and foresters conduct classes.[7]

– 1934 –

In 1934 the Army had an official nationwide education program for all the camps and an education advisor was hired for each camp.[8]

Projects

The Eighth Annual Report of the Department of Agriculture, 1934 reported that the CCC under the Emergency Conservation Work program erected four new fire towers bringing the total of towers in RI to nine. One of the four placed in service in 1934 was in the Wickaboxet State Forest. Three of the four towers constructed by the Washington camp in 1934 did not go into service till 1935. One tower was in the George Washington Memorial Forest in Glocester. This tower would later be moved in 1937 to Escoheag Hill in Exeter. Another tower was on Buck Hill in Burrillville. These towers were helpful in the early detection of forest fires and helped to reduce the number of destroyed acres of forests. The RI towers cooperated with two towers in nearby Massachusetts and one tower in Connecticut.[9]

Albert Klyberg wrote: "Until 1935, with the arrival

of four additional camps, Camp George Washington's forest work, which included timber stand improvement, the creation of truck trails for forest fire suppression, water hole construction, and blister rust eradication extended throughout all of the northern Rhode Island and as far south as Goddard Memorial State Park on East Greenwich Bay."

– 1935 –

Projects

The 1935 January Session of the Thirtieth Annual Report of the Metropolitan Park Commission reported that the Washington Camp worked at Lincoln Woods in the northeastern section of RI where they reconstructed about ½ mile of Olney Road. They widened it to twenty feet and surfaced it with 8 inches of gravel. They worked with crews from the Civil Works Administration (CWA) and Emergency Relief Act (ERA).

Once the camp at Primrose in N. Smithfield was established in June 1935, the Washington camp

Enrollees Al & "Goosy" by an Army Chevrolet stake-body truck with canvas top that protected enrollees from inclement weather. Roland N. Bisaillon (1933-34) Robert Bisaillon

concentrated its work in the northwestern part of the state and the river valleys that separated Rhode Island from eastern Connecticut.[10]

In his research of the George Washington Camp, Albert Klyberg stated: "It was frequently cited for innovations that were adopted for the entire New England Region. A book-keeping practice for accounts in the Canteen is one example. Another was its introduction of educational programs both for enrollees addressing remedial needs and also promoting conservation ideas to visiting groups that used its educational building on the shore of Bowditch Reservoir. It is now in the camping section of the forest. This facility, still standing, can accommodate 100 people for meetings, has a large fireplace, and, once, a fully-furnished kitchen. It was available to community groups for events during the CCC years, provided they were willing to hear a talk on modern forest conservation practices."

Rhode Island camps were among the first to stop working with just hand saws when they moved to using power saws (buzz saws) for making cordwood. The Washington supervisory personnel were complimented for this innovation by Major General Fox Conner, Commander of the First Corps.[11]

Recreation

In the December 16th, 1935 issue of the camp's monthly newspaper The Washingtonian it reported that on Thursday, Nov. 14 the La Salle Dramatic Society directed by Brother B. John presented two one act comedies. The members were so impressed by the polished performance of the group that they asked the administration to start their own dramatic group.

In November, the basketball team began practicing at the Big Cedar Inn. They also got some practice playing a high school team, the Pascoag Maroon Seconds (village in Burrillville). Co. 142 basketball team played in a league of six Rhode Island CCC camps.[12]

The basketball team had its first game of the season on Dec. 18 at the Foresters' Hall in Arctic. When they arrived, however, the opposing team didn't show and the Washington team won by forfeit. The boys were upset that they had to drive all that way without playing a game.[13]

Education

The first issue of the new camp newspaper The Washingtonian debuted in December 1935. It replaced the Pine Tree News.

The Dramatics Club presented a one-act play entitled "Guppy's Folks" on Dec. 19th. The play was directed by Foreman Bob Tetu who had plans to do more plays in 1936.[14]

Camp Improvements

July: New Army and forestry Mess Hall

August: Built walks and benches on the knoll

December: Constructed truck grease stand; redecoration of Army and forestry quarters

The August 31, 1937 issue of The Washingtonian camp newspaper showing an enrollee leaving camp and going out into the world a better person.

There was a large cook staff headed by the Mess Officer or Sergeant (Top row, 2nd from left) who was either in the Army or a Leader. He was responsible for ordering food, storage, menu planning, and the supervision of workers and mess hall. Glocester Heritage Society

– 1936 –

Staff

Commander: Lt. Newell A. Peavey

Mess & Canteen Officer: Lt. Phillip D. Thayer

Camp Physician: Dr. Benjamin L. Nadelman, MD

Superintendent: Arthur C. Cole

Assistant Super: George Anderson

Foresters: Joseph Burns, Stanton Cull, Willard Hall, George Holleran, Thomas Knox, Robert Tetu, and Fred Whitcomb.

Truck Master: George Bell [15]

There were a few improvements in the camp in January. An addition to the mess hall provided space for a more equipped ice box and larger supply room. A work crew tore out the old kitchen floor and installed a new cement floor. The arrangement of the mess tables was changed to two rows running the length of the room that allowed for three aisles one of which was for the men to line up inside before meals instead of standing outside. Work on a new latrine was postponed due to cold weather. [16]

The February 11, 1936 Washingtonian reported the new latrine was completed. It was well insulated and had good ventilation. It also had a well-stocked library of magazines and books. "It will make an ideal hangout in sub-zero weather for the goldbrickers. But the administration will see to it that there will be no congestion of traffic in the aisles."

Education

During the 1936-37 Winter, the National Youth Administration (N.Y.A.) of RI scheduled speakers for Camp Washington. The first was L. Ralston Thomas of the Moses Brown School in Providence, on Jan. 9. [17]

Raymond Tolbert of the U.S. Forest Service gave a lecture to 15 enrollees from camps Washington, Primrose, and Mt. Vernon on Jan. 15th at the Cranston St. Armory in Providence. On the return trip to camp, The Washingtonian newspaper reported: "In the drowning rain, but snugly covered under watertight tarpaulins, the boys returned to camp. A couple of unfortunates who slipped across the street to guzzle an ice cream soda, were left behind. The penalty of their indiscretion was a long trek back to Glocester largely afoot. They couldn't find a taxi driver who would extend them a line of credit. However, in spite of these mishaps the lecture was enjoyed by these that ventured forth on this miserable night." [18]

The next lecture was on Monday, Jan. 13 at which Brown University wrestling coach, Richard Cole, spoke on his trip to the Olympic Games in Los Angeles four years ago. Then he showed several movies some of which were in slow motion that showed his Brown team in action in 1932. [19]

On the 23rd W.H. Cotter of the RI Dept. of Ag. & Conservation gave a talk on bacteriology and chemistry. [20]

The last lecture in January was on the 30th that featured H.F.A. North of the RI College Experimental Station who gave a lecture on "Grasses." [21]

The February lectures started on the 6th with Alonzo Quinn, Instructor of Geology at Brown University, who spoke on glacial deposits in RI. He used lantern slides to show the great ice cap that thousands of years ago covered all of New England and removed an immense amount of boulders and soil. [22]

The camp Library had a good supply of books, magazines, and newspapers. Many of the books were donated by local libraries and organizations. It was also a quiet place to write letters for family, friends, or girlfriends. Glocester Heritage Society

The Washington Recreation Hall (c.1933-34) with a baby grand piano that was used by the enrollees and for entertainment programs. Two enrollees are seated in Adirondack chairs and enjoying the warmth of the wood burning fireplace. Roland N. Bisaillon (1933-34) Robert Bisaillon

Army Chaplin Nuzum made his monthly visit in February and brought five movies some of which were cartoons and others were educational. He also gave a straight talk on the evils of drunkenness, gambling, and licentiousness.[23]

Educational films were shown bi-weekly in the rec hall during February. By the end of the month, approx. 40 were shown. One week ice cream was served at the end of a showing and the attendance swelled that night.[24]

On January 27, the Dramatics Club was formed with the title "The Washington Forest Troupers." Then on February 4th they presented their first play "Crime Conscious" in the rec hall. The organization had 13 members.[25]

The Dramatics Club led by Forester Bob Tetu spent January practicing plays for the coming year. The group was scheduling performances with church and club organizations in Pawtucket.[26]

A Catholic retreat was held on February 5-6 with Fr. Greenan. There were morning and evening services and confessions.[27]

The first Spelling Bee was held at camp in February and 29 people entered. A large crowd watched the contest. The contestants were vying for the top prizes of two cartons of cigarettes: 1st place won five packs, 2nd four packs, 3rd three packs, 4th two packs, 5th-10th each one pack. During the first round all contestants made it but as the words got harder the boys dropped like flies. There was hope that other contests would be held in the future.[28]

The Washington Forest Troupers were busy during February. They performed "Crime Cautious" at the Primrose camp on the 10th and at the Douglas, Mass. camp on the 13th. (The Washingtonian, Feb. 22, 1936, 5.) On Feb. 26, the Troupers traveled down the road to nearby Harmony and entertained the PTA in the hall of the new school building. After the play the camp Hillbilly Orchestra led by foreman Stan Cull provided music for a dance. All enjoyed the entertainment.[29]

The Providence Journal ran a favorable story about the education and recreation programs at Camp Washington in its Saturday, February 22nd issue. It also included photos of activities at the camp.[30]

On the next Friday the Troupers, stage-hands, production managers, stage door Johnnies, and Hillbilly Band traveled to the Providence YWCA. It was the first time an all-male group entertained at the Y. The Camp Washington entertainers were invited by Mildred E. Lister of the N.Y.A. This gig spurred the boys to develop another play and the adventure of acting and traveling.[31]

The Educational Program in February had a large number of teachers and wide selection of classes. There were four WPA teachers along with members of the camp staff. Here are some of the courses: Metal Work, Modeling, Freehand Drawing, Pastel Drawing, Elementary Electricity, House Wiring, Wood Carving, Elementary Reading, Writing, Arithmetic, Leather Works, Typing, Business English, Commercial Law, Commercial Arithmetic, Marine Engineering, High School Math, German, French, Algebra, Tree Surgery, Linoleum Floor Laying, Carpentry, Radio, Cartooning, and Etiquette.[32]

Also in February Bob Hilson's Radio class assembled an amplifier kit and installed a public-address system for the camp. Now Top-Kick Batchelder was heard at 6 am gently reminding the boys to get up.[33]

The March issue of The Washingtonian stated that Miss Adelaide Patterson, a dramatics and public speaking professor at RI College of Education, did a series of dramatic readings. She used a variety of dialects such as Irish, Negro, and Italian. The boys enjoyed her humorous and serious presentation. This was a positive influence in spurring the boys' interest in acting.[34]

The Hillbilly Band participated at two amateur nights in Putnam, CT and General Motors at Rhodes-on-the-Pawtuxet in Cranston. They won 3rd place in Putnam, CT but didn't place in the latter. They then traveled to the Firemen's Circus in Harmony and entertained.[35]

On Thursday, April 2, the Troupers and Hillbilly Band entertained 200 members of the PTA from northwestern RI and performed at the auditorium of the Harmony School. After their performance, the boys were treated to homemade cakes and cookies and then enjoyed dancing by their camp band. These performances throughout the state were great publicity for the CCC camp.[36] The Troupers had their last performance of the spring season when they performed for the PTA of Abington, CT.[37]

The Summer Education Program began in June and most of the classes were scheduled for outdoors. The Agriculture Class made many trips to nearby poultry farms. A few of the basic classes such as English and Math along with the Radio, Leather Craft, Biology, and Photography were offered.[38]

Twenty-five members of the Farming Class visited the Langenfeld Poultry Farm on Snake Hill Rd. in July. It was one of the outstanding White Wyandotte breeding facilities in the U.S. On July 14 the club visited the Houghton Farm in East Putnam that was an excellent Rhode Island Red farms in New England. From these experiences the boys were ready to order chicks for their new chicken house and see if they could make a profit.[39]

The 12-week Fall Education Program began on September 21 in which all enrollees were required to take at least 2 courses thus stressing the importance of broadening each member's education that would help when they went searching for a job. The faculty was composed of Education Advisor, three WPA instructors, two Army officers, and all of the forestry staff. These classes were offered:

Elementary: English, Arithmetic, Geography, History; Intermediate: English, Arithmetic, Algebra, Hygiene, Current Events, Geometry, Trigonometry, Chemistry, First Aid; Vocational: Steam Engineering, Carpentry, Cabinet Making, Art Metal, Cartooning, Auto Mechanics, Mimeographing, Photography, Leather Work, Block Printing, Clay Modeling, Drawing, Typing.

Work Projects

- Pest Control
- Cement & Stone Work
- Truck Trail Construction
- Tree Surgery
- Dynamiting, and
- Food Handling [40]
- Blasting (Education-Safety Procedure)

The Washingtonian issue on March 20, 1936 had an article written by the supervisors on safety while using dynamite. It described an accident in Vermont in which an enrollee stood 300 feet behind a tree during a blast. He thought he was safe but a rock glanced off the tree and hit the man over his heart and killed him. The article went on to state these two important rules: a man should stay no less than 500' from the blast and second never return to the scene of the blast until the "all over signal" is sounded. Dynamiting work was often used at the Washington camp in road and trail construction.

Driving

For many of the CCC boys this was their first time driving and these were the rules they had to abide by: Must drive 25 mph. while transporting people and never exceed 30 mph. They should make sure passengers are seated while traveling, and no one should ride the fenders, bumpers, running boards, or cab roof.[41]

Recreation

The basketball team had its first game of the year scheduled for January 7 at the LaSalle Academy in Providence. The next day they played Beach Pond.

In February the basketball team was at the top of their Western Division CCC League. They beat the Mt. Vernon team 27-22 at the Foresters Hall in Arctic [West Warwick].[42]

On February 25, the Washington basketball team beat the Arcadians in a close game, 32-29 at the Big Cedar Inn. The next day the team traveled to the Foresters' Hall in Arctic and defeated the Primrose five 12-9. At their final game Co. 142 defeated Beach Pond 20-12. The Washingtonians were the undisputed champions of the Western CCC League.[43]

The basketball team ended their season competing in Newport for the Fourth District Championship, but they lost to the Milton team. They did, however, win the Championship of Rhode Island CCC camps.[44]

The Washington camp baseball team that played other CCC camps and sometimes local town teams. Roland N. Bisaillon (1933-34) Robert Bisaillon

On June 1 Camp Washington celebrated the Third Anniversary of the CCC with a dinner and dance. The celebration took place in the rec hall and music for the dance was provided by the Premier Orchestra from Pascoag. Ladies came from Webster, Putnam, Pascoag, Chepachet, and Providence. Twenty-five Co. 142 enrollees, however, were busy fighting a fire in Johnston but there were 150 enrollees to keep the ladies entertained.[45]

During the summer the boys switched to baseball, volleyball, horseshoes, track, and swimming at Pascoag Reservoir (about 3 mi. east of camp). Swimming lessons and instruction in life saving were given by an able and certified swimmer from camp.[46] The baseball team practiced at the Chepachet field. The Fourth District was divided into three leagues. The Washington team competed with Primrose and the two Mass. teams of Upton and East Douglas.[47]

In June, the WPA Vaudeville group made their second appearance of the year at Camp Washington. The reporter for the June 26 issue of The Washingtonian stated: "The standout act of the evening was put on by Miss Olive Lopez, blues singer and shimmy dancer par excellence. She gave just the merest hint of what she could shake and how she could shake it, and the audience howled vociferously for more and more. As one member remarked: 'There is nothing like this classical stuff after all.'"

On Tuesday, June 16 the camp track team held its first meet in the camp's history at the Burrillville Trotting Park (in nearby Pascoag on Money Hill Road). Our lieutenant donated prizes and the owners of the track made it available to our Co. 142. Approx. 35 enrollees entered the five events.[48]

The N.Y.A. Camp for Young Women on the Kiwanis Reservation (Spring Grove Rd.) in Chepachet hosted weekly dances during July and August and the boys from the Washington Camp were invited. In August, the boys reciprocated by inviting the girls to a dance at their rec hall when the girls camp was closing in August. The boys hoped the girls would come back again next summer.[49]

In the March 20th issue of The Washingtonian, there were rumors that Camp Washington was to close in April 1936 and enrollees were wondering what would happen. Luckily for them the camp continued to function.[50]

In March as boys were making their decision to sign for another six months, the Army announced that volunteers were needed to go out West to Oregon. Thirty-five camp members seeking adventure signed up but only 12 were chosen. They left the last day of March and traveled to Fort Adams. From there they were taken to a railroad and traveled about five days on a train to their new camp.[51]

Another education project that was completed by Washington enrollees in 1936 was the building of a 20-foot model of the camp. The project was displayed at many of the sportsmen's club conventions in Hartford, New Haven, Philadelphia, Boston, and New York City.

Sports

In the early years of the CCC many boys drowned while swimming because a lack of proper supervision and no one was trained in life saving. Since then a few boys from each camp were sent for life saving skills and then came back and taught the enrollees. These new camp rules in RI were stressed:

- Regular hours of supervised swimming were enforced
- Water used for diving must be 6' deep and free of objects
- The Buddy System must be followed at all times – Every swimmer must have a partner
- At least one qualified person well-versed in artificial resuscitation must be present
- All swimmers must wait 2 hours after eating to avoid stomach cramps[52]

In July, the Volleyball & Baseball teams were busy competing in the Northern Division that included Blue Hills (Milton), East Douglas and Primrose.[53]

Company 142 competed with the other five CCC camps at the Kingston Fair in the fall 1936. The Washington camp won 1st place in the Forestry Exhibit. It was a large-scale model of their forestry project that covered more than 60 sq. miles showing every pond, brook, road, trail, and building. The enrollees also had a model of their camp with all the buildings built to scale. Enrollees also displayed the crafts and photography made in their classes.[54]

Projects

In the spring 1936, the staff and enrollees were busy sprucing up the camp. The lower half of the walls in the mess hall were painted grey. The hospital was repainted and a new floor installed in the first aid room. A new grease trap was constructed by the kitchen. The oil room got a new cement floor, and a new truck [jack] stand was constructed. The walkways were re-graveled and thousands of paving blocks were installed for sidewalks. Gardens were spaded near the entrance and buildings and flowers were planted.[55]

In April enrollees were constructing Angell Trail along the northwest border of RI and Mass. This would help in preventing fires from coming across the border and is similar to the Border Trail (between CT & RI) and the Richardson Clearing Trail to the State Line.[56]

The RI Highway Association visited the camp on September 16 for their regular fall meeting. The Camp Superintendent escorted the group on a tour of the trails that the camp had constructed: Olney Keach, Richardson Clearing, Munyan, Border, and Durfee trails. The Highway Association praised the camp for their excellent work.[57]

Superintendent Arthur C. Cole commented on the new challenges from the Federal Govt. with regard to their road and water hole construction:

"The completion of the Durfee Hill Trail marks a milestone in the development of the work projects of the CCC.

"At the start of the camps the objective was to get as many miles of trail broken open and as many holes in the ground for water in the shortest time possible.

"This was sound practice at the time as our primary job was conservation and any quick steps we could take to cut fire losses were taken.

"Little attention was paid to the looks of the job or to the long life of a trail or water hole. There was not time to do this as there were thousands of acres and woodland beyond reach of motorized fire vehicles.

"Gradually the Forest Service tightened up on specifications, each year setting higher standards. At the same time the foremen and enrollees kept adding little touches here and improvements there. Now we are required to build durable trails designed for long life and water holes with capacity and of sturdy construction. We are not required to do this but most of the foremen and enrollees in this work desire to build better and better trails, water holes, etc."[58]

Superintendent Cole stated in November his crew was working on the Wilson Trail (approx. 3 mi. north of Camp Washington). He said it was one of the most important for fire protection because it was "…a connecting link in the chain of beautiful trails built by this camp."[59]

These 15 trucks were very important in transporting workers in stake-body trucks while dump trucks were used in transporting materials. The photo also shows the trained drivers by their assigned truck. Glocester Heritage Society

The Washington camp entrance with stone pillars built by enrollees. Roland N. Bisaillon (1933-34) Robert Bisaillon

The mess hall had two rows of tables that sat eight. The kitchen and serving area were in front and the building was heated by two coal stoves plus heat from the kitchen stoves. The room was kept spotless or the enrollees would be in trouble. Glocester Heritage Society

The Recreation Hall provided enrollees a place to relax: play pool, ping-pong, cards, read, entertainment shows, dances, and a Canteen (at the far end of the building) that sold: ice cream, candy, soda, etc. Glocester Heritage Society

The July 31, 1937 issue of The Washingtonian reported that construction of the Wilson Trail began in 1936 and completed about a thousand feet in July 1937. The trail was built under new specifications that stressed that it be more attractive. It called for a "turnpike surfacing that was a wider travel surface. The banks and slopes were carefully graded; debris was removed or covered. Five men spread the gravel that was transported from the Munyan gravel bank (southeast of Wakefield Pond).

As of July 1937, Camp Washington was proud of its safety record doing construction work and driving record. For the past year they did not have one serious accident of loss of life.[60]

Camp Improvements

February: Repainting of mess hall and new tabletops.

May: Built horseshoe and volleyball courts; graded and landscaped campgrounds; built new floor and stage in the rec hall; constructed new grease trap and incinerator; built a new school building; painted library and canteen.[61]

October: Outside wiring revamped; hot water supply doubled; new wash stands installed; root cellar demolished and new one built under mess hall; all barracks painted; new storm entrances installed; barracks #5 divided into 3 sections (two schoolrooms and a reading room).[62]

Camp Accomplishments

The March Issue of The Washingtonian boasted of the camp's past accomplishments:

Tree Diseases

Dutch Elm	• 10,624 trees removed • 453 man-days • 380 miles of roads • 119,462 acres covered
Blister Rust	• 12,438 ribes plants removed • 43,225 acres scouting
Gypsy Moth Control	• covered 3,507 acres • 3,234 man-days
Mapping	• 59,016 acres

State Forest Improvement

Project	Man-Days
Thinning and cleaning: 374 acres	9,782
Cords of wood cut: 1,060	n/a
Pond improvement: 8	969
Experimental plots: 4	68
Fireplaces (Johnston, RI): 3	130
Planting: 158 acres	578
Type mapping: 232 acres (Shows the distribution of tree types)	6
Signs: 54	150
Construction	1,445
Truck trail maintenance: 20.1 mi.	6,316

There were originally 5 barracks with approx. 40 enrollees in each when there was a total of 200 men. Notice how the head placement in each bunk was staggered and the large room was well-kept. It had three coal stoves to keep the men warm in the winter. This photo was in 1939 when it was harder getting recruits and the #5 barracks was converted into a schoolhouse. Glocester Heritage Society

Truck trail construction: 47.4 mi.	43,877
Foot trail construction: 0.3 mi.	200
Grading the camp's site: 350 yd^3	413
Power line construction: 1 line	178
Telephone line construction: 0.7 mi.	98
Landscape work: 0.6 mi.	847
Beach improvement: 9 acres	622
Fighting forest fires	350
Forest fire pre-suppression	200
Fire hazard reduction (trailside)	845
Fire lane construction	1,929
Waterhole construction	3,226
Hunting missing persons: 4.998 acres	763
State Park improvement: 14.1 acres	1,339 [63]

– 1937 –

Staff

Commander: Lt. Atkins Mickerson, USNR
Welfare Officer: Lt. Guy L. Colson, CAS Res.
Camp Physician: Benjamin I. Nadelman
Education Adviser: Joseph A. McCaull
Camp Superintendent: Arthur C. Cole

Assistant Superintendent: George Anderson
Foremen: Fred Whitcomb, Robert Tetu, George Halloran, Joseph Burns, & Joseph Higgins
Truck Master: George Bell

Education

The January/March Education Program boasted its enrollees were all signed up for 3 classes. Most of the students are taking English, Arithmetic, and one project course. The Technical Staff was handling the project classes. The classes ran from 6-9 pm in 45-minute periods from Monday to Wednesday. On Wednesday and Thursday, the WPA teachers were available for tutoring while the officers were in charge of recreation.[64]

A 20' x 20' model of the Washington CCC camp was made by camp enrollees for the 1936 RI State Fair and then chosen by the National Forestry Service and displayed at the Sportsmen's shows in Boston, New York, and Hartford in 1937. (The Washingtonian, Feb. 28, 1937, 6.)

With the end of the enrollment date of March and new recruits coming to camp, the Spring Education Program began on March 20th. New classes were offered besides the basic classes: Tree Identification, Tree Surgery, Outdoor Sketching, Photography Field Trips, Auto Mechanics, Greenhouse Management and Flower Plants. The average age of the new recruits was a few months over 17 years old.[65]

The Summer Education Program scheduled a majority of classes outside. Here are some examples: Tree Surgery, Gardening (flowers and vegetables), and Farm Animals (100 baby chicks). The birds were all cockerels and sold off in approx. 13 weeks. Enrollees fed the chicks kitchen scraps and looked forward to a learning experience and a profit, too.[66]

Recreation

From January 1st Co. 142 was the only CCC camp that was invited each week to dances at the Betsy Williams N.Y.A. Camp on Pulaski Road in West Glocester. One truck load of enrollees left each Thursday at 6:45 pm loaded with boys who needed dancing lessons and a second truck left at 7:45 with expert dancers for the dance that started at 8 pm. The dances ended at 10:30 pm. The

LIEUT ATKINS NICKERSON, *USNR.*, COMMANDING

SECOND LT. HENRY H. BAKER, *Inf.-Res.*, EXCHANGE OFFICER

Roster

JOSEPH A. McCAULL, *CEA*

DONALD BLACKWOOD, WINTHROP CULBERT, *WPA Teachers*

TECHNICAL PERSONNEL Arthur C. Cole, Supt.; George R. Anderson, Fred Whitcomb, George Bell, George Holleran, Robert Tetu, Joseph Burns, Joseph Higgins, Raymond Birman.

LEADERS Alfred Arruda, Middletown, Rhode Island; Carlton B. Baker, East Providence, Rhode Island; Mathew Baur, Newport, Rhode Island; William H. Becker, Chepachet, Rhode Island; Howard Briggs, East Greenwich, Rhode Island; Vernon King, Chepachet, Rhode Island; John N. Matthews, Providence, Rhode Island; Ernest H. Piette, Woonsocket Rhode Island; Joseph G. Silva, East Providence, Rhode Island.

ASSISTANT LEADERS J. Brusso, Chepachet, R. I.; E. E. Burdick, West Warwick, R. I.; W. N. Castaldi, Woonsocket, R. I.; F. J. Connors, Providence, R. I.; J. B. DiMuzio, Providence, R. I.; B. Gimber, Lonsdale, R. I.; A. W. Lamoureux, Woonsocket, R. I.; J. Giardino, Providence, R. I.; A. L. Mandeville, Providence, R. I.; H. Perron, Central Falls, R. I.; F. Procaccini, Central Falls, R. I.; C. A. St. Andre, Central Falls, R. I.; J. Starsiak, Central Falls, R. I.

MEMBERS

Barry, L., Pawtucket, R. I.
Bowie, J. G., Providence, R. I.
Boudette, A., Chepachet, R. I.
Callahan, J. J., Pawtucket, R. I.
Carello, R. A., Providence, R. I.
Carr, E. M., Pawtucket, R. I.
Christie, R. F., Providence, R. I.
Coletti, D., Providence, R. I.
Cleary, W. H., Newport, R. I.
Cole, A. A., Cantredale, R. I.
Cote, G. D., C. Falls, R. I.
Coutu, A., Central Falls, R. I.
Davis, A. J., Portsmouth, R. I.
Demeo, A. T., Providence, R. I.
Denault, W. D., Warren, R. I.
Desroches, J., Providence, R. I.
Desmond, D., Providence, R. I.

Dionisi, E., Providence, R. I.
Doane, V. J., Central Falls, R. I.
Dolloff, R. P., Providence, R. I.
Doran, J. T., Bristol, R. I.
Duarte, A. M., Providence, R. I.
Edmonds, M. T., Bristol, R. I.
Famiano, J., Providence, R. I.
Favro, E. R., Bristol, R. I.
Fournier, N. J., Providence, R. I.
Galinelli, J. N., Barrington, R. I.
Gauthier, R. G., Pawtucket, R. I.
Germano, I. R., Pawtucket, R. I.
Gaumond, J. E., C. Falls, R. I.
Gaumond, H. J., C. Falls, R. I.
Gregory, H. L., Riverside, R. I.
Howard, F. E., Providence, R. I.
Howcroft, T., Lincoln Park, R. I.
Hull, R. A., Conimicut, R. I.
Hutchinson, J. H., H'sgrove, R. I.

Hannagan, W. F., P'idence, R. I.
Hesketh, K., Pawtucket, R. I.
Hill, W. T., Scituate, R. I.
Hines, R. H., Providence, R. I.
Johnson, A., Pawtucket, R. I.
Juaire, R., Pawtucket, R. I.
Kabbaze, L. I., Central Falls, R. I.
Keenan, F. J., Pawtucket, R. I.
Knight, H. E., E. G'wich, R. I.
Kosacz, B. S., Pawtucket, R. I.
Kulacz, R., C. Falls, R. I.
Lambert, A. J., C. Falls, R. I.
Lambert, L. H., W'socket, R. I.
Lambert, J., Woonsocket, R. I.
Lamphear, L. L., C. Falls, R. I.
Lavallee, N. J., Centredale, R. I.
Layden, F. F., Jr., P'dence, R. I.
Leduc, E., Woonsocket, R. I.

Leduc, A. H., Woonsocket, R. I.
Leduc, H., Woonsocket, R. I.
Leduc, O. A., W'socket, R. I.
Leonard, G. F., Providence, R. I.
Lucidi, A., Providence, R. I.
Lynch, T. M., Providence, R. I.
Macaruso, A., Providence, R. I.
Machado, M., Newport, R. I.
Manning, J. F., Pawtucket, R. I.
Marciezyk, E., Providence, R. I.
Marshall, A. S., Hoxsie, R. I.
Matthews, M. R., P'mouth, R. I.
Mastrofine, T., Providence, R. I.
Matano, J., Pontiac, R. I.
Mederios, F. V., Bristol, R. I.
Miller, R. A., Pawtucket, R. I.
Misewicz, J., Pawtucket, R. I.
Mollerberg, R. A., E. P'ence, R. I.
Mulholland, A. W., P'ence, R. I.

Murphy, W. C., Newport, R. I.
McCarthy, H. P., Providence, R. I.
Nadeau, N., Central Falls, R. I.
Namejko, J., Providence, R. I.
Normandin, G., Pawtucket, R. I.
Oxley, K. M., Providence, R. I.
Prignano, U., Providence, R. I.
Proulx, E., W. Warwick, R. I.
Pacheco, F. T., Tiverton, R. I.
Pettis, P. G., Johnston, R. I.
Piechocki, A., Providence, R. I.
Poirier, G. C., Pawtucket, R. I.
Potenza, R. J., Providence, R. I.
Raposa, A. L., E. P'ence, R. I.
Reilly, W. J., Bristol, R. I.
Renshaw, S. I., Central Falls, R. I.
Repoza, A., Providence, R. I.
Rebello, E. G., Providence, R. I.
Robidoux, R. G., Pascoag, R. I.

Roderick, P., E. P'dence, R. I.
Rose, F. P., Newport, R. I.
Rose, J. F., Providence, R. I.
Rose, S., Providence, R. I.
Rubino, F., Bristol, R. I.
Russo, F., Newport, R. I.
Sirois, Romeo, Pawtucket, R. I.
Sirois, Robert, Pawtucket, R. I.
Sawyer, N., Pawtucket, R. I.
Silvia, C., Pawtucket, R. I.
Silva, J. J., Providence, R. I.
Slocum, R. A., Providence, R. I.
Smith, C., Providence, R. I.
Smith, I. A., Lakewood, R. I.
Sullivan, G. A., Providence, R. I.
Sweet, C. J., Pawtucket, R. I.
Szczez, W., Artic, R. I.
(See back page for additional names)

This 1937 photo of the Washington Company 142 Staff and Members from the Third CCC District First Corps Area, 1937, Yearbook

reporter for the paper stated: "…if members do not get enough dancing in the course of the evening, he only has himself to blame."[67]

On Monday, June 14 the WPA troupe from NY entertained the enrollees with the play "Murder in the C.C.C." that involved inserting two-dozen of the camp enrollees as characters. The boys had fun learning the parts and acting. The play was enjoyed by all.[68]

During the summer, Camp Washington was able to use the new pool the town of Putnam had built in the spring. The pool was built by damming a nearby brook. The pool was emptied every evening and refilled with fresh water in the morning. There was a shallow area and a deep part for diving. The boys had free access to the bathhouse. Several boxing team members participated in an exhibition that raised money for the pool.[69]

The volleyball team moved from the old court in back of barracks #1 to Higgins Park where inter-barracks competition was staged.[70]

Projects

By 1937 Washington camp built 2,000 water holes and 40 miles of truck trails and covered 50,000 acres in blister rust and gypsy moth eradication.[71]

In August, a chemical treatment plant for kitchen wastewater was constructed on the site where the wastewater had been deposited for the past four years.[72]

Planned Projects

The April 30, 1937 issue of The Washingtonian listed these projects:

- Build 19 waterholes in Burrillville and Glocester
- Construct 4 miles of truck trails
- Scout and eradicate ribes bushes to control blister rust on 8,262 acres in Burrillville and 84,848 acres Glocester
- Spend 90 man-days mapping white pine and ribes
- Scout and creosote gypsy moth egg masses in Burrillville, Glocester, and North Smithfield
- Remove and dispose of debris on a 20' wide strip on either side of 50 miles of trails and roads in Burrillville, Glocester, and North Smithfield
- Use 890 man-days for maintaining some of the already constructed trails

The Munyan Trail was expected to be completed in June. This trail connected the Border Trail and the Richardson Trail. One could now drive to and from Wakefield Pond from different routes. The Richardson Trail was named for an early settler whose home was between the Border and Munyan trails. He raised his family in that area and made a living by making charcoal that was later used by jewelry manufactures in Providence.[74]

The May 31, 1937 issue of The Washingtonian describes the history of the area: "The Wakefield family did a flourishing sawmill business at the site of 'Mickey's Bridge' on the Munyan Trail, near the RI/CT line. Not far from this point the Ross family tilled the ground and pastured their livestock, hence the name 'Ross Pastures.'

The Washingtonian reporter stated: "Changes that come with the passing of time have erased all but a few of the signs of human habitation but with keen eyes and some imagination; you can reconstruct these homes in the wilderness. As you pass the Wakefield Pond you may even see a real Indian casting his line in hopes of catching some of those five-pound pickerel that lurk in the protection of the grass along the shore."

In June Mr. Higgins' waterhole crew were busy constructing a waterhole on the Putnam Pike just east of the cemetery from camp Washington. When the crew arrived at the site, the area was inhabited by thee cows that had to be moved. The crew used trail builder #4 to help dig the 4' deep hole. As the machine dug deeper, water and mud slowed the machine and pumps were called in to remove the water and mud. Finally, the machine was

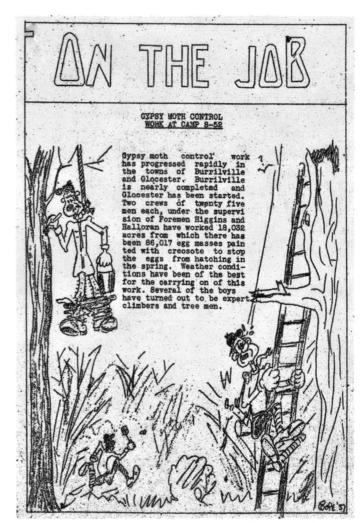

The February 28, 1937 issue in The Washingtonian had this humorous cartoon to describe the camp's work of controlling the Gypsy Moth in RI.

The Infirmary/Dispensary attendant wearing a white coat, Roland N. Bisaillon, with the ambulance driver who took seriously ill patients to the nearest Army hospital at Fort Adams or even to Fort Wright on Fisher Island, NY near New London, CT. Roland N. Bisaillon (1933-34) Robert Bisaillon

Waterholes

Forester Joe Higgins led a crew of 10 men in building waterholes. In the spring 1937 their goal was to construct 25 waterholes. The average amount of man days to construct one hole was 75 man-days. Waterholes were strategically located to allow for protection of about one square mile.

The average waterhole was approx. 18' x 18' wide and 4' deep and held approx. 7,500 gallons of water. The sides of the walls were lined with stone arranged in steps that permitted animals to escape.

Space for parking and turn around were located close to the waterhole for fire trucks.[73]

A group of CCC boys by a waterhole that was built to fight fires. Podskoch collection

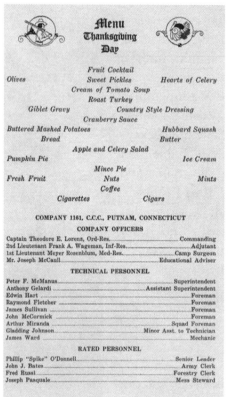

After going through the terrible '38 Hurricane and working on cleaning up in the towns and forests, the camp had time to be thankful for being alive and together with their leaders and friends. Gary Potter

able to extricate itself. Once the water was removed work on the stonework commenced.[75]

In August a new doctor, Edmund Sydlowski, arrived at camp. He initiated some new rules for the Dispensary (clinic). If a person is sick, they should report to the Dispensary from 7-7:45 am or 4-5 pm. Loitering was strictly forbidden during the day and visiting hours were 7-8 pm. Sydlowski stated: "Talk quietly in the Dispensary and refrain from the use of obscene language. Smoking, as in every clinic, is strictly forbidden."[76]

In 1937, Rhode Island's six camps were reduced to four. The Greene/Mount Vernon was closed in September and in December the Washington camp closed. At this time the George Washington Forest had 244 acres.[77]

– 1938 –

In 1938 Washington camp got a reprieve. Since there were many uncompleted projects in the Washington Memorial Forest, CCC enrollees from the Woonsocket/Primrose (N. Smithfield Co. #1161) camp were transferred to Glocester. When the Primrose camp transferred to Glocester it continued to operate as Co. 1161.

On the Friday after the storm the Washington camp was called out to help the public utilities to clear their wires in the North Providence and Westerly areas. There was a need to restore communication and electricity to the dairy farms.[78]

– 1939 –

Staff

Commander: Capt. T.E. Lorenz

Assistant: 2nd Lieut. Inf. Res. F.A. Wageman

Doctor: 1st Lieut. Meyer Rosenblum

Education Adviser: Joseph A. McCaull

Superintendent: Peter F. McManus

The 1939 the State Annual Report described the George Washington Memorial Forest:

"244 acres - Town of Glocester.

"Natural forest with winding trails and ponds. A gift to the State from various organizations. It is used for general forest demonstration purposes. Recreational building is available for picnics and parties, [there are] also outdoor picnic grounds and fireplaces. There is a heavy growth of oak, pine, and maple on most of the area. It is the site of a United States Forest Service CCC Camp. Located in the northwestern part of the State, six miles from the Rhode Island/Connecticut line.

"Improvements needed: Timber stand improvement. Rebuilding roads and trails. Additional fireplaces and parking areas. Repairs to recreational building and additional latrines."

The Hurricane of 1938

Historian Albert Klyberg had this to say about the '38 Hurricane: "The great September hurricane drove a twenty-foot wall of water up Narragansett Bay and toppled thousands of trees. Loss of life and property damage convulsed every aspect of state life. Instead of the focus on fire-fighting and tree protection, the agenda for the four remaining CCC camps was recovery and the rescue of 84 million of useful board feet of downed lumber. The first jobs of the enrollees was road clearance and restoration of power line service. Then they attacked the devastation in the forests and parks. The recovery took at least nine months, using 2,600 WPA workers and 600 young men from the remaining CCC camps."

A CCC crew working to clean up the damaged tree caused by the 1938 Hurricane. Podskoch Collection

– 1940 –

In 1940 the State of Rhode Island acquired leases from the Federal Government for approx. 10,000 acres of sub-marginal land in Exeter, West Greenwich, Westerly, Richmond, Glocester, Hopkinton, and Burrillville – most of it from north to south as wooded land adjacent to the border with Connecticut.

The 1938 Hurricane caused extensive damage to the towns of Glocester and Burrillville near the George Washington Forest. Most of the lumber was salvaged and what remained in 1940 was of little value. Both the CCC and WPA workers thinned out the hardwoods and removed diseased or dead trees in the state forest and converted them into cordwood. They also carried out fire hazard reduction along the roads and trails. They planted over 5,000 white and red pine seedlings around and near Peck Pond.[79]

One of the tracts in Burrillville contained Peck Pond, now part of the Casimir Pulaski State Park that adjoins the George Washington Memorial State Forest. The George Washington camp was building a service and recreational road that was 4.5 miles long and 19' wide that went from George Washington Forest to the Peck Pond Recreational Area. Work on the road continued in 1941. CCC workers then constructed a bathhouse, parking area, and picnic grounds that would be open to the public in 1941. In the George Washington Memorial Forest workers built 20 new fireplaces and latrines. Finally, enrollees repaired fireplace and the chimney in the cabin that was used for recreational purposes.[80]

– 1941 –

CCC workers continued working on the service and recreational road that was 4.5 miles long from George Washington Forest to the Peck Pond Recreational Area. In May of 1941 the Washington camp was one of the last operating CCC camps in Rhode Island. In May a new crew of workers, Co. 1116-V from the Arcadia/Hope Valley camp, came to work at Camp Washington. The Veterans' companies were composed of WWI unemployed 'veterans.' This probably explains why they were the last to work while most of the young CCC boys were drafted into service during WWII.[81]

By the end of the year Camp Washington and all the other camps in RI were closed.

Over almost a nine year period the Washington camp accomplished these tasks: carried out forest stand improvements, fire hazard reduction, controlled insects and diseases, fought forest fires, built waterholes, truck trails, fences, fire places, campgrounds, telephone lines, parking areas, built and repaired forest fire towers, and did some fire tower restoration work.[82]

RI historian Al Klyberg said: "It is interesting that George Washington Memorial Forest provides a set of bookends to the CCC story in Rhode Island. The Edgewood Women's Club's gift kicked RI's first forest in 1932. Then, the CCC story at George Washington continued into 1940 when the other CCC camps headed towards close-out. The last task of the CCC was building the Central Trail connecting the original George Washington area with Peck Pond in the newly acquired Casimir Pulaski State Park. This occurred after Pulaski was conveyed by the Federal government to Rhode Island as part of the 10,000-acre transaction from the U.S. Soil Conservation Service."

LEGACY

The George Washington State Management Area

Located within the 4,000-acre George Washington Management Area, and on the shores of Bowdish Reservoir, the 100-acre George Washington Memorial Camping Area is an overnight, primitive camping facility offering a multitude of opportunities to enjoy the outdoors.

There are 45 well-spaced gravel sites suitable for tents, trailers, and RVs. Electrical hookups are not available; water is available from the various shared spigots throughout the campground. Bathrooms are either outhouses or pit toilets, and there are now shower facilities. There are two Adirondack-style shelters available by reservation, for group camping (limited to 20 persons each). The campground is open from the second weekend of April to the end of October.[83]

Through the hard work of the CCC, there are many miles of roads and hiking trails that provide hiking, horseback riding, biking, and in the winter there are trails for snowmobiling and cross-country skiing. The Bowditch Reservoir and Pulaski State Park and Recreational Area's Peck Pond provides fishing and boating.

Enrollees built this Education Building in the 1930s. The building is used my many community groups. Podskoch

Retired RI CCC Alumni who were members of the National Association of Civilian Conservation Alumni (NACCA) Chapter 109, placed this memorial stone in front of the Education Building on the banks of the Bowditch Reservoir to honor the work of the CCC in Rhode Island. The memorial stone lists the seven RI CCC Camps. Podskoch

One of the 45 beautiful campsites built by the CCC at George Washington Memorial Camping Area. RI DEM

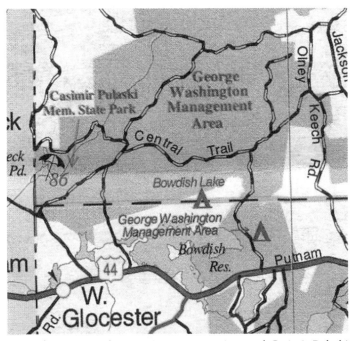

Map of George Washington Management Area and Casimir Pulaski Memorial State Park. Albert Klyberg

Peck Pond in Pulaski State Park has beautiful beach for swimming, fishing, and picnicking. Podskoch

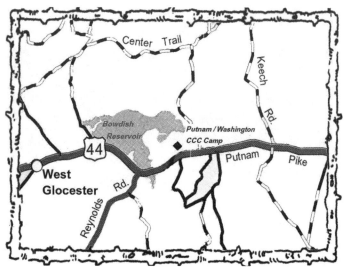

Camp Washington Map by Paul Hartmann

(L) Dispensary/Infirmary attendant, Roland N. Bisaillon, beside the entrance to the dispensary door. (R) Roland assisted Dr. Henstell in taking care of patients at the Washington Dispensary. Both photos Robert Bisaillon

Directions

From Pawtucket: Take Rt. 44 W for approx. 20 miles to the entrance of the George Washington Campground & the RI DEM Division of Forest Environment Office.

From Westerly: Take I-95 N for approx. 10 miles. Then take Exit 5 B towards West Greenwich and go 13 miles on Rt. 102. At Foster Center turn left onto Rt. 94 and travel 12 miles N to Rt. 44/Putnam Turnpike. Turn right on Rt. 44 E and go about 1 mile. The RI DEM Division of Forest Environment Office and G. W. Campground are on the left.

From Newport: Take Rt. 138 W to Rt 1. Go N for approx. a mile and turn left onto Rt. 4 N. After 10 miles take I-95 N and then go on I-295 to Rt. 44. Then go W for approx. 18 miles to the entrance to the George Washington Campground & RI DEM Division of Forest Environment Office.

MEMORIES

Roland N. Bisaillon

On May 12, 2019 at the dedication of the CCC Worker Statue at Chatfield Hollow State Park in Killingworth, CT, Robert Bisaillon came up to me and told me that his father, Roland, had been in the CCC in Rhode Island. My ears perked up when he said Rhode Island because I was gathering information on the CCC camps there. Then he said: My father kept a photograph album of the camp. Would you like to see it?"

I enthusiastically said yes and we agreed on a date when he would come to my home and I'd scan the photos. That is why this chapter has a lot of Roland's photos of the Washington camp.

I asked Robert for information about his dad's life. Robert said: "My father, Roland N. Bisaillon, was born in Pawtucket, Rhode Island in 1916. His parents died when he was young. He lived in Woonsocket with his aunt and uncle Gingras' family. He lived with them on an off and was also living at the Our Lady of Victory Orphanage in Lackawanna, near Buffalo, NY.

"When he was about 17, he joined the CCC (1933) and was sent to the Washington camp in the George Washington State Forest in Glocester. From the photo album I can see my father worked as an attendant in the Dispensary/Infirmary helping the doctor to take care of patients.

"After working in Rhode Island for about a year my dad was transferred out West to Trask, Oregon in 1934. The camp was located near the Trask River and Tillamook was the nearest town.

After the CCCs he worked as a chauffeur and butler for different people. He worked for Major Bowes

An outside view of the Dispensary, or as Roland called it the 'Hospital,' where he was an attendant. It had two entrances. It also had a large center fireplace and a ladder for access to the roof as the chimney needed to be cleaned regularly to prevent chimney fires. Robert Bisaillon

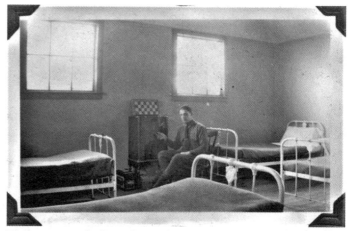

There were six beds in the Washington Dispensary/Hospital ward. For entertainment there was a radio and games like checkers. Robert Bisaillon

who had the radio show "The Amateur Hour." My dad also worked for Muriel Hubbard, who was one of the Rockefeller/Whitney descendants. She owned an estate in Middletown, CT. It has since been torn down.

"During WWII, I believe he went into the service in the Army Air Force. He was in the 15th AAF 781st Bomber Squadron in the Medical Unit.

"He served in the European theater.

"After WWII my Dad went back to do domestic work for a short time.

"When Pan American Airline was just starting up my father applied and was hired to work as a Bursar that basically was a male steward. He graduated from Pan Am's first class of cabin attendants. I guess his experience in domestics made him a perfect candidate for the job.

"He married Eileen Burkimsher on April 26, 1947. They had two children: Roleen on Aug. 28, 1951 and myself on Nov. 29, 1954.

"I'm not sure how many years he worked for Pan Am but after being in two crashes, if my memory is correct, on a DC 10 Constellation, one accident was at Shannon Airport in Ireland, my mom got him to move on to a safer job.

"My dad was on the maiden flight from New York to Cape Town, South Africa. I have a picture of him with the entire crew. He called it the Obit picture as it was used by the company if the plane went down.

"After Pan Am my dad got employment at the Royal Doulton English Bone China Company in New York City. He worked there for 35 years until he retired.

"My dad passed on October 3, 1996 from complications of a stroke.

"We often spoke about his days in the CCCs. He told me about the logging roads that were built and the huge trees that were cut down. Although I don't remember a whole lot, he was very proud of the work he did in the CCCs. He was a life-long Democrat and thankful to FDR for a chance to work and send some money back to my great uncle and aunt Gingras in Woonsocket."

Stanley P. Malikowski

On May 30, 2014 I met Stanley P. Malikowski at the West Greenwich Town Hall when I was doing research on the seven CCC camps in RI. I was accompanied by historian Al Klyberg of Lincoln, RI and Mike Wilk of CT who was searching for his father's CCC camp. Stanley told me he worked at the Washington camp in the George Washington State Forest and proudly showed me his discharge paper.

Two years later after speaking at the Greene High School in West Greenwich on Dec. 19, 2016, I visited Stanley at his home in Coventry, RI and interviewed him.

"I was born in Coventry, RI on October 30, 1919. My father Felix worked at the Anthony Mill, a textile factory in our town. My mother was Martha Kowalski. She had seven children: Dorothy, Rudy, Bernadine, Blandine, me, Teddy, and Joseph.

"In 1937 I graduated from Coventry High School and worked in a sawmill and then at Berkshire Fine

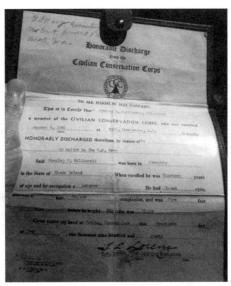

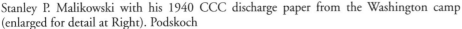

Stanley P. Malikowski with his 1940 CCC discharge paper from the Washington camp (enlarged for detail at Right). Podskoch

Stanley Malikowski shared his life stories and experiences in the CCC in Rhode Island.

Spinning cloth factory in Anthony.

"I knew about the CCC from my brother Rudy who was in the CCC in Connecticut. Things were tough getting jobs so I went to Providence and joined on January 4, 1940. I was sent to Camp George Washington in Glocester. Our captain was T.E. Lorenz. He thought he was God. We got paid a dollar a day. My mother got $22.00 that was sent straight home and I got $8.00.

"My first job was working as an assistant to the tool room clerk. My job was keeping track of the tools and doing maintenance work. I also did odd jobs in camp. I painted fire extinguishers and Indian water tanks.

"Then I became a truck foreman. I gassed up the trucks and kept track of how many gallons were used.

"At supper the food was excellent. Pork chops were my favorite. Six guys sat at each table. The KPs brought out the food and placed it on the tables. When we got to the table we stood in silence as the sergeant said grace. While he prayed everyone had their eyes on the chow looking for the largest pork chop or other piece of meat to grab. There was no fighting for food.

"After dinner I sometimes went to the rec hall and shot pool or read, but most of the time I went to the radio shack and used the shortwave radio.

"At night I took classes in camp. There was a radio building where I studied about the radio. We had our own station W1NPG. I learned how to get on and do Morse code. There was a civilian who taught classes and I helped him. At night we went on the air and I tried to contact other CCC camps. I also talked to other parts of the world.

"There were sports teams if you wanted to join. I played on the basketball team and we practiced at the Putnam High School gym in Connecticut. We played local teams in Putnam. When it got warmer, I played on the baseball team.

"On many of the weekends I hitchhiked home. I'd get a weekend pass, skip supper, and start hitchhiking around 4 or 5 o'clock.

"I decided to leave the CCC and signed up for the Navy on May 20th, 1940. When I got back to camp after signing up, our captain was happy because the military was looking for men. I was sent to Newport, RI for basic training and stayed till August. Then they assigned me to the destroyer USS Madison in Boston. We did convoy duty escorting ships to Europe that was part of the Lend Lease Program. We also searched for enemy submarines. After the invasion in Africa, we came back to the U.S. for repairs in Brooklyn, NY in January 1943. I heard the Navy was looking for submarine men so I joined the submarines corps.

"In my last year in the Navy I was stationed in New London. One time I came home and met Doris Caron. We dated and got married on July 31, 1948. We had a son Gary.

"After I got married, I got a job as an electrician in Providence. When they went on strike, I joined the Army in February 1949. They sent me to the White Sands

Proving Grounds that is also called the White Sands Missile Range. Here I worked with over 300 German scientists in New Mexico. I lived in an old Army barracks in El Paso, Texas. Each day a bus took us to work.

"Every week one of the German scientists gave a speech to the Army workers. Sometimes the famous scientist Wernher Von Braun spoke. I worked there as an electrician.

"In 1950 my missile command group moved to the Red Stone Arsenal in Alabama. I was there till 1951.

"Then from 1951-53 I was sent to Korea and was in charge of the signal maintenance. After two years I requested to be sent back to Alabama.

"My request was granted and I was in charge of missile maintenance. They then sent me to the Officer's Missile School where I graduated in 1954.

"The Army made me a warrant officer and sent me back to El Paso with the 4th Ordnance Co. My company was then sent to Germany in 1957. I stayed there till 1961. Then I was assigned to Philadelphia, PA in the missile shop.

"I went back to Europe in 1964 in missile maintenance. I stayed till 1965 and I came back to the U.S. I retired in January 1966. I came home to Coventry and built my home. Then I got a job at Raytheon Co. in Portsmouth, RI. I worked in the instrument repair section. I retired in 1984. In retirement I work around my home and help my son Gary.

"I thought my experience in the CCC was good for me because I learned how to get along with people and how to better myself."

A year later Stanley died on Wednesday, November 8, 2017.

"The Grease Pit Accident"

"Ray Morin making a detour by the back end of the kitchen, fell into the grease pit one evening last week. An ambitious K.P., who had been doing the skimming, left momentarily and forgot to replace the cover during his absence. It was Mr. Morin's misfortune to saunter by in those few fateful moments and plunge in.

"Hank Briggs was sore as a boil at Morin. Hank accused him of doing the job on purpose, with an eye to splashing grease all over the side-walls of the trap and to extend discrediting his otherwise efficient supervision of

the mess hall and all its ramifications. All this Mr. Morin vehemently denied. He insisted it was all an accident, with no element of malice or prearrangement.

"His story probably has some truth to it because it was known that he was going out that evening on a very serious date involving love and romance and all that sort of thing. He made the date, it is reported none too sweet. It is said on good authority that he remained for only a short spell at the young lady's house, and has never been back since.

"Moral: If you really must fall in a sewer, be sure and pick an appropriate night."

- The Washingtonian, January 1936

"For Sale"
by Anonymous

A Pontiac car with one piston ring;
Two rear wheels, one front spring;
Carburetor busted half way through;
Engine cracked and hits on two;
Nine years old, – ten in the Spring;
Has shock absorbers n'everything;
Radiator busted, how it leaks;
Body all rusted and full of squeaks,
Ten spokes missing, front all bent;
Tires blown out, – ain't worth a cent,
Down long steep hills, goes like a deuce;
Burns either gas or tobacco juice;
Tires all off, been run on the rim;
A good Pontiac, for the shame she's in.
Price $1.69
- The Washingtonian, February 11, 1936

"Camp Washington Enrollee's Dream House"

"Member Wilfred Cote is setting an example in enterprise, initiative, and foresight that should serve as inspiration to every member of the company. With his limited savings, he purchased a small tract of land on the State Road below the Camp. The owner of the land had an old Essex lying hopeless and helpless on the dump pile. Wilfred went to work on it and put it in good running condition. The owner, in gratitude, agreed to haul the second-hand lumber which Wilfred had obtained from an old house in Pasebag [Pascoag], that was given to him for the tearing down and trucking away.

Wilfred Cote (1906-1949) grave in St. Patrick's Cemetery in Burrillville. Podskoch

"With the materials on his lot, he set out single handed and started his house. In his spare hours, in rain, snow, or icy blasts he may be seen hammering and sawing away. The house is slowly taking shape.

"A week ago Sunday, in a snowstorm, Wilfred was up on the ridge pole, boarding in the roof. Someday soon, the State is going to build a two-lane cement highway right by his door. By that time, he hopes to have his little house completed, along with a repair shop; with gas pumps out front.

"Wilfred and his sister are orphans. They are now separated but he looks to the time when he may be able to take care of her in his own little home, with a business of his own, and an assured future.

"This is a lesson in a lot of things. Without help from any source and without asking aid or favors from anyone, he has set out to make a place for himself in the world. He is not going to wait for someone to make a place for him.

"If Wilfred's project can be matched by anything in the CCC Camps of the country, we would like to hear it. Given the breaks, there is no question that he will realize whatever goal he may set before himself. He has the stuff of which success is made."

- The Washingtonian, February 22, 1936

"The Skunk Hunters"

"Returning home from the basketball game at Arctic a week ago Wednesday, were Lieuts. Peavey, Guibault, and Mr. McCaull, enrollees Johnson and Lamoureux, and Mr. McCaull's terrier, Blackie. Just out of Hope Village someone spied a skunk making his slow and dignified way over the snow and into the woods. The car halted and Blackie bounded out in pursuit, closely followed by Lt. Peavey and the other passengers. Blackie cornered the wee beastie, cunningly keeping out of range of its powerful artillery. Lt. Peavey in an effort to help Blackie, advanced with a stick, but Mr. Skunk must have sensed the maneuver. Before the coup de grace could be delivered, Mr. Skunk had let go a powerful salvo.

"The skunk was carried to the car at arm's length by Mr. McCaull and placed on the running board of Lt. Guibault's car. With powerful fumes trailing for miles behind, the party proceeded home, with all four windows open wide.

"A stop at the Chepachet Diner for a cup of coffee, and in less time it takes to tell, they had the place to themselves, barring the counterman, who had to stay and serve the coffee. When they left, the counterman omitted his customary cheery, 'Come again.'

"Lt. Peavey had his uniform out on the line all the next day. Despite the discomfiture and embarrassment suffered by all concerned, he felt gratified that his cohorts refused to be intimidated by a lowly wood pussy.

★ **GRAND OPENING** ★

Under New Management

I have taken over the Canteen business of the late Mr. Red Hogan, lock, stock and barrel.

This store will be open for business seven days a week, morning, noon, and night. (And in between times)

We will do what we can to merit your patronage and service is our motto.

-Albert Gagnon

The Camp Canteen ran the above ad [not original design] in the February 22, 1936 issue.

"Leader Baker, who knows his skunks, did the skinning next day. He is planning on a new fur cap, but needing a little more fur, he has placed his order with the C.O. for another skin." [84]

- The Washingtonian, April 30, 1936

"Former CCC Camp Busy Site as Monks Take Over Quarters"

The following story appeared in the April 6, 1950 issue of the Woonsocket Call newspaper:

Some 90 monks of the fire-razed Abbey of Our Lady of the Valley, Cumberland, took up residence yesterday in the former CCC camp on the George Washington state reservation in West Glocester.

The monks arrived at the new site in buses, automobiles, and trucks from the temporary refuge at Portsmouth Priory, a private school for boys operated by the Benedictine Fathers at Portsmouth.

The brown clad brothers and the white and black robed priests were greeted by a sign which reads, "Our Lady of Refuge," as they turned from Putnam Pike into the site of what is to be their residence for the time being. In front of the sign is a five-foot statue of the Blessed Mother.

The monks filed from the vehicles and entered the central office building where they were greeted by a fire glowing in a huge fireplace.

Wonderfully Renovated

The Rev. Fr. M. John OCSO (Order of Cistercians of the Strict Observance), prior who has assisted the Rt. Rev. M. Edmund Futterer, abbot, in the rehabilitation work of the past two weeks, reported that the former

ANNOUNCING
LAUNDRY REOPENS

G.I. Pants washed ....10 cents
G.I. Pants washed + pressed ....10 cents
G.I. shirts washed ....10 cents
G.I. shirts washed + pressed......................10 cents
Summer pants washed + pressed ....15 cents
Summer shirts washed + pressed..............15 cents
Summer shirts & pants washed + pressed.. 25 cents
Jersey and shirts washed (a set) .... 08 cents
Towels washed ....05 cents
Socks washed (per pair)..........................02 cents
Civilian pants pressed................................10 cents
Civilian suits pressed .... 25 cents
White shoes cleaned ....05 cents
Black or brown shoes polished.................05 cents
G.I. pants widened ....50 cents

All types of clothes repaired at low cost.

Suits stored per week................................25 cents
Suits stored per month .... 75 cents

(One FREE press if stored a month)

We aim to please,
ARRUDA & STARSIAK

QUICK SERVICE • CLEAN SERVICE

The August 31, 1937 issue of The Washingtonian ran the above advertisement [not original design].

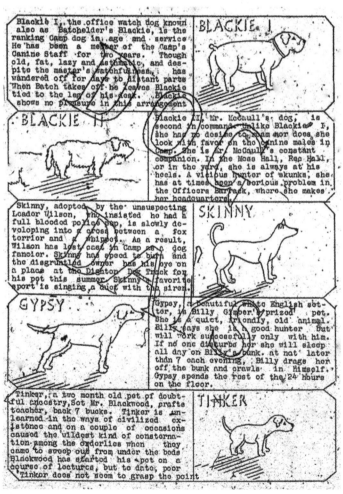

The April 30, 1936 issue of The Washingtonian had this description and drawings of the five dogs that graced the lives of the staff and enrollees of Camp Washington.

CCC camp had been "wonderfully renovated" to provide new accommodations for the monks.

The old military terms which were used to identify the buildings of the CCC camp were being changed yesterday by the green signs with yellow lettering. For example, what was formerly "barracks" are now dormitories; where a sign once said, "Commandant" one now reads Abbot: one-time officers' quarters have been

A montage containing an aerial view of the Putnam CCC camp where the Trappist monks and laybrothers were kindly received after a disastrous fire that destroyed their monastery in Cumberland, RI on March 21, 1950. Their temporary home was called Our Lady of Refuge. The statue of St. Bernard (c.1091-1153) was centrally responsible for the early expansion of the Cistercian Order. St. Joseph's Abbey

combined to provide an infirmary and chapel; the "mess hall" is now the refectory (religious term for communal meals).

The renovation work will continue for another week as the monks strive to make the buildings more suitable for their needs. Austere requirements of the Trappist order were relinquished somewhat yesterday to facilitate and speed the work. Usually the monks do not speak with one another except by sign language.

All the monks seemed enthused with their new quarters with one of the older monks commenting jokingly, "I feel like a Boy Scout again." The camp was a beehive of activity. The roads of the camp were continuously filled with monks yesterday afternoon, some carrying firewood for the pot stoves, some with heavy loads of blankets, others with carpentry tools.

Only the aged monk in the shoe repair building was idle while on the bench in front of him stood about 50 pairs of shoes awaiting the attention of his nimble fingers. Questioned about his idleness he turned slowly and answered in broken English: "I not even have my hammer and nails since the fire. My machines and all my equipment were destroyed." And tears filled his eyes.

Asked if he thought any good had come of the fire, the old monk hesitated a moment and then declared, "I think it has drawn us still closer together...if that was possible." He had gathered firewood a few minutes before and put a few pieces in the pot-bellied stove before he turned towards the shoe bench once more and shook his head sadly.

Trappist monks and priests praying in one of the Camp Washington buildings that was converted into a chapel after their monastery in Cumberland was destroyed by fire. St. Joseph's Abbey

The Trappists converted the CCC rec hall/canteen into a chapel. St. Joseph's Abbey

Fr. David Holly working in the refectory, the converted CCC mess hall. St. Joseph's Abbey

Once Defeated Champion

The other monks praised his work incessantly. "He can make a beautiful shoe by just starting with a piece of leather," one of them said. "And did you notice his muscled body?" another said, "He once defeated a Polish wrestling champion in his younger days."

The skills and crafts of the older monks were paying an important part yesterday in readying the camp for their way of life. The elders could be seen here and there advising the younger members of the order on how to tackle the various jobs. The carpentry shop was probably the busiest place at the camp with benches, clothing racks, partitions, and chapels to be constructed.

The camp treasurer reported that the total sum of gifts now stands at $6,600. "But what is that," he said, "when you consider that building a chapel such as we

had in Cumberland costs about $900,000 to $1,000,000. However, don't think we are not grateful for all the donations that have come in so far. We are, but I was just thinking," he went on wistfully, "if all the 40,000 people or so who visited the monastery fire ruins had contributed a little something, wouldn't that be wonderful?"

In the Army type mess hall last night, supper was being readied for the first time. Mess kits were being used instead of plates. On the menu for each monk, was the following: stewed prunes, pea soup, one potato, and a variety of vegetables and rye bread.

In the tailor shop and supply house, near the dormitories, several monks were still sorting and repairing clothes that were thrown in a heap outside the monastery the night of the fire. Beds were being made in the dormitories. The monks sleep on straw mattresses with boards instead of a spring. The beds were separated by plywood partitions which formed individual cells.

The monks plan to occupy every one of the 23 or so buildings on the camp site. The camp is off Route 44 and is sheltered by trees and bushes from the main road providing solitude and privacy which the monks desire.

Work was being rushed on the canteen building yesterday, which will serve as the church. Two altars already had been erected and liturgical books stood in the benches in two rows.

Feet Washed

Though Holy Week observances are to be somewhat curtailed, the usual Maundy Thursday service of the

During Easter Holy Week the Trappist priests and monks formed a procession as they left the former rec hall that had been converted into a chapel. St. Joseph's Abbey

The Easter procession of Trappists walk past the old Putnam CCC garage. St. Joseph's Abbey

washing of the feet was observed this morning with the abbot and a few monks chosen by him, washing the feet of the other members of the community, in a traditional act of humanity,

However, there is a shortage of liturgical books at the moment and the monks had to couple-up to sing the services. Some of the books were destroyed in the fire, and some of those which were saved were in need of repair.

Meanwhile, about 30 monks remain at the abbey in Cumberland where the work of reducing the fire-scarred walls and carting away rubble continued today.

Father John pointed out that William J. Halloran, rigging contractor, whose aerial boom has been used in the demolition work and Fred Egan, a steeplejack and contractor, have been very helpful to the community in directing the cleanup of the fire.

The General Assembly received a letter yesterday from the abbot in acknowledgement of the Legislature's resolution of sympathy in the abbey's loss on the fire of March 21.

The abbot pointed out that the loss of the guest house and chapel was a "cruel blow" to the community but he expressed hopes "that provisions be made so that it will be possible for us to remain in Rhode Island." It is still a matter of conjecture whether the monks will remain in Cumberland or the site purchased in Spenser, Mass. last year.

The Glocester camp was put at the disposal of the Trappist community by Gov. John O. Pastore shortly after the plight of the monks became known in the wake of the disastrous fire.

The main body of monks will remain at Glocester until accommodations are available either in Cumberland or Spencer. No decision has been announced by the abbot yet as to where the community will eventually settle permanently.

"The Monks at the Glocester CCC Camp" by Father Gabriel Bertoniere of St. Joseph's Abbey, Spencer, MA

The history of the community of Our Lady of the Valley harks back to the monastery of Petit Clairvaux in Tracadie, Nova Scotia, which was founded around 1825 by French monks fleeing from the aftermath of the French Revolution. In 1900 this monastery was transferred

Brother Jerome is one of the three survivors of the monastery fire and he lived for a time in the Camp Washington CCC camp in 1950. St. Joseph's Abbey

to Cumberland Rhode Island when Bishop Harkins of Providence offered to the monks a farm property facing onto Diamond Hill Road as a future home.

After years of modest growth, on the night of March 21, 1950, the church and the principal wing of the monastery itself were destroyed by fire. Then Governor of Rhode Island, John O. Pastore promised the State's aid, generously offering the monks the use of the Glocester CCC Camp as a temporary refuge. This turned out to be an ideal solution as a first move for the monks while they pondered their options for the future. At the time of the fire there were approximately 150 persons living in the monastery. [All documents in the archives were totally destroyed, and the exact number of monks and guests present during the fire is not known.] Fortunately no one suffered serious injury. The source of the fire is not known. It seems to have begun in or near the entrance foyer of the monastery near a staircase leading to the second floor of the building.

The monastic life is the oldest form of religious vocation in the Catholic Church consisting of self-commitment to God in a community characterized by the mutual support and love of its members. Prayer, spiritual reading, and work are given pride of place. Initially, self-support centered on agriculture. Today the preparation of food and other products has become more common. While the members of the community do not participate in religious ministry outside the monastery, the monastic guest house makes it possible for visitors to share in some measure in the life of the monks.

There are still three brothers in the community of Spencer who are survivors of the fire and who lived for a period in the camp. Unfortunately due to infirmity they are no longer able to easily communicate. Here, however, is what one of these men, Br. Jerome Collins, had to say in an early interview about the experience of those days:

The Monastery of Our Lady of the Valley was about as austere as you could possibly get. In one sense, the fire was a pleasant interlude; there was a sense of excitement, something new. We never thought it was going to be so disastrous; there wasn't a sense of sadness or foreboding. There was rather a sense of euphoria, the sense that we were going to make good, do something to overcome the loss. The fire wasn't a heartbreaking thing; at least I didn't feel that way. People had a sense of beginning something new. Spencer was a new beginning; the fire was all forgotten when we came up here. We just wanted to work and get the place built."

A broader expression of the reaction of the Camp and of the monastic vocation that it helped to save was the fact that a number of young men became novices at the camp and many of them stayed on to make their vows.

Length of Monks' Stay at Camp

The monks arrived on April 5, 1950. A first challenge was the adaptation of the existing camp buildings to the needs of the community: Church, kitchen, refectory, infirmary, dormitories, etc. One of these would be set aside as office of the Father Abbot. By April 22 some space in a wing of the old monastic building at the camp had already been cleared of debris from the fire, and 27 monks were able to take up temporary residence there. Records also show that by the same date 115 monks were already lodged at the Camp itself! Though some of their monastic activities had to be curtailed, the lives of the monks at the camp reflected the age-old rhythm of prayer, reading and work. But It was also a time to decide where their future home would be.

A New Superior

After years of great dedication as superior of the community, Dom John O'Connor offered his resignation, and in late November Rome approved the election of Dom Edmund Futterer as O'Connor's successor. His sabbatial blessing took place on October 2. At the same time the Holy See elevated the monastery itself to the rank of Abbey, and Dom Edmund became its abbot. The dynamism of his commitment to the community in following years was to become legendary.

High on his list of concerns would be the question of where the community would find their definitive home. At first some study was devoted to the possibility

Trappist Monks heading for daily work. St. Joseph's Abbey

Trappist Monks reading in the library. St. Joseph's Abbey

of rebuilding the monastery in Cumberland, but this was eventually ruled out, in part because the growth of the neighborhood on Diamond Hill Road did not jibe with the monks' need for seclusion and peace. It is reported that not far from the monastery itself there were a number of entertainment establishments such as a bar with a juke box, a polka parlor, and a race track for small automobiles. The new Abbot General of the Order during his first visit to Our Lady of the Valley made it clear that he too wished for a change to a more secluded site.

A first move in the right direction came from the archbishop of Santa Fe, NM, who had been hoping that the monks would found a monastery in his own diocese. The archbishop now informed Dom Edmund that a suitable farm site near Pecos, NM was up for sale. Dom Edmund was interested, and after appropriate preparations some 30 founding monks were able to set forth in April 1948. This meant that space had suddenly opened up for new vocations in the group at the Valley.

Looking toward the needs of future vocations, the search continued. Dom Edmund sent Brother Leo as far afield as California. It was also in the year 1948 that a family-owned dairy farm in Spencer, MA was put on the market. Learning of this Brother Blaise was sent to see the property, and came away mightily impressed. From that time on, all the community's efforts were directed to planning, seeking financial support as well as permissions from the Holy See and from the Order to transfer the community once again. As it had been transferred to Rhode Island from Nova Scotia, this time it would be to transfer it from Our Lady of the Valley to Spencer, MA. An important step along the way was the agreement to sell, signed on May 27, 1949 between the Owners of the Alta Crest Farms, Inc. and the CISTERCIAN ABBEY OF THE STRICT OBSERVANCE, INC., a Rhode Island Corporation, but no one could foresee what lay ahead on March 21, 1950, and this brings us back to where we started—with the Great Fire. Thanks to newly found benefactors of the Grace family in the New York area and of Harry John of Milwaukee as well as others, it turned out that even after the fire there would still be hope for the Spencer solution. Two monks were soon sent to take possession of the property, but gradually existing buildings were reworked into a temporary monastery, and on December 23 most of the community was on hand for Christmas. Afterward a small contingent of 30 novices

had to return to the Camp once more to close things down and to bid a grateful farewell to the temporary home offered to them by the generosity of Rhode Island.

Today most of the original CCC camp Washington buildings have been removed, but there are some concrete foundations and steps. The only remaining CCC building is the log Education Building on the shore of Bowdish Reservoir and can be reached by driving through the campground and following signs.

CHAPTER 10
WESTERLY / BURLINGAME

The 1934 Camp Burlingame Co. 141 group photo. John MacDonald

HISTORY

After a few weeks of orientation and conditioning at Fort Adams, RI, Co. 141 left on May 24th, 1933 and arrived at the Burlingame Reservation in Charlestown. The camp, however, was called Camp Westerly because Westerly had a post office in the nearby village of Bradford with a railroad station a few miles from the camp.[1]

CCC camps were of two types: forest and park camps. At first, Burlingame was a forestry camp under the direction of the United States Forest Service. The

One of the waterholes that Co. 141 built so that fire fighters could have a nearby source of water. It was located by the Pasqusset Trail by Rt. 2. John MacDonald

park camps came under the domain of the Dept. of Interior, National Park Service, and after a couple of years Burlingame morphed into a park camp when the other park facility, Beach Pond, came on line in 1935.

Forestry camps, as their name suggests, focused on building truck trails throughout their domain enabling rapid deployment of equipment in the case of forest fires. These 'in-roads' had numerous convenient roadside waterholes installed along their courses.

Other work of the forest camps was divided between clearing out deadfalls, reforesting burned out areas, and treating tree diseases like gypsy moth infestation, Dutch Elm, and pine blister rust disease. Not all work took place at the camps and state lands. There were parallel Federal programs of buying up marginal woodlands that CCC men could improve.

Projects

Most of the projects were on or near the 3,100-acre reservation that surrounded the 500-acre Watchaug Pond except the 9-acre Kimball Bird Sanctuary the Audubon Society of Rhode Island maintained.[2]

Col. Cyril L.D. Wells planned and supervised the Westerly Camp projects. While awaiting the arrival of

Historical Description of Burlingame CCC Camp
Albert Klyberg, RI Historian

"The Burlingame Reservation, comprised approx. 2,000 acres of woodland and Watchaug Pond. It represented nearly half of all the state park holdings in the entire State of Rhode Island. At the time, there were no state beaches along Rhode Island's southern coast. The first of these, Scarborough, came along in several purchases in the next years, 1935 to 1937.

"Burlingame, on the other hand came about in a series of woodland acquisitions/condemnations, beginning in 1927 and continuing through 1930. The Metropolitan Park Commission, the state body empowered to manage state public parks, followed the lead of the adjacent Audubon Society's acquisition, a bequest of Walter Kimball. Kimball of Providence, like other successful Rhode Islanders, had taken to the woods of southern Rhode Island and built a bungalow-style cottage on the south shore of Watchaug Pond. The Audubon Society converted his gift to the Kimball Wildlife Sanctuary of 29 acres.

"The recent history of the Charlestown lands dated back to the years, 1880 to 1884 when the Narragansett Indians disbanded, and their centuries-old lands went to the State of Rhode Island. The tribe had never fully recovered from the effects of King Philip's War, two centuries earlier. Subsequent to the detribalization, large parcels of land in Charlestown went into private ownership. Many, like the Kimball lands, became summer camps of wealthy Rhode Island entrepreneurs from the Providence metropolitan area.

"The conservation and early environmental movement of the first decades of the 20th century motivated some of these folks to consider preserving woodlands and wetlands for wildlife habitats, and a few, like Kimball, made gifts of property to non-profit nature organizations like the Rhode Island Audubon Society founded in 1897. This upland, running parallel for miles along Route 1, originally the Queen Anne's highway of 1703, had not been part of the broad plains and salt ponds along the shoreline that had comprised the world of the original Narragansett Planters, who raised sheep and cattle in South Kingstown, Narragansett,

Charlestown, and Westerly. They were the breeders of the famed Narragansett Pacers.

"To the north, beyond their coastal plain was the stony upland, a place of many acres of coniferous species, dotted by small ponds and small streams – land that was not easily adapted to agriculture, but was well-suited for woodland recreational purposes, either public or private. It was into this environment that the unemployed single men, between the ages of 18 and 25 signed up for the forest jobs.

"The recently acquired Burlingame Reservation and the new state forests of George Washington Memorial and Wickaboxet (near West Greenwich) were logical places to put the CCC men to work.

"Stimulated by the establishment of the CCC camp in 1933, the following year Burlingame increased to 3,100 acres. It was named for Edward Burlingame, long-time chairman of the Park Commission.

"The Commission's early vision had been the creation of a ring of public parks and 'reservations' in an eight-mile radius of the Rhode Island State House. Scenic drives, or parkways, like spokes in a wheel, linked the parks to the urban concentrations of Providence, Pawtucket, and Central Falls. Most of the urban/industrial workers, for whom the park system was designed found their way to the woodlands, ponds, and picnic groves by the electric trolley. Almost all of the early parks were available for a nickel a ride.

"The original metropolitan scope of a ring of parks changed, however, with the philanthropic gift of Goddard Memorial Park, with more than 400 acres in 1927, on the Bay, in the Potowomut section of Warwick. The Kimball Wildlife Sanctuary of the Audubon Society came to life the same year, and eyes turned to the south coast of Rhode Island for the expansion of the Metropolitan Park Commission's holdings. With the twin arrivals of Burlingame and the CCC, that vision became anchored in a state-wide system of preserves and reservations. The year 1932 also saw another twin gift of the state's first forests: George Washington Memorial in Glocester and Wickaboxet State Forest in West Greenwich."

Federal government heavy equipment, the recruits at Burlingame used borrowed tools and trucks from the state of RI as they widened the entry road into the Sam Bailey Hoxie farm on the shore of Watchaug Pond. Going into a nearby cedar swamp they cut white cedar trees and floated poles a mile down Watchaug Pond to a place where they were loaded on state trucks. The poles were then used to support and carry telephone and electrical service lines one and a half miles from Sam Bailey Hoxie farmhouse to their camp. The boys also graded a small part of the beach and a recreation field. About thirty to thirty-five men did work in the park while the rest of the men worked on projects outside of the reservation.[3]

At Rhode Island State College in Kingston CCC enrollees performed these work projects: cut wood, constructed fire lanes, cleared and thinned woods, did fire hazard reduction and trail side burning, constructed telephone line and water holes, built bridges, planted White Spruce and Red Pine trees on burned-over areas, and cleared acres of land.[4, 5]

CCC camp Forester Eric Jacobson stated in an article of the February 1937 issue of the camp newspaper, *Wahoo*, that the enrollees did salvage cutting which was the removal of all the dead trees from the burned areas and used the wood in the camp for fuel. They also piled the brush and burned it in the open.

Co. 141 men had other projects such as fighting tree diseases such as blister rust by destroying gooseberry bushes and doing gypsy moth eradication by searching for and destroying the insect's egg masses. They constructed waterholes and roads, developed camp grounds, and improved beach sites.

During the fall of 1933 enrollees helped construct

CCC boys taking a break from working on a road with a tractor and compressor. Frank Fields

Col. Cyril L.D. Wells

Camp Burlingame Superintendent Col. Cyril L.D. Wells. Undated Providence Journal

Col. Cyril L.D. Wells served as Superintendent of the Burlingame Camp for seven years. He was born on June 9, 1883 in the West Indies. His father James was a prominent civil engineer and contractor.

He came to the U.S. and began doing construction work in Providence. He took up special classes in concrete and steel engineering at Brown University. Wells took many jobs with construction companies. He joined the RI National Guard and rose to major in 1917. During WWI he served with the 72nd Artillery, Coast Artillery Corps. He continued to advance in rank and in 1922 he retired as a Brigadier General.

Wells did extensive construction work in the Providence area. Some of his projects were: Commercial High School, Emery (Carlton) Theater, the Summerfield building, Temple Beth-El, the Museum in Roger Williams Park, and numerous other industrial and school buildings.

In 1933 he began working as superintendent at the Burlingame CCC camp and continued till he died in 1940 at the age of 57.

(L – R) Four barracks where the boys lived and slept. Frank Fields | An aerial view of Camp Burlingame. The road on the lower left is the entrance road leading to the circle. The pond is in the right corner and the long garage is right below the circle. The four barracks are next to each other on the lower right. ridemgis.maps.arcgis.com | The road in front of the camp buildings and gas pumps. John MacDonald

The Burlingame CCC boys enjoyed relaxing in their rec hall where they played pool and cards and also saw movies, had dances and enjoyed music and plays.

Six boys seated in the mess hall. Frank Fields

permanent wooden camp structures so that the men could move in before winter: barracks, mess hall, administrative building, washrooms, rec hall and other support structures.

Enrollees also built fire places, camp sites, and picnic areas. They also made recreational improvements to the beaches of Watchaug Pond.

- 1934 -

In the spring of 1934, nineteen-year old Alexander Krupka painted two beautiful murals in the mess hall that were admired by his fellow enrollees and by visitors such as U.S. Senator Theodore Francis Green who also was Governor of RI and frequently hiked to the Westerly camp. About the same time, Co. 141 was awarded the best camp in District 4 that included RI and Cape Cod camps.[6]

At the end of 1934 the Burlingame Reservation consisted of 1,988 acres and 10,000 people visited the park.[7]

Recreation

During the evenings and on weekends the Army provided recreation activities for the enrollees after work. There was inter-camp competition in baseball, volleyball, basketball, boxing, soccer, swimming, and horseshoe pitching. There was also intramural competition in touch football, track, skiing, tennis, hockey, ping-pong, and pool.[8]

- 1935 -

In 1935 the Park Commission purchased 103 acres of burned-over land in the vicinity of the road near the camp that enters into the Hoxsie Farm. Approx. 50 men from the camp were to work on clearing the land. Twenty-five men each in two groups worked clearing forest lanes and improved 80 acres of burned land. They also widened firebreaks from 60 to 120 feet and improved several miles of trails. Another project was the widening of the road into camp and covering the road with cinders and oil. The caretaker's house was also wired for electricity.[9]

The Burlingame camp continued to do fire suppression and forestry sanitation program on both public and private land.[10]

By the end of 1935 the Commission added 889 acres to the Burlingame Reservation. Workers constructed 6-1/3 miles of 150' wide fire lanes, improved 131 acres of forest, and improved the landscape of their CCC camp. They also improved the picnic area near Watchaug Pond by constructing five fireplaces and an overnight campground. Water and toilet facilities were now open to the public.[11]

At the end of 1935 the Burlingame Reservation consisted of 3,100 acres and had 10,000 visitors.[12]

– 1936 –

On April 18, 1936 the camp changed from a Forest Camp under the U.S. Forest Service to a State Park (SP-2) under the National Park Service. The CCC camp was asked by the Tercentenary Committee to establish a temporary overnight campground with toilet and water facilities. The future projects were for the development of the beach, a new entrance road, hiking and bridle trails, three Adirondack lean-tos, and an overlook shelter. They also worked on reducing fires by building waterholes, firebreaks, and truck trails.[13]

The 1936 Co. 141's basketball team had a very successful season and came in second place in the District Championship. That same year the soccer team easily won the District championship. In 1935 the company's swim team came home with a trophy.

In September 1936 Co. 141 won first place for its educational exhibit at the Rhode Island State Fair in Kingston.[14]

The Second Annual Report of the Department of Agriculture and Conservation 1936 reported that the Burlingame Park had 3,100 acres and attendance jumped to 20,00 visitors.

– 1937 –

The Burlingame Reservation (State Park) was the largest in the state and drew over 20,00 visitors who enjoyed picnicking, hiking, and swimming the clean fresh water of Watchaug Pond. It was one of the most popular spots and many days it was full to capacity. The parts of the reservation that were burned over a few years ago have improved greatly due to the intensive work of the CCC.[16]

There was a change in the camp newspaper title in January 1937 from The Wayfarer to the Wahoo. The old title meant a person who travels on foot. Now that they were in a group in a camp they were not alone. The title came from the Hebrew "The Burning Bush." It was chosen because the CCC boys were like the Hebrew youth of the past who were faced with strange and distressing circumstances. The camp editor stated: "Most of us are trying to escape from circumstances which we do not like. But don't run from them. Stand up and fight to better yourself, no matter how hard the battle, you can win."

On Jan. 27th a variety show was held. A group of

The roster of the Burlingame camp supervisors and enrollees.[15]

The cover of the monthly Wahoo Burlingame camp newspaper was written and illustrated by the CCC boys under the supervision of the Education teacher.

Girls in training at an N.Y.A.-run summer camp in Chepachet. The CCC boys often got together with the N.Y.A. girls. National Archives

Throughout the year ministers and priests visited CCC camps and gave religious instructions and sermons. In June 1937 Rev. Francis Patrick Keough, Bishop of Providence, visited Burlingame and some enrollees received Confirmation. John MacDonald

25 entertainers from the Federal Theater Project featuring dancers, singers, comedians, acrobats, and a torch singer performed to an enthusiastic audience of CCC boys and their leaders.

The Carpentry & Woodworking Class made a scale model of a wooden building that was 27" x 27" and 15" tall.[17]

On April 4, 1937 the camp held an "Open House" to celebrate the 4th Anniversary of the founding of the CCC. The camp was open for inspection from 2-5 pm and a program was held in the rec hall where refreshments were served.[18]

Later in the month on the 26th a band concert was held at the improved baseball field that was dedicated to Edmund Baxter who was the first enrollee that died at the Burlingame Camp.

On June 2nd Co. 141 was invited to a dance at the N.Y.A. (National Youth Administration) Chepachet camp by its supervisor Miss Stone. Two weeks later a Company Dance was held on Wednesday, June 16, 1937. The camp invited ladies from the N.Y.A. camp and other young ladies from surrounding towns.

During the summer of 1937 the camp emphasized safety when swimming. Camp Doctor Lt. Sulman taught the entire company artificial respiration. The camp rule was that no one could go swimming unless they passed a distance swimming test. Another rule was that each enrollee should always swim with a "buddy."[19]

Even as a 'park' camp, however, men from the 141st fought forest fires in 1936 and 1937, which occurred along the Wood River and in Westerly.[20]

– 1938 –

Co. 141 was called to help when the Hurricane of '38 hit Rhode Island on September 21st. It downed and destroyed thousands of trees and disrupted roads and public improvements. One of the enrollees' distasteful chores after the '38 Hurricane was the recovery of 28 bodies on the South County beaches on the night of the 21st and the next day. Enrollees also cleared roads and removed fallen trees in the forests. Boys from Burlingame Camp were later joined by CCC boys from Beach Pond and Arcadia camps for additional search work. They were complimented by the State Police for their efficient and effective work.[21]

The Division of Forests, Parks and Parkways acquired the 36-acre site of the Great Swamp Fight from the Hazard Associates of South Kingstown. Great Swamp Fight or "Great Swamp Massacre" was fought on December 19, 1675. It was a critical battle of King Philip's War, in which Native Americans fought English settlers and their Indian allies in one of the bloodiest conflicts (per capita) in U.S. history. It took place in the area of West Kingstown, RI. The Burlingame boys began constructing the entrance road and parking area in 1938.[22] A grand opening was held a year later on October 18, 1939.

Major projects by the CCC on the southeast shore of Watchaug Pond were the construction of a parking area that accommodated 250 cars, a recreation building and field house, a large latrine and septic tank with a sewage disposal system.[23]

The Burlingame CCC camp helped remove trees damaged from the 1938 Hurricane. Postcard from www.newenglandhistoricalsociety.com

CCC crews did fire hazard reduction work, repaired roads, improved picnic and beach areas. Workers also began working on a large log shelter with two fireplaces.[24]

Recreation

As in all the camps for young men, ages 18 to 25, sports filled weekend hours. Among the opportunities offered were baseball, basketball, boxing, soccer, and swimming. Many of these were team sports against nearby camps. Burlingame won several championships. It also won prizes in the nearby Kingston State Fair for various displays and demonstrations. It was once rated the best camp in the 4th District of the 1st Corps of CCC. The Fourth District embraced all the Rhode Island camps, plus those on Cape Cod.

– 1939 –

The following is a list of the Co. 141 staff: Commanding Officer Lt. James L. Wiggmore who was assisted by 2nd Lt. Constant L. Simonini and 1st Lt. Gordon E. Menzies. The Education Dept. was led by E.O. Peckham. Camp projects were led by Superintendent Cyril L.D. Wells. His foremen were: Walter Johnson, Pacifico Colicci, Oscar Mageau, and Frank Pierce; John Bernowich, engineer; Harry Blanchard, mechanic; John Sullivan, blacksmith, and Lemuel MacDonald, carpenter.

Company 141 accomplished many projects. They constructed fireplaces, shelters, guard rails, roads, truck trails, a picnic ground, beach campground, wash room, lavatory, and a septic tank and disposal field. Enrollees planted trees, removed old structures, and did fire hazard work on state and private properties.[25]

The camp baseball team ended their season with a record of 16 wins and 4 loses.[26]

All members of the camp had to enroll in a job training course. The education program was enhanced with new equipment. The woodworking shop located in the "Black Cat" building received a new Delta 24" scroll saw. There were plans to move the printing press into the schoolhouse that made room for a table saw and jointer. In the Black Cat building the dark room was re-equipped and with running water.[27]

On Wednesday, October 18, 1939 The Rhode Island Historical Society dedicated a monument in the

Great Swamp Fight commemorating the war between King Phillip's Indian tribe and the combined forces of the settlers of the Plymouth Colony, Rhode Island and Connecticut. Rhode Island Governor William H. Vanderbilt III (1938-39) commended the work of Co. 141 for their work in building the road to the rotary and the footpath to the monument. There were approx. 300 people that attended the event along with four members of the Narragansett Tribe that were in native dress. The parking area had approx. 80 cars. Members of Mr. Colicci's work crew were dressed in their new green CCC uniforms for the occasion.[28]

Also, in October 1939, enrollees began working on the road in front of the camp quadrangle. The job was supervised by Philip Tyler of the state department of roads and bridges who also brought some of his men to help Mr. Mageau of Co. 141 and his men. Work began on Oct. 23, 1939. They completely regraded and graveled the road. The state used their graders and steam rollers for the job. This work was a great help in improving drainage. The road was to be eventually tarred.[29]

In December 1939 two new pieces of equipment were installed in the woodworking and plastics shop. The first was a miter saw and the other was a motor to drive the lathe. Wood turning tools and a supply of different woods were also purchased.[30]

That same month, enrollees were busy fighting old man winter. The men were removing snow around the camp and as far as the caretaker's house. This consumed 144 man-days of work. The other important job was cutting and hauling wood to camp to keep the stoves going. This took 736 man-hours of work.[31]

By the end of 1939 the Burlingame Reservation had 3,100 acres that were purchased from many owners at a cost of $72, 836.[32]

– 1940 –

In January 1940, the Education Dept. made arrangements with the RI Civil Service Dept. so that the CCC camp would be on the mailing list of all exams that would be coming up so that enrollees would be aware of the testing for job vacancies. The announcements were then placed on the camp bulletin board.[33]

The camp softball team was in a softball league of 12 teams from Westerly. The league started playing on May 20th, 1940.[34]

Projects

During the month of January work continued on the construction of the Senator Green Road that was begun on Dec. 15, 1939. A work crew of approx. four men supervised by Mr. Johnson first cleared the area of brush, trees, and stumps. They then graded the roadbed. When completed the road would be 2.1 miles long and connect the rotary north of the camp with the Buckeye Brook Trail. It was hoped the road would eventually encircle Watchaug Pond and eventually connect with Prosser Trail near Prosser Beach.[35]

Three crews composed of approx. 90 men were doing fire hazard reduction and clean-up work caused by the large number of damaged trees caused by the 1938 Hurricane. The crews were supervised by Mr. Mageau, Mr. Pierce, and Mr. Colicci. The latter's crew of 11 men were busy on other land owned by the state.[36]

In January 1940, the camp newspaper Wahoo announced the completion of the beautiful log shelter at

The road around the quadrangle containing the flag and buildings. Frank Field

One of the roads built by Co. 141 at Burlingame State Park. Frank Field

Prosser Beach. The work originally began on April 13, 1938 but due to a few delays kept being postponed. The first problem was the Hurricane of 1938 that necessitated all of the camp enrollees to work on the clean-up. The next delay was securing the logs. Once the logs arrived, 15 bundles of shingles for the roof were stolen. After this delay work was completed. It is still in use today.[37]

The April 1940 Wahoo camp newspaper regretfully announced the passing of the former Superintendent, Col. Cyril L.D. Wells, of the camp. He began his work at the Burlingame camp in 1933. For the past seven years he guided all of the work at the camp and tremendous improvements were made to the Burlingame State Park. John Barnowich was named new Superintendent.[38]

The 141st Co. was called out on April 29, 1940 to fight a fire at Usquepaug (in the towns of Richmond and South Kingston). Over 600 acres of woodlands were destroyed. The speedy action of the enrollee crew prevented the fire from destroying the village.[39]

The Burlingame Camp celebrated the 7th anniversary of the CCC with an Open House in April. The public was invited and a slide show was held describing all of the projects completed by Co. 141. Then a fire fighting demonstration was held.[40]

In May 1940 a group of enrollees invested in a farm project in camp. They purchased 125 baby chicks. The boys also built a chicken coop and placed it beyond the volleyball court. The chickens were making steady progress despite a weasel, heavy rains, and cold weather. The reporter for the Wahoo jokingly stated: "The rest of the company is looking forward to a chicken dinner some Sunday when all the chicken farmers are on a weekend pass.[41]

The Sixth Annual Report of the Department of Agriculture and Conservation 1940 stated the National Park Service CCC camp did a great job of work at the 3,100-acre and 800-acre pond forest park area in Charlestown. They developed an area for camping, bathing and picnicking in a confined area of the shoreline. Here are the improvements:

- A 45' x 26' log shelter containing two built-in fireplaces and picnic tables
- A 29' x 19' latrine building containing a septic tank and drainage field
- Installed an artesian well and pump house for a

future bath house
- Constructed 159 rods of guard rail along the camp entrance roads
- Completed 608 acres of fire hazard reduction work.
- Scouted for blister rust on 3,100 acres of the Reservation
- Planted 68,350 forest tree seedlings and installed a weather station

– 1941 –

The Seventh Annual Report of the Department of Agriculture and Conservation 1941 stated that the Burlingame CCC camp installed two water systems, "... one at the camping area west of Watchaug Pond and one at the Prosser Beach area. Connections have been laid to the toilet building, completing a much needed improvement. The CCC Camp at Burlingame is now closed, thereby depriving us of valuable help in the development of this park. The closing of the camp leaves uncompleted the road which was under construction for about two miles in the westerly part of the reservation."

In 1941 the Burlingame CCC camp closed and many projects went unfinished. The two-mile road under construction in the western part of the reservation was not completed.[42]

All CCC work in the U.S. ended in 1942 and many of the CCC boys were needed for the WWII effort. During the War the Burlingame Park was used to house Naval personnel that were training pilots at the nearby Charlestown Naval Air Station. There were also times the CCC camp was used to house U.S. Army and also by British Navy personnel as a rest stop. It also was used to house prisoners of war.

After the war from 1946-61 part of the park was used by the American Legion for a summer youth camp called "Legion Town."

For quite a few years the state used park trees at Christmas time to decorate the State House.

"Beginning in 1991 a four-phase upgrade of the camping sites, sanitary infrastructure and maintenance amenities was undertaken. Using a combination of National Park Service grants and the state's Recreation Area Development Funds much needed improvements to facilities, some dating back to the 1930s, commenced."[43]

Bathers at Watchaug Pond Beach. www.visitrhodeisland.com

One of the most impressive structures built by the CCC at the Burlingame State Park is the beautiful log picnic pavilion that has stone fireplaces at each end. Podskoch

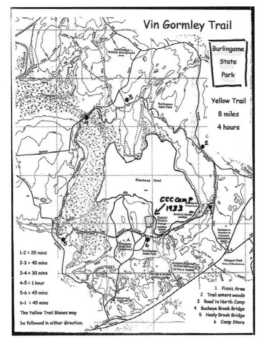

The CCC boys built the Gormley Hiking trail that goes around the Watchaug Pond. Albert Klyberg

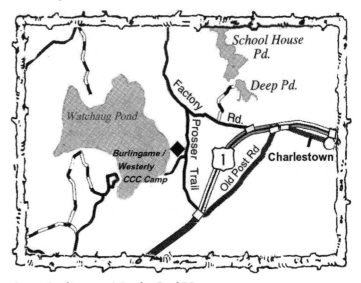

Camp Burlingame Map by Paul Hartmann

LEGACY

Over an eight-year period the tremendous work of Co. 141 cleared and restored farmland and burned forest at the park. They also built 755 campsites for fishing, swimming, picnicking, boating and hiking. The area north of Buckeye Brook Road, abutting the Pawcatuck River, is primarily a hunting area."

Directions

Directions: Set your GPS to 25 Sanctuary Rd., Charlestown, RI.

From Westerly go approx. 10 mi. E on Rt. 1/Post Rd. to Prosser Trail Rd. on your left. Go .8 mi. on Prosser Trail Rd. and make a left on Sanctuary Rd. Burlingame

State Park is on the right and the original site of the Burlingame CCC camp.

From Providence: take I-95 S for approx. 12 mi. to Exit 9 Rt. 4 S. Go approx. 9 mi. on Rt. 4 to Rt. 1. Go S on Rt. 1/Post Rd. travel approx. 17 mi to Prosser Trail Rd. on right. Go .8 mi. on Prosser Trail Rd. and make a left on Sanctuary Rd. Burlingame State Park is on the right.

MEMORIES

Lemuel J. MacDonald
Leader & Teacher at Camp Burlingame

John MacDonald came to three of my CCC talks in Rhode Island and shared his stories and photos of his dad who worked at the Burlingame CCC camp. I interviewed John on Dec. 7th, 2017 at a Dunkin' Donuts restaurant in John's home town of Westerly.

(L) Lemuel J. MacDonald joined the CCC in 1934 and worked at the Burlingame Camp Co. 141. He is standing near his barracks. (R) On May 1, 1936 MacDonald was promoted from Asst. Leader to Leader of Barracks C and his job was to make sure the boys behaved, listened to orders and kept the barracks clean and orderly. John MacDonald

Tell me about your dad's early life.

"My father Lemuel J. MacDonald was born on July 5, 1903 in the small town of Bear River on Prince Edward Island, Canada. His parents were John and Margaret. My father was the eldest child, followed by his brothers Francis and Tom and a sister Margaret. My father came to the United States in 1924 when he was approximately 21 years old. He lived in Boston with other Canadians and then moved to Providence, RI where he did construction work. This is where he learned his carpentry skills. When the Depression came, he continued to do construction work although it was getting harder to find jobs."

John then showed me excerpts from his father's journal.

July 9, 1932. Returned to Providence. Went to work at St. Pius Church remodeling classroom.

This period between July 9, 1932 to April 26, 1934 has been a very discouraging one. No steady work.

April 26, 1934 My lucky day. Answering an ad that was in the Providence Journal. I received a job in the CCC'S, Co. 141, Charlestown, RI as a carpenter. On June 1st, 1934 I was appointed Asst. Leader and Acting Leader in Barracks on Oct.1st, 1934.

I was appointed Leader as of May 1st 1935 and as of this writing I am still in the CCC'S. It has been one of the most fortunate incidents in my life. Unemployed and discouraged this was a God send. It has also given me a deeper sense of appreciation of Army Officers and the service in general. Time of this writing, Sunday July 28, 1935, 10:50 am.

"Now I don't know how he was able to sign up since there was an age limit of 25 but maybe he was hired as a Local Experienced Man (LEM) since he had construction and woodworking experience. He was assigned to the Burlingame camp. At that time work was hard to get and it was a godsend when he got to work in the CCC.

"After six months of work, he resigned and this time he was listed in his discharge papers as an 'L.E.M. Carpenter' and his performance was listed as 'Excellent.'

"My father had a few jobs at the camp. During the day he would work with a group of boys and they did construction work for the future state park. He built the concession stand and the shower building. The latter had burned down sometime in the past. Later my parents would often take us three boys to the park that he helped build. The buildings were made out of cedar wood from the state park forest. He and his crew also built log structures like the beautiful pavilion that has two fireplaces and is used by visitors for picnics, etc. Another job was teaching a carpentry class at night.

"My father lived in the barracks along with the CCC enrollees and sometimes on weekends he went to visit his brother Tom who lived in Cranston. He also went with the other CCC boys on the weekends to the town of Westerly where one day he met my mother. They were married in approx. 1942. They had three sons: Bruce, Tom, and me."

We then went to John's home because he wanted to show me a sewing cabinet that his father built at the CCC camp. Near the staircase of the living room the sewing

MacDonald (L) teaching house building in his carpentry class. John MacDonald

(L – R) The sewing cabinet that MacDonald made was displayed at the September 1936 Tercentenary State Fair exhibit. John MacDonald | John MacDonald by the sewing cabinet his father made at the Burlingame CCC camp. Podskoch | Lemuel J. MacDonald in his retirement years. John MacDonald

cabinet had a plaque proudly displayed and it said: "This cabinet was built by leader Lemuel J. MacDonald, a member of the 141st Company CCC at Burlingame Reservation, Charleston, Rhode Island. Pop Taylor, a fellow CCC carpenter and I picked up dead cedar logs. We brought them into our carpenter shop in camp, allowed them to dry, and sawed them into boards 1 inch thick. From those boards, we each built a cabinet. We made the knobs out of cedar since we could not find suitable ones in the store. We finished the cabinets by applying seven or eight coats of varnish, allowing each coat to dry and rubbing down smooth each time before applying the next coat. The glue used in building this cabinet was the cold water type."

Then John showed me his father's CCC discharge papers. Under remarks it stated: "Official commendation given September 17, 1937 for superior work over and above regular duties. Not indebted to this company in any way. App't. Ass't Ldr. Per S.O. #12 7/1/34. Promoted to leader per S.C. #15 5/1/35." John was very proud of this.

John also showed me two certificates his father received for taking evening classes in "Journalism" and "Building and Estimating."

"On September 30, 1937 my father left the CCCs after 3½ years. He got a job at the New London sub base in Groton, Conn. He worked in the carpentry department doing public works projects. Eventually he was appointed a superintendent at his job. In around 1969 he retired after working in Groton for 32 years. He died in 1987."

John then showed me a bunch of letters praising his dad's work and performance at the camp. One was for making a special size typewriter table, another for making the company Honor Roll for his Superior work as a Leader, and another for rebuilding the interior of the Burlingame Clubhouse.

"My father did a lot of projects at the CCC camp with another enrollee, Walter Bell. He was a good friend of my father. I believe he was originally from Providence and settled in Westerly after the CCC."

John also had a certificate of Recognition of Service that his father received from the Navy for his work at the U.S. Submarine Base, in New London during WWII. I wished that I could have met his father before he passed. He really benefited from his time in the CCC where he was a leader and teacher. These experiences helped him to secure a very good job at the Submarine Base.

The Burlingame Dispensary/Infirmary

The hospital is open day and night and is always ready in case of an emergency. This means the hospital orderly must be on duty 24 hours a day.

The hospital orderly is a regular enrollee who was chosen for this job because he wants to learn the medical business and has a fair idea how any wounds should be treated. Because he has such an important job, he is a rated man which means he gets six extra dollars and has the right to order men into doing things.

The hospital orderly has an assistant who takes over when he is out. The main duty of the orderly is to conduct sick calls every morning at seven o'clock and every afternoon at four o'clock. This means that any men that have cuts, bruises, or rashes are treated,

The orderly never treats any serious wounds or ailments.

The orderly sleeps in the hospital and must keep the place spic and span. The orderly also records all treatments that are made in the hospital.

The hospital has always taken care of their patients in grand style and will continue to do so in the future.[44]

Camp Doctor's Recommendations to Stay Healthy

In many of the camp newspapers the camp doctor had an article about ways to stay healthy. In the December 1937 issue of the Wahoo Dr. Menzies gave advice on the common cold. He advised the enrollees that super-heated rooms and little ventilation harbor germs that could cause colds. Colds are often initiated from sneezes that spread the germs.

Persons with a cold are recommended to cover their mouths while sneezing and coughing. The doctor said enrollees should refrain from going to church or movies where there are crowds and where they might spread their colds.

The doctor recommended that those who just got a cold should do the following: take a hot bath, a glass of hot lemonade, a cathartic (laxative), and go to bed.

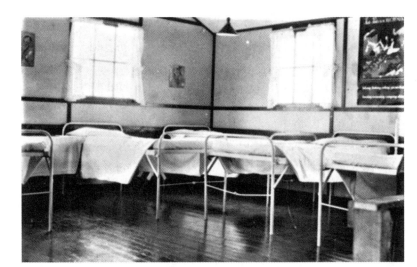

(Clockwise from L) Inside the infirmary/dispensary there were approx. five beds where enrollees were treated by the camp doctor. Frank Fields | The Burlingame Infirmary/Dispensary was staffed by an attendant and an Army doctor. John McDonald | The attendant's infirmary job was to stay in the building for 24 hours and take care of the ill and also bring them meals. He had his own room for sleeping and he had to keep the wood/coal stove going. Frank Fields

131

CHAPTER 11
WOONSOCKET / PRIMROSE

A 1936 aerial view of the Woonsocket/Primrose Camp in North Smithfield. North Smithfield Heritage Association & Larry Smith

HISTORY

The Woonsocket/Primrose Camp was established on June 1, 1935 when Capt. Webster L. Simons led a cadre of 22 men from the 130th Co. in Alfred, Maine. They arrived in Primrose, a section in North Smithfield, and pitched their tents on farmland the government leased from the Cesario family. It was near the Primrose train station that was a stop on the Providence and Springfield Railroad. The railroad came from Providence on its way to Pascoag (a village in the town of Burrillville). The men

The cadre of enrollees from Alfred, Maine set up tents near the Providence and Springfield Railroad crossing on Black Plain Rd. Lorenzo Harry Frisiello & Kathleen Duxbury Collection

lived in tents while work progressed at a rapid rate on the buildings.[1]

Although the camp was in the hamlet of Primrose in North Smithfield, the Army named it the Woonsocket camp. Rich Keen the President of the North Smithfield Heritage Association stated that the Army designated the Woonsocket name because the Primrose part of North Smithfield used the Woonsocket Post Office Rural Free Delivery #2 as their mailing address in those days.

[Author Note: To avoid confusion I will refer to the camp as the 'Primrose Camp' since the locals and CCC boys referred to as such.]

On July 27, 1935 one hundred and sixty-nine men arrived from the District Headquarters at Fort Adams. The enrollees lived in Army tents for about a month and moved into completed buildings on Sept. 1st.[2]

– 1935 –

Projects

Work projects were under the direction of Superintendent Peter F. McManus. He was assisted by foresters: Anthony Gelardi, Alfred Jones, Raymond Fletcher, Gladding Johnson, Charles Jones, and James Sullivan. John McCormick was the mechanic. The

After a hard day's work on the Primrose camp site and a hearty meal these young men had the task of washing their mess kits. Lorenzo Harry Frisiello & Kathleen Duxbury Collection

Tents were on both sides of Black Plain Road for the whole complement of Company 1161. There are also five buildings that look completed in the rear of the camp This photo was during the summer of 1935. Lorenzo Harry Frisiello & Kathleen Duxbury Collection

A hungry group of boys have their mess kits ready for dinner at the tent camp in the summer of 1935. Lorenzo Harry Frisiello & Kathleen Duxbury Collection

All the camp buildings were built on posts instead of stone or concrete foundations. Construction has begun on the posts for the barracks. This was a fast way of construction and low cost, too. Lorenzo Harry Frisiello & Kathleen Duxbury Collection

Two barracks under construction in August were ready for the enrollees in September. Lorenzo Harry Frisiello & Kathleen Duxbury Collection

(L – R) The inside the barracks where 40 enrollees lived. The large room was heated by three wood stoves and enrollees had to make sure they kept the room clean and orderly. North Smithfield Heritage Association & Larry Smith | The Primrose Mess Hall where enrollees sat at picnic tables and were served their meals "family-style." This meant the components of a meal were put on the table in bowls or plates so everyone can serve themselves. They could eat as much as they wanted. Many boys gained five or more pounds, much of it was muscle from their hard, physical work. North Smithfield Heritage Association & Larry Smith | After supper and on weekends the boys at the Primrose camp relaxed in their Rec Hall where they could play pool, ping pong, cards, read or even play one of the two pianos. The room was heated by a wood stove and a huge fireplace. At one end was the canteen where they could buy soda, ice cream, candy, cigarettes, etc. North Smithfield Heritage Association & Larry Smith.

The Primrose entrance and buildings in winter. Lorenzo Harry Frisiello & Kathleen Duxbury Collection

Enrollees in uniform at retreat and lowering of the flag in the camp courtyard. Lorenzo Harry Frisiello & Kathleen Duxbury Collection

Education Adviser was Charles Whittaker and Lt. H.B. Worden (USNR) was the Junior officer.[3]

Historian Albert Klyberg described the early projects: "Work began in August of 1935 with the building of the Black Plain Trail at the entrance to the camp. Then in September, the fire lane known as the Whortleberry Trail in North Smithfield was done. In order to safely store the dynamite used in construction projects, an explosive magazine building was constructed and the road to it was called the Dynamite Trail."

The Second Annual Report of the Department of Agriculture and Conservation, 1936, reported a donation of 235 acres on Diamond Hill: "…located in the rugged Cumberland section of the state which should provide among other recreational uses, a place where a real winter sports program may be developed." The Primrose camp was close to the mountain and was assigned the work.

– 1936 –

I was only able to locate one copy of the April 17, 1936 issue of the Primrose camp newspaper, the Winchell in Woonsocket. It probably was named after Walter Winchell (April 7, 1897 - February 20, 1972) a syndicated American newspaper gossip columnist and radio news commentator.) Just like Winchell the newspaper had hard news but also some gossip. The logo in the newspaper was a microphone. I added information from the newspaper throughout the 1936 section.

The newspaper reported that Camp Superintendent Peter McManus had talked with Governor Theodore Francis Green who said he was very enthusiastic about the boy's physical development from their work projects and sport activities but also the education they were gaining. The Governor said he looked forward to visiting the camp in the near future.

It was announced that retreat and lowering of the flag would begin each day at 4:45 pm and the O.D. (order of the day) would be wearing the complete uniform instead of the winter outfit. The newspaper also reported that the Primrose camp was the only company in the District where every man, including the foresters, attended the flag exercises.[4]

Mr. Whittaker studied landscaping at Harvard. He mapped out the area in the camp for planting. He planned on using evergreens, bushes, and native plants. He was contacting growers in the area to obtain shrubbery. It was hoped that by summer the camp would be in bloom.[5]

Education

Lieut. Worden and Mr. Durfee with his radio class were busy installing a public address system. They wired all the buildings with speakers so that messages from the administration would be a lot easier. They also hooked up a two-way radio set to communicate with Fort Adams. The reporter concluded: "…all that is needed to complete the picture is television."[6]

The camp began organizing an orchestra with a piano, two trumpets, drums, guitars, clarinet, and violin. They were ready to play in the camp and for outside parties.[7]

Carpentry teacher Mr. Picard, a first-class carpenter, had a fully equipped shop to teach his students useful skills. They were working on a model of the camp that would be used for exhibits.[8]

The education adviser had his students raising chickens and he planned on adding rabbits and ducks.

He also began having his students do landscaping by transplanting pines and native bushes.[9]

The camp planned on running classes during the summer. Here were some of the topics: typing, carpentry, forestry, photography, plant identification, nature study, and landscape planting.[10]

In April the camp library received a loan of 50 books from the Woonsocket Library. Enrollees could sign a list stating what type of books they were interested in and each week the list was taken to the Woonsocket Library and the librarians tried to fill the requests. If some of the books on loan were not used, they were sent back and new books returned thus keeping a total of 50 books on loan.[11]

The newspaper praised the camp's school building as one of the best CCC camps in Rhode Island. Over 65% of the camp enrollees attended one or more of the 22 classes. Mr. Costello did an excellent job in teaching history. Mr. Irving taught the photography class. The men learned how to take photos, then Costello showed them how to develop the photos and even color them.[12]

On April 29, 1936 Camp Primrose celebrated the 3rd Anniversary of the founding of the CCC. A dance was held at the American Hall from 8-12 pm. The music was provided by a 14-piece orchestra from Providence. There were several vaudeville acts and enrollee entertainers also spiced up the evening.[13]

Captain Simons congratulated members of Camp Primrose for coming in second place in the monthly District ratings with a score of 936.1 that was only 1.9 points behind the 1st place winner.

Enrollees in the carpentry class made this model of a house. Lorenzo Harry Frisiello & Kathleen Duxbury Collection

The camp had a quiet section for reading and writing letters. Lorenzo Harry Frisiello & Kathleen Duxbury Collection

(L – R) The Primrose basketball team and their coach. They played other CCC camps in RI and neighboring MA. Lorenzo Harry Frisiello & Kathleen Duxbury Collection | The Primrose Hospital/Infirmary was staffed by an enrollee/attendant and an Army doctor. North Smithfield Heritage Association & Larry Smith | The Primrose camp was adjacent to Primrose Pond, a great place for the boys to swim. Great stylish swimwear. Lorenzo Harry Frisiello & Kathleen Duxbury Collection

The c.1936 Primrose group photo showing the approx. 200 enrollees. Seated in the center row are the state and military supervisors and foresters and LEMs. Behind them are the cooks in white uniforms. North Smithfield Heritage Association & Larry Smith

1161ST. CO. CCC, CAMP P-56, PRIMROSE, R.I.

W.L.SIMONS CAPTAIN.ENG.-RES..COMMANDING **P.F. MC'MANUS, CAMP SUPERINTENDENT**

H.B.WORDEN,LIEUT. -JG-CV -S-USNR
H.SHERWIN,CAPT..MED-RES.
C.MC CORMICK,EDUCATIONAL ADVISER

W.P.A. INSTRUCTORS
ALFRED PICARD
F.COSTELLO
L.C.IRVING

C.JANES O.W.JOLLEY R.FLETCHER
A.GELARDI J.MC CORMICK J.SULLIVAN
A.DAVENPORT J.WARD

PHOTOS BY
SPENCER & WYCKOFF
DETROIT

P.J.O'DONNELL,SENIOR LEADER	J.DICHRISTOFORO LEADER	N.BOULAY	W.DICHRISTOFOR	O.HACHADORIAN	G.MAGNOLE	D.PEARSON	J.SOKOLSKI
BILL AMES,MESS STEWARD	W.O'ROUKE, "	R.BOUSQUET	J.DENISEWICZ	J.HARKNESS	J.MARINO	J.PELLAM	F.SPINK
K.DAVIS,FIRST COOK	DICK PICARD "	L.BRANCONNIER	W.DENSMORE	N.HOULE	J.F.MAY	C.PELLET	A.ST.GEORGE
J.TABELLO,FIRST COOK	C.FREIBERGER "	W.BREAULT	P.DINOLA	R.JACOB	O.MAYER	A.PERRON	G.STABILLE
MCPECK,SUPPLY STEWARD	M.DUMAINE, ASST.	A.BRODEUR	E.DU BOIS	J.J.JOYCE	R.MC DERMOTT	A.PFEIFFER	E.SUROWIEC
E.V.MILLER,COMPANY CLERK	BILL GRAFFIUS .. "	T.BURKE	C.DUBUQUE	G.KAWAM	P.MC ENENAY	A.PHANEUF	A.SWISKA
DANNY LANDRY,FORESTRY CLERK	H.MARZINI, " "	T.CAMERON	W.DUGUS	J.KENT	J.MISHANETZ	A.PRATT	W.TAILLON
GEO.COTA,TOOL ROOM	H.PIERCE, " "	L.CAMPENELLI	D.DUPHINEY	W.KOGUT	J.MONTERIO	M.PRIMIANI	F.THERRIEN
DUQUETTE,MECHANIC	W.ROMBLAD, " "	F.CARLE	T.DZIOK	W.KORENIOWSKI	S.MONTERIO	P.REIS	C.THORNTON
FRISIELLO,UTILITY MAN	V.SANZI, " "	T.CARPENTER	R.ETHIER	B.KOSYK	J.MORAWIEC	V.RIVERS	A.TIRIOCCHI
IMBARO,ARMY TRUCK DRIVER	FRED LEMIRE " "	F.CASTELLI	A.FAVREAU	J.KOZAKA	L.MORIN	J.J.RODERIC	A.TURCOTTE
E.HURLEY,ARMY TRUCK DRIVER		R.CHARBONNEAU	R.FOUNTAINE	R.LABONTE	J.MURPHY	A.ROSSI	N.UCCI
J.S.LUSZCZ,BAKER	**MEMBERS**	C.CHARETTE	A.GARCIA	E.LAMARINE	D.NADEAU	W.RUSSI	W.VADNAIS
C.J.PASCIK,PX STEWARD	R.ALLARD	A.CONTI	P.GARZONE	E.LANGLOIS	J.NICHOLS	F.SALISBURY	J.WALTON
G.PAQUIN,2ND COOK	R.ALLEN	N.COREY	E.GAUDETTE,ASST.ED.ADV	A.LANNON	W.NICHOLS	G.SANTOPIET	A.WARZYBOK
PETROSKI,HOSP.ORDERLY	H.APPOLONIA	J.COSTELLO	R.GAUTHIER	N.LAROQUE	T.NOWAK	A.SASSO	L.WELLS
JOHNSON "	X.J.ASSIS	E.COTE	O.GENEREAUX	G.LARROW	J.O'BRIEN	A.SILVA	A.WHELPLEY
SAVOIE,ARMY "	R.BALLOU	G.CROCHETIERA	J.GIBBONS	E.LAVALLEE	J.O'NEIL	P.SMITH	A.WOLOWIEC
ASSELIN,FORESTRY ORDERLY	L.BILODEAU	G.CROWLEY	H.GOULD	L.LAVOMODIERE	B.PALAZZO	W.SMITH	J.ZYDOK
BENNY SCOTT,TRUCK FOREMAN	M.BILLAO	M.DALTON	D.GREGORY	E.LAVIN	N.PALOMBO	A.SOARES	A.ALMON
REDELSPERGER,BLACKSMITH	S.BILOTTI	R.D'ANESE	M.GUANARI	LEDUC	G.PAQUIN	E.SOARES	GUILLEMETTO
THIFAULT,2ND COOK	M.BOBBY						

Primrose camp staff and members. North Smithfield Heritage Association & Larry Smith

Sports

Lieut. Worden was also the Athletic Director and in charge of organizing two squads of baseball teams. He started practicing at Mowry Field every evening. (Historian Rich Keene said the field was about a mile away at the intersection of RI Route 104 and RI Route 5) Then Worden began negotiating to get uniforms for his team.

The Primrose team belonged to the Central CCC League of 12 teams that played at 6:15 pm at a Woonsocket field.[14]

In April inter-barracks volleyball matches were to begin while some boxers had matches and a couple enrollees wound up in the infirmary with their battle scars. Some enrollees were hoping to have a track team to meet with other CCC teams.[15]

Staff

Commanding: Capt. W. L. Simons, Lieut. H. B. Worden

Physician: Capt. H. Sherwin

Forestry Superintendent: Peter F. MacManus

Foresters: Raymond Cote, John McCorrmack, James Sullivan, Allen Lavenport, Anthony Gelardi, Charles Jones, Albert Barden

Staff Technicians: L. Wells, W. O'Rourke, J. Kent, J. Gibbons[16]

Colonel Thomas J. H. Pierce, head of the U.S. Department of Forests & Parks, had a plan to make the newly donated land on Diamond Hill a great place to attract sports enthusiasts from this section of New England by having Camp Primrose develop the mountain into a summer and winter playground. Pierce noticed a big trend in people wanting winter sports and many had to travel on "snow trains" on weekends to go skiing in other states.[17]

The plan for the Primrose camp was to construct a 2,880' toboggan slide 100' wide. The project would be located between Fisher and Diamond roads. There would also be a ski jump.[18]

Another project called for the damming of Sylvy's Brook to create a pond near Grants Mills and the New York, New Haven and Hartford Railroad. This would make a large area for swimming in the summer and skating in the winter.[19]

Another project Company 1161 was going to work on was with the R.I. Fish & Game Division in doing a stream correction project on Mowry Brook in North Smithfield. The Woonsocket Sportsmen's Club had worked to get rights to this stream for RI residents. The state stocked the stream but the fish had always left the area without being caught.[20]

The Primrose camp planned on completing the road projects that were already in progress and they planned on finishing them by the end of the year.[21]

Superintendent McManus had approx. 100 men working in controlling gypsy moths in the Lincoln Woods Reservation and also working on a road project on Whortleberry Hill in N. Smithfield.[22]

Camp engineers were working on two other road projects. The first was the construction of an access road to the fire tower on Woonsocket Hill. The other was an approx. 1.8-mile road in the Spring Lake section (in Burrillville).[23]

Mr. Littlefield's crew was constructing a waterhole at the rear of the camp. Mr. Sullivan was helped in the construction by blasting some of the ledge.[24]

Education

The camp planned on running classes during the summer. Here were some of the topics: typing, carpentry, forestry, photography, plant identification, nature study, and landscape planting.[25]

Projects

From 1936-1937 the Primrose camp worked at Diamond Hill in Cumberland constructing a slalom course, ski jump, a slide, a cross-country ski trail, toboggan and bobsled slides and a place for children to sled. Enrollees also constructed two Adirondack lean-tos and several fireplaces and toilet facilities.[26]

(L – R) Primrose boys dammed Mowry Brook creating a pond at the Woonsocket Sportsmen's Club that prevented fish from swimming away. Larry Smith | The overflow pipe and grate at the Mowry Brook Pond at the Woonsocket Sportsmen's Club. Larry Smith | In road construction, the camp superintendent needed to find a gravel pit close to the road construction site. These enrollees were taking a rest from the arduous job of loading the dump trucks with shovels. There were no loading machines. Lorenzo Harry Frisiello & Kathleen Duxbury Collection

Diamond Hill

Diamond Hill, located on Diamond Hill Road in the town of Cumberland in northeastern Rhode Island is 14 miles north of Providence. The hill is a huge outcropping of white quartz with a 350' vertical drop. The hill was named in Colonial times because of its sparkling and shining appearance. On a clear day from the summit one can see the skyline of Boston.

The Diamond Hill Granite Company was founded in 1877. Copper was also mined on the hill. In 1935 Philip Allen, C. Faulkner Kendall, and Henry Munroe Rogers donated 235 acres on the hill to the State of Rhode Island.

When the CCC came to Primrose they brought winter sports activities to the area when they built the Diamond Hill Ski Run and the Toboggan slide. Work started in 1936 and was completed at the end of 1937.

On January 16, 1938 the Diamond Hill Ski Area opened. Approximately 17,400 people came to ski and watch events and about the same number were turned away. Traffic jams were also reported in the area for the next few hours.[29]

Here is a list of groups that attended the event: Brown University Ski Club, the Appalachian Ski Club, Agwam Hunt Ski Club, Rhode Island Ski Runners Club, and the Hoch Popo (Thumbs up! Back to top) Ski Club, and many other spectators and skiers. These were some exhibitions that were demonstrated: down-hill skiing, christies, telemarks, stem turns, and jumping and down-hill races.

The following story was from the R.I. Ski Runners Club: 'The first time that skiers raced under the banner of the Rhode Island Ski Runners Club: "A throng of 17,245 showed up to watch. Say what? In Rhode Island, the Ocean State, where there isn't a single mountain, 17,245 people spent a Sunday watching a ski race? Yeah, right. But it's true, sort of. That first race, on Jan. 16, 1938, coincided with the official opening of Diamond Hill Reservation in Cumberland. That huge crowd arrived on a sparkling winter day to watch skiing demonstrations and racing and to play in a sports park with ski trails, a ski jump, and a toboggan slide.

"Winter sports enthusiasts went early and stayed late. Police started turning cars away at 2 o'clock. Late arrivals parked on Diamond Hill Road and walked as far as three miles to the slope. They parked on Wrentham Road almost to the Massachusetts line in one direction and to Woonsocket in the other. They left their vehicles on Sneech Pond Road and walked two miles from Cumberland Hill.

"Lt. Ernest Stenhouse of the State Police said the traffic jam was worse than any tie-up at Narragansett Park in East Providence during the thoroughbred racing season.

"On the snow, founding members of the R.I. Ski Runners (RISKI), formally organized earlier that month, were the stars. Robert Chase won the cross-country run and the downhill, Homer Green the slalom and Paul Anderson the jumping. Members of ski clubs from Agawam Hunt and Brown University, the Appalachian Mountain Club and Hoch Popo, as well as unattached skiers, also competed. The slopes were lighted, and people were skiing and sliding until 10:30 p.m." [30]

In 1940 Diamond Hill Mountain experienced a heavy snowfall and people enjoyed a longer period of skiing and tobogganing. Work began on constructing a new 900' exit road.[31]

After the CCC left the area in 1937, the hill contained two small ski areas. At Ski Valley (1939 to 1981) skiers had to hike-up and ski-down. Later rope tows and a T-bar were constructed and eventually multiple two-person chair lifts were added. The second ski area was Diamond Hill Reservation that operated from the mid-60s to the mid-80s when skiing came to an end. In 1997 the town of Cumberland acquired Diamond Hill from the State. The hill is now a 373-acre town park and is the starting point of the 33-mile hiking trail, Warner Trail, to Sharon Mass. The park contains picnic areas, athletic fields, 3.8 miles of hiking trails and a bandstand near the pond.[32]

These two photos show the huge crowds that watched skiers compete on January 16, 1938 and did exhibitions on the new Diamond Hill Ski Area constructed by the Primrose CCC camp.[27,28]

Enrollees water their award-winning flower garden. Lorenzo Harry Frisiello & Kathleen Duxbury Collection

This is one of the award-winning projects, a garden and pond with a fountain behind the rec hall. Lorenzo Harry Frisiello & Kathleen Duxbury Collection

Awards

Company 1161 received awards for its excellence. In August 1936, it was selected as the top camp in RI and second best in the whole First Corps Area. One of the accomplishments of the Primrose camp was the beautiful landscaping of their camp where they planted over $5,000 worth of shrubs and flowers.[33]

On April 4, 1937 over 2,000 people visitors were entertained at the camp in celebrating the 5th Anniversary of the CCC.

– 1937 –

Inaccessibility to the Mowry fire tower, on Woonsocket Hill in North Smithfield, was corrected when the Primrose camp built the Fire Tower Trail. It was completed in February, 1937. This road also increased fire protection for the surrounding area during the dry seasons. Directions: From Rt. 146 in North Smithfield take Woonsocket Hill Rd. to the tower.[35]

Closing

In December 1937, as part of a pull-back by Congress on Emergency Conservation Work, Camp Primrose was caught in a national reduction of camps and closed after two years of service. Rhode Island went from six to four CCC camps.

The enrollees were fortunate, although their camp closed in North Smithfield in December, the Company 1161's staff and enrollees were transferred to the George Washington Memorial State Forest in Glocester.

LEGACY

During its brief existence of 2½ years (1935-37), the biggest accomplishment of the Primrose CCC camp was the creation of the ski slope at Diamond Hill State Park. For over 40 years thousands of people enjoyed skiing and sledding on the ski slope visitors also enjoyed swimming in and ice skating on the pond they created in the park by damming Sylvy's Brook.

Some of the other lasting effect were the construction of roads in the surrounding area. Enrollees also built fireplaces at both Lincoln Woods and at the Peter Randall State Park in North Providence.

(L) The Mowry fire tower, on Woonsocket Hill in North Smithfield.[34]
(R) The road built by the Primrose camp to the Woonsocket Hill fire tower is still in beautiful shape. Larry Smith

Two enrollees are working on the stone edging of the road. The beautiful courtyard and walkways have been completed. In the center will be a clock. A lawn will complete the work. Lorenzo Harry Frisiello & Kathleen Duxbury Collection

Senior leader Philip O'Donnell (right) won a Happy Days newspaper nationwide essay contest entitled "What the CCC Has Done for Me." O'Donnell was invited to NYC to be on the radio with Philip Lord. He also traveled to Washington D.C., where he met President Roosevelt. Albert Klyberg Collection

(L – R) North Smithfield Heritage Society President Rich Keene explores the Diamond Hill Ski Slope where he skied in his youth. Podskoch | At the top of Diamond Hill, Valley Breeze reporter Lauren Clem & Rich Keene explore the old tow rope machine. It was made from a truck or car transmission and axle that powered the wheels that pulled a rope that pulled skiers up the hill. Lorenzo Harry Frisiello & Kathleen Duxbury Collection | The Primrose CCC boys dammed up Sylvy's Brook (under the walking bridge) that flowed near the base of Diamond Mountain, and diverted the water to large man-made pond on the left behind the bridge. The water to the right continued flowing downstream. Podskoch

(L – R) The CCC made a dam under the bridge that diverted water to the pond area the CCC boys created. Lauren Clem & Rich Keene are above the dam. The pond and band shell are to the right of Lauren & Rich. Podskoch | The Primrose CCC boys created the space to form the pond and encircled it with a beautiful stone wall. Water from Sylvy's Brook flowed in from an opening to the right of the band shell and exited at a spillway to the left of the band shell. This created a place for swimming in the summer and ice skating in the winter. Today it creates an amphitheater-like venue for concerts. Podskoch | Four miles northwest of Pawtucket in the town of Lincoln the Primrose camp boys built this unusual four-sided fireplace and many other fireplaces in Lincoln Woods State Park. Podskoch

CAPT. WEBSTER L. SIMONS, *Engr.-Res.*, COMMANDING

FIRST LT. LOWELL A. MILLIGAN, *C.A.-Res.*, EXCHANGE OFFICER

Roster

CAPT. HERBERT SHERWIN, *Med.-Res.*, SURGEON

CHARLES C. McCORMICK, *CEA*

TECHNICAL PERSONNEL P. F. McManus, Supt.; A. Gelardi, R. Fletcher, C. Janes, A. Jones; J. E. McCormick, J. A. Sullivan, G. Johnson, J. Ward, Mech.

LEADERS William Ames, Newport, Rhode Island; Kelsau W. Davis, Malden, Massachusetts; John DiChristofero, West Warwick, Rhode Island; Charles W. Freiberger, Providence, Rhode Island; George A. McPeck, Quincy, Massachusetts; Philip J. O'Donnell, Everett, Massachusetts; Richard J. Picard, West Warwick, Rhode Island; Wilfred W. Russi, West Warwick, Rhode Island; John Tabello, Providence, Rhode Island.

ASSISTANT LEADERS R. Danese, Woonsocket, R. I.; L. Frisiello, Everett, Mass.; W. Grafius, N. Smithfield, R. I.; W. Korzeniowski, Woonsocket, R. I.; F. Lemire, Woonsocket, R. I.; J. Luszcz, Woonsocket, R. I.; H. Marzini, Woonsocket, R. I.; E. V. Miller, Warren, R. I.; A. Petroski, Cambridge, Mass.; H. J. Pierce, Providence, R. I.; G. E. Pratt, Oakland Beach, R. I.; V. Sanzi, Providence, R. I.; J. Sokolski, Woonsocket, R. I.; A. Thifault, Woonsocket, R. I.

MEMBERS

Allard, R. A., Central Falls, R. I.
Anderson, V. A., Edgewood, R. I.
Applegate, L., Providence, R. I.
Bagalini, L., Allendale, R. I.
Bates, J., Providence, R. I.
Bentley, T., Providence, R. I.
Bigbie, F., Woonsocket, R. I.
Billao, M., Providence, R. I.
Billodeau, L., Warren, R. I.
Bilotti, S., Warren, R. I.
Boudreau, L., Woonsocket, R. I.
Boulay, N., Woonsocket, R. I.
Bousquet, R., Central Falls, R. I.
Boyajian, S., Providence, R. I.
Branconnier, L., W'ket, R. I.
Breault, W., O. Beach, R. I.
Britto, J., Providence, R. I.
Cameron, T., Providence, R. I.

Cardoza, J., Bristol, R. I.
Carlson, A., Hillsgrove, R. I.
Carpenter, T., N. Smithfield, R. I.
Carol, R., Providence, R. I.
Castelli, F., Thornton, R. I.
Cerbo, L., Providence, R. I.
Charette, C., Woonsocket, R. I.
Charlotte, D., Woonsocket, R. I.
Cheney, F., Cranston, R. I.
Church, M., Cranston, R. I.
Clark, W., Pawtucket, R. I.
Corcoran, J., Providence, R. I.
Corey, N., E. Providence, R. I.
Cowsill, W., Providence, R. I.
Crocheteire, G., W'socket, R. I.
Crowley, G., Providence, R. I.
Cullen, J., Providence, R. I.
Dalton, M., Woonsocket, R. I.
Dandeneau, R., Providence, R. I.
DeLuca, C., Providence, R. I.

Densmore, W., W'socket, R. I.
DeSanto, V., Valley Falls, R. I.
DiNola, P., Cranston, R. I.
Dziok, T., Woonsocket, R. I.
Ethier, N., Woonsocket, R. I.
Favreau, A., Woonsocket, R. I.
Ferland, H., Central Falls, R. I.
Ferriera, M., Bristol, R. I.
Fontaine, E., Central Falls, R. I.
Fontaine, R., W. Warwick, R. I.
Gammino, A., Warren, R. I.
Garcia, A., Providence, R. I.
Gaudette, E., Providence, R. I.
Gauthier, W., Woonsocket, R. I.
Gibbons, J., Providence, R. I.
Gould, H., E. Providence, R. I.
Guillemette, A., W'socket, R. I.
Gudeczaukas, J., Cranston, R. I.
Hachadorian, O., P'idence, R. I.
Harkness, J., Westerly, R. I.

Harrington, J., Providence, R. I.
Houle, N., Woonsocket, R. I.
Iachei, J., Providence, R. I.
Jackson, W., Providence, R. I.
Jacob, R., Woonsocket, R. I.
Joyce, J., Central Falls, R. I.
Kawam, G., Central Falls, R. I.
Kelly, J., Providence, R. I.
Kent, J., Everett, Mass.
LaBonte, G., Boston, Mass.
Labonte, R., Woonsocket, R. I.
Lannon, A., O. Beach, R. I.
Larrow, G., Providence, R. I.
Laurence, A., Central Falls, R. I.
Lavault, N., Central Falls, R. I.
Leaver, R., Providence, R. I.
Leduc, E., Woonsocket, R. I.
Lisi, F., Providence, R. I.
Maher, C., Oakland Beach, R. I.
Martel, L., Pawtucket, R. I.

Martin, E., Valley Falls, R. I.
Masse, M., Woonsocket, R. I.
McCloud, T., Apponaug, R. I.
McDermott, R., C. Falls, R. I.
McGuirl, T., Providence, R. I.
McMullen, J., O. Beach, R. I.
Mederios, M., Bristol, R. I.
Mederios, S., Bristol, R. I.
Migliozzi, F., Johnston, R. I.
Miller, F., Lonsdale, R. I.
Miller, I., Providence, R. I.
Mishanetz, J., Woonsocket, R. I.
Moody, F., Woonsocket, R. I.
Morawiec, J., Woonsocket, R. I.
Morin, J., Central Falls, R. I.
Mozol, A., Woonsocket, R. I.
Mulkerrin, R., Providence, R. I.
Murray, B., Providence, R. I.
Nadeau, A., Woonsocket, R. I.
North, E., Pawtucket, R. I.

Nowak, T., Woonsocket, R. I.
O'neill, J., Lakewood, R. I.
Padula, A., Natick, R. I.
Palombo, N., Lymansville, R. I.
Paquin, L., Olneyville, R. I.
Pellet, C., Washington, R. I.
Perron, A., Woonsocket, R. I.
Phaneuf, A., Woonsocket, R. I.
Pinault, G., Providence, R. I.
Preaster, R., Providence, R. I.
Ravenelli, R. Woonsocket, R. I.
Reis, P., Providence, R. I.
Rivers, V., Woonsocket, R. I.
Santopeitro, G., Johnston, R. I.
Salisbury, F., Johnston, R. I.
Sasso, A., Woonsocket, R. I.
Savoie, R., Pawtucket, R. I.
Scarmuzelli, F., Providence, R. I.
(See back page for additional names)

The Roster of enrollees and staff of the Primrose camp in the 1937 Third CCC District First Corps Area Yearbook.

MEMORIES

A member of the North Smithfield Heritage Association recommended that I contact Ms. Betty Cesario whose family owned the land where the Primrose CCC camp was located.

On February 25, 2014 I called her to learn about the history of the Primrose CCC camp and about her family who owned the land where the Army built the camp in 1935. She said: "I would be delighted to talk with you about the camp and our farm. It was on our land that my dad purchased from the Providence & Worcester Railroad. My father grazed his cows on the land where the CCC camp was built. My father rented the land to the Army for the camp.

"My grandfather and his brother Vincheso were the original owners of the farm. They bought the land for $1,500. My grandfather raised vegetables in the summer and each day he drove his horse-drawn wagon to Providence to sell his produce. Then he planted a lot of apple trees and from this orchard he hoped to sell apples. When the Hurricane of 1938 hit Rhode Island, the trees were uprooted and his orchard was destroyed. He & my father went into the dairy business and used the land for corn. Later my dad bought all the land on Pond Road. My father was quite a guy.

"Suddenly Roosevelt put a ceiling on the milk price and dairy farmers like my dad lost money. From then on Dad was a Republican.

"I was born in 1928 so I was 7-9 years old when the camp was running. Down the street from the camp my friend's mother ran the Breezy Knoll, a store where

(L) Betty Cesario at her home and farm where she was raised. Podskoch (R) Betty Cesario by the last remaining structure from the Primrose CCC camp, a chimney from the rec hall. Podskoch

the boys went for ice cream. I remember one boy had a guitar and played on the store steps. I also remember boys walking by my house and my father warned them not to bother his girls.

"There were five children in my family and it was hard on families during the Depression. Then Dad died and Mom split up the land. I got 18 acres, 13 of which was where the CCC camp was. Then my sister died and her land went to her boys. The only things left from the camp is a chimney and an artesian well. My nephew is going to build a house there.

"The CCC boys worked on several projects: conservation work, bridges and the fire tower road on the way to Wright's farm."

I then arranged to meet Betty on June 1, 2014. It was also on that day that I met Albert Klyberg, the Director of the Rhode Island Historical Society. Al wanted to visit all of the CCC camp sites because he was writing an article for the state on the great work projects that the CCC did for Rhode Island's state forests and parks.

Both Albert and I met at Betty's farm and she took us to the location of the camp. What we saw was a development of homes and at the rear of one was a large stone chimney that might have been a remnant of the rec hall. We then walked through the woods and looked for some remains of the camp but just found some slabs of concrete.

Lorenzo "Harry" Frisiello

Most of the pictures of the Primrose camp came from a photo album that CCC historian, Kathleen Duxberry of New Jersey, purchased on Ebay. Fortunately, Kathleen learned that I was doing research on Rhode Island camps and she shared it with me. The album contains not only the Primrose camp but three other camps.

Harry, as most people called Lorenzo, was born in Boston, Mass. on Dec. 28, 1915. His parents were Pasquale and Maria? (La Russo) Frisiello. The amazing part of Harry's life in the CCC is that he served for seven years and worked in five different camps. In 1934 he joined the CCC and was in Co. 130 in Alfred, Maine. That same year the company moved to Millenocket, Maine where it stayed till 1935. Harry then was transferred to Co. 1161 in Rhode Island and he helped set up the Primrose CCC camp in June 1935. While at Primrose he was listed as an Assistant Leader and his home was Everett, Mass. After two years his Company 1161 was transferred to the Putnam/George Washington camp in Glocester where he remained till Feb. 22, 1941.

After the CCC Harry joined the Navy during WWII. When he was discharged, he worked as an electrician for the Whitins Machine Works in Whitinsville, MA. Harry worked there for 38 years and retired in 1979.

He was married to Rita (Chagnon) and they lived

Here is photo of Lorenzo "Harry" Frisiello around 1990 when he was a member of the North Smithfield Volunteer Fire Department. Rich Keene

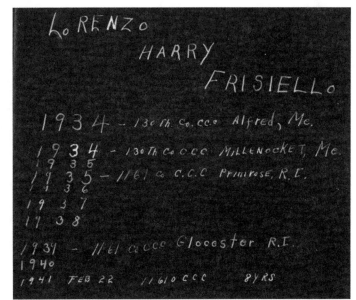

A page from Harry's photo album listing all his CCC camps he worked. Lorenzo Harry Frisiello & Kathleen Duxbury Collection

in North Smithfield, RI. He was active in the VFW and a Charter member of the Primrose Fire Department.

Harry died on July 1, 1995. He had a stepson, Robert Chausse of North Smithfield; a stepdaughter, Lorraine; a brother; three sisters, Mary Radosta, Rose Polizzotti, and Ann Anzivino.

The following was found in the April 1936 issue of the Winchell in Woonsocket newspaper:

***

The Primrose Platform

To Mold Manhood

To Construct Character

To Maintain Discipline of Mind and Body

To Work Together in Strength and Spirit

To Make Primrose THE Camp in The CCC

***

Benjamin Godon
Stone Mason, Built Rec Hall Fireplace

After reporter Lauren Clem wrote an article in the May 6th, 2020 issue of The Valley Breeze newspaper, I received this email on the next day from Peter Godon, Burrillville.

"I just read the story in The Valley Breeze about the CCC camp known as Primrose on Black Plain Road. I was shocked to read that the fireplace remains. I grew up knowing that my grandfather made that. He was not a youth at the camp but was hired to build it for them. His name was Benjamin Godon from Woonsocket. He died years before I was born. He also made the stone "entrance" to the Spring Lake area off of Spring Lake Road at Black Hut Rd. The lake's first name was Herring Pond. I'm wondering if there was ever another CCC camp there. It's in the Glendale area of Burrillville. I would love to see the fireplace at Primrose."

I was very excited to find information on someone who worked at the Primrose CCC camp especially since he built the stone fireplace that was in the Rec Hall. I immediately called Peter Godon and he told me about his grandfather.

"Most of the information about my grandfather who worked at the Primrose CCC camp came from my father. Dad was born in 1924. I assume the CCC camp at Primrose was built in the mid to late 1930s which would

Benjamin Godon and his wife Anna with their sons (L-R). Raymond and Roger by the dump truck he used to sell and deliver coal from. Peter Godon

have made him a teenager at the time the camp was built.

"My grandfather Ben was born in the mid-1880s in northern Rhode Island. There were about 12 kids in the family. His older brothers & sisters were born in St. Prosper, Quebec, Canada between Trois Rivers and Quebec City. Then his parents moved to RI where my grandfather & younger siblings were born.

"When my grandfather Ben was in 3rd grade his father died. At that time, he was removed from school in order to work in a mill to help support the family.

"When he was older, he struck out on his own and worked for himself. He became a self-taught stone mason. He bought a dump truck and delivered coal in the winter as a subcontractor for the gas company which sold coal in addition to gas.

"My grandparents had three children: Cora followed by Raymond, and then my father, Roger.

"When my grandfather built his house in Woonsocket, he built an ice house under the side porch. He would buy ice in bulk and store it in the ice house. When coal sales were down during the summer, he would sell the ice. My father, Roger, said that when he was a kid during the Depression, his family always had food on the table. It wasn't always the best food but they never went hungry.

"After a hard life my grandfather died in 1951. He and my dad were doing stone work on a new house when he felt ill. He sat under a tree for the rest of the day. Later he was taken to the hospital where he was told he had a heart attack. He died a day or so later. He was about 63 years old.

"I finally got to see the chimney this spring. I was very pleased to see that the chimney was still standing. Although his work was on the crude side, it was strongly built. That chimney has seen many hurricanes come and go. It withstood them all. Like the Roman aqueducts, real masonry lasts the test of time. The art of real masonry is all but gone these days."

Rich Keene
North Smithfield Heritage President

"The Primrose CCC boys did a lot of work at Lincoln Woods where they worked on many projects. The gravel road they built to the summit of Woonsocket Hill fire tower is in remarkably good condition.

"From a humanity perspective, the CCC boys left an indelible imprint on Primrose demographics. Bill Ames was the Primrose Camp Supply Sergeant at one time. He eventually married Grace Carpenter and settled less than a mile from the camp. His daughter's family lives in his former house and his grandson built a house next door. Bill joined with Harry Frisiello and others in 1959 to form the Primrose Volunteer Fire Dept. Bill later became a full-time firefighter and rose to the rank of captain. Bill's great-grandchildren still live a half-mile away from the camp. Bill and Harry Frisiello were charter members of the Primrose Volunteer Fire Department in 1958. Bill Graffius' granddaughter still lives in town as does Frank DiChristophero's son. I know of at least five CCC boys at the Primrose camp who met local women and then settled in town. Their legacy lives on."

Benjamin Godon's chimney is the last standing structure of the Primrose CCC camp. Podskoch

CHAPTER 12
RI BOYS IN OTHER STATES

Paul Perkins
Danbury, NH

Paul Perkins used his photo album to describe his experiences at the Danbury CCC camp in New Hampshire. His wife Eileen and daughter Eileen Edel enjoy hearing his CCC stories at their home in Wakefield, RI. Podskoch

On Thurs., Dec. 7, 2017 I traveled to Wakefield and visited Paul Perkins and his family. I was greeted at the door by his daughter, Eileen Edel, who had contacted me because her breakfast friend had heard me speak at the Charlestown Library and that I was searching for CCC boys and families. Paul's wife, Eileen, invited me to their dining room to interview. On the dining room table was a large photo album. Paul began telling me about his life and experiences in the CCC.

"I was born on Jan. 15, 1923 in Dorchester a section of Boston, Mass. My parents were John and Mary McCarty. My father worked at the Boston Globe newspaper as a linotype operator. There were six boys and one girl in my family. The eldest was John followed by me, Joseph, Richard, Philip, Thomas, and Mary. I graduated from high school in 1940. It was hard getting work. One of the jobs I had was delivering newspapers.

"My neighbor got me a job working in Boston on Atlantic Ave. in a foundry where they worked on big scales that were in trucks. The job involved working on repairing the parts of the scales. My job was going underneath these big trucks to remove damaged parts.

"While working something set me off. I realized I was interested in trees and woods. One day I saw boys coming home on weekends. They said that they worked in the CCC and did a lot of work in the woods.

"When I was traveling in the woods one day, I saw a CCC camp of veterans of WWI in the town of Milton. I was stimulated again with the idea of working in the CCC. I was looking for something else to do and I thought I'd like to join the CCC for a spell. Someone told me that if I wanted to join, I should go to the welfare office in town.

"I went inside the office and said I had to get a job and would like to join the CCC. They asked me: 'How much does your dad get paid.' When I told them they said: 'Sorry you can't join the CCC because he gets paid too much.' But then he thought for a while and said: 'I think it'll be okay and you could go.'

"A few days later I went to Boston and met a group of 30 or so boys who were also joining the CCC. We took a train to Fort Devens where we had our physical exam and training.

"Then we were sent on a Boston and Maine Railway train to Danbury, New Hampshire. We then got in a

Three CCC enrollees by their Danbury New Hampshire camp 1123 Company sign. Perkins

Two camp Danbury boys with their barracks and camp in the background. Perkins

(L – R) Paul J. Perkins early into his arrival at the camp. He was issued an Army work uniform and later issued a CCC uniform. The pants were made of thick olive-green wool. Perkins | A work crew loading the truck with tools for a day in the woods. The most important item on the truck was lunch. Perkins | A crew carrying their tools down a path that was damaged by the Hurricane of 1938. Perkins

truck that took us to camp. There were four barracks and I was assigned to barracks number one. When I walked in there was a big potbelly stove that turned out to be the most important thing because it kept us warm during the winter. There were about 40 bunks on both sides of the room. Our commanding officer was Capt. Batchelder. Most of the boys in camp were from Massachusetts. Some guys didn't like living in the country and they went over the hill. Sometimes the police went after them to get their clothing and any other materials they didn't turn in.

"The first things I wanted to be was organized and prepared. Did I have enough clothes, razors, a toothbrush, comb, toiletries, etc.? Did I have enough money to buy cigarettes? We were alerted that most of our pay was going to be mailed home and I'd be lucky if I got money to buy cigarettes. I had all these questions swirling in my head and I didn't even smoke. The one thing that I really wanted were candy bars.

"I met one guy who was from Boston and was a $36 man. That meant he was an assistant leader and he was

paid six dollars extra per month. He told me the company was looking for truck drivers. It just so happened I was the only one at camp with a license. Then the guy said: 'Come with me. We went to the wood yard and he said put your face in front of mine and he punched me right in the face. It was very similar to a college hazing. He wanted to see how I would react to being hit. If I took the punishment without reacting, then I was qualified to drive the truck. He later became my friend. I was so surprised I didn't know what to do. He then said: 'You're going to have to drive to the railroad station and pick up supplies. Then I found out that the lieutenant was coming with me because he wanted to see how my driving was. As I came to the railroad station, I stopped on the railroad tracks because there was no other place to stop. The lieutenant blew his stack. 'Why are you parking on the railroad tracks? Don't you know this is dangerous! Then he yelled: 'Don't do that again!'

"The truck drivers were responsible for taking care of the trucks. The lieutenant would inspect the level of the oil and other important parts of the engine. The trucks were always kept in a garage. In the shop our mechanic had a big picture of Franklin Roosevelt on the wall. Each day I walked in I looked at it and said: 'Hello Pres. Roosevelt.'

"I had this job for a few months. Then I got assigned to filling the coal and wood in the barracks to keep the buildings supplied. One time while backing up to the barracks with a load of wood I skidded into part of the building and put a hole in the box part of the truck. I didn't want anybody to know what happened so I went to see the camp carpenter who patched it up.

"I also had the job of taking the camp doctor who worked not only our camp but a WWI Veterans camp nearby. Sometimes the doctor spent a couple days with each camp. One time on the trip to this camp the roads were icy and there was a really steep hill I had to drive up. I asked the doctor to help man the brake. The both of us worked together and I was able to go up this mountain very slowly.

"I was taken off the truck driving job and I worked in the woods. I worked with another boy and we use the two-man saw. Our camp had a big job of trying to cut up a lot of the wood that had been destroyed by the Hurricane of 1938. When I was in the CCC the U.S. was in the period of training for war. One of the things the Army needed was wood to build barracks for the soldiers and sailors that were being trained. Every state was assigned to cut logs into 8' lengths to get lumber. The state had what they called Buddha trucks that had an extra set of wheels to carry the weight of these logs. One day while walking and carrying the saw I hit my knee with the sharp blade.

I went to the infirmary and the medic only put a bandage on it. I know it should have had stitches because when it healed I had this terrible scar for years.

"In the springtime I had another job that of forest fire protection. The state gave us training in fighting fires.

"Then we did light work repairing wooden bridges. We also built water holes so that when there was a fire the men could use them to fill up their tanks to fight a fire. We were given boots when working since our job was to walk in the holes and shovel out the mud to make the hole larger. There were many times when our boots got stuck in the mud and we had a hard time getting out. There were water holes all over the state of New Hampshire that were very important in fighting fires.

What did you do after work?

"We went to the mess hall and the food was very good. The cook was an Army man. The mess sergeant was very strict. He wanted everyone to eat properly. Nobody was to act like a pig. You had to wait for the food and have manners. The Army taught us young fellows what was important in life.

"After dinner it was our free time. Sometimes I went to the canteen in the rec hall and bought soda, soap, or candy. It was also a time that I did reading or wrote letters. I enjoyed looking out the window at the large mountain near our camp to see if anyone was climbing it. When it was a time to wash our clothes, we used the old washboards to scrub the dirt out.

"Then we had the chance to take night classes. I took a math class and another in forestry. Our classes were held in a special room where the foresters gathered."

I asked Paul what he did on the weekends?

This photo of the boys who were part of the Boston District crew was taken using a Brownie Box camera. Perkins

This truck was used on Saturday nights' liberty trips. One Saturday night the truck slipped off the road with 35 boys in the back. These two boys survived the accident but two other boys were killed. Perkin

"On Saturday nights a truck drove guys to the nearby town. It was my first or second week that I heard a truck was going to the movies. It usually left camp in the early evening but I told my friend I didn't want to go. My friend, Fred said: 'Ah let's go. We'll have fun.' I replied: 'No, I'm too tired.' Later that evening I heard that the truck had 35 boys riding in the back when it ran off the road and two boys died. The camp called everybody out to help. The ambulance took boys to the Fort Devens hospital. I knew one of the boys that died. The reason for the crash was that the truck was going around a sharp corner and the boys who were sitting in the rack truck shifted their weight to one side causing the truck to tip over and roll down into a ditch."

Do you remember any tricks that guys played on each other at camp?

"That same guy who hit me did a trick on his friend's mother. He drove the camp ambulance to his friend's mother's house in Boston. He loaded his friend in the back to make it look like he was sick. He stopped at the house and knocked on the door and when the boy's mother came to the door he said; 'Your son's in the ambulance and really sick. She went out very sad and upset and when he opened the back and saw her son lying in the stretcher. She thought he was really sick but then her son got up and said: 'Oh, it's just a joke.'

"One interesting part of payday was when the guys went into the office and the captain had money to pay the boys. They were lined up and on the table near the captain was his .45 revolver. He didn't trust anybody with the money.

"After six months I decided to leave. I worked in Boston again and then decided to join the Navy. I went to the Boston recruiting office where they tested me and gave me a physical exam. The doctor said: 'You have a hernia and we can't take you.'

"I went home and told my father what happened. My dad said: 'I don't think you have a hernia but we'll go to our doctor and see what he says. The doctor gave me a physical and said I didn't have a hernia. My father asked him to sign a letter saying I was okay. He did and my dad said to wait for a few months and then try again.

"One day I went by a drugstore and saw the headlines in the paper that said: 'Pearl Harbor Attacked.' I said to myself: 'I'll bet they'll take me now.' I had a friend who also wanted to join. I got papers from the Navy that required a parent's permission to join so my dad signed them. We had to take an oath at the office. Then we got into the elevator and a guy stopped the elevator and said: 'I'm giving you guys your last chance to get out of the Navy if you want but we all stayed and joined.

"Then a train took us to New London. Our boot camp was in the building on the State Pier. I was assigned to a sonar school on a ship. After that I was assigned to a sub chaser for a year. I got tired of it. I wanted to go to a submarine school. I did something nobody had done before. While our sub chaser was tied up for liberty for the weekend and the captain and most of the other guys left the ship. There was only one officer who stayed on board. I decided to also stay. I went to the office of the yeoman who had a typewriter. I decided to type a letter requesting that I be transferred to a sub school. I took the letter to the officer who was a lieutenant in the reserves. He looked at it and said okay and signed it. Then I took the letter to the mailroom and a man mailed it.

"A week later the commander said to me: 'You are being transferred to a sub school. I don't understand it. I didn't sign it but it says the lieut. signed it. So sorry you have to leave.' Boy, was I happy.

"After training our group sailed on the SS Lurline

Paul Perkins (R) receiving commendation from Rear Admiral Elton Grenfell, in Pearl Harbor, Hawaii. Eileen Perkins Edel

from San Francisco, California to Honolulu, Hawaii and then transported by bus to Pearl Harbor. I was assigned to a WWI mine sweeper. Our job was to test for torpedoes and recover and refit them for the submarines. Having graduated from the first sonar school class in New London, CT, I was assigned to teach on board several vessels over the next few years. My first permanent submarine was the USS Bluegill, as the chief sonar man.

"After the war I continued in the Navy. In 1949 I went to Hawaii. Then I worked at the Naval Electronics Laboratory in San Diego. I retired on Sept. 29, 1961. Then I got a job at the University of Rhode Island's School of Oceanography. They hired me and I worked on their research vessel. They were collecting sounds of fish and whales. I worked there for 20 years. Then in 1981 I got a job working at the Newport Naval Underwater Lab. I stayed there till 1989 when I retired for good.

"I met my wife Eileen Gray when I was delivering newspapers. Her mother was my customer. We also went to the same high school and we saw each other in study halls and some of our classes. I think our first date was when we were 14 years old. We got married in 1944 and had four children: Eileen, Paul Michael, James, and Thomas."

Did the CCC help you in any way?

"A person who was in the CCC was always looked at as being worthy of higher esteem. When the Army and Navy men were making decisions, CCC boys were always given a higher level or position. I also learned to enjoy being in the woods. I liked to look for snakes and berries, and had an appreciation of the importance of nature. I also learned the importance of fire control, how to get along with people, and the love of flowers and plants."

Paul J. Perkins died on August 14, 2019 at the age of 96. He and his wife Eileen (Gray) were married for 75 years.

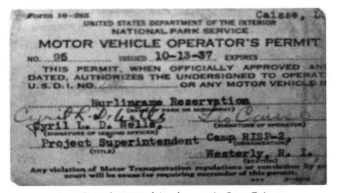

Leo Caisse's 1937 driver's permit. Leo Caisse

Leo Caisse
Burlingame, RI / Triangle Lake, OR / Casper, WY

Leo Caisse at the Fort Casper CCC camp in Washington state. Leo Caisse

I first learned about Leo Caisse and his interest in the Rhode Island CCC camps after reading a story [on www.smallstatebighistory.com] he wrote for the Online Review of Rhode Island History called "Small State Big History." Leo's story was entitled "The Civilian Conservation Corps in Rhode Island, 1933-1942. Leo also wrote a book about the great works of the CCC in Rhode Island entitled *The Civilian Conservation Corps: A guide to their works in Rhode Island* that was published in 2019 by Stillwater Publications.

Leo Caisse's interest in the CCC goes back to the stories his father told him about his adventures working in CCC camps in Rhode Island and two Western states. He also describes the history of the Rhode Island CCC camps and how they contributed greatly to the landscape across the state.

Leo lost his father when he was young and has spent years researching those contributions by the CCC Here is an excerpt from his writing:

"Here is the story of a Warren, Rhode Island, seventeen-year-old who joined the CCC on July 2, 1934. He was assigned to the 141st Company when headquartered at Burlingame in Charlestown. There the teenager learned to drive a truck, earning a license issued by the Department of the Interior.

"At Burlingame, the teenager and other CCC

(L) A view of the Triangle Lake CCC camp near Junction City, Oregon. Gary Nenninger (R) A Triangle Lake camp enrollee driving a bulldozer while building a road in a rugged mountainous area in Western Oregon. Gary Nenninger

A 1936-37 photo of CCC boys at the Triangle Lake camp taking a break while working in the forest. Gary Nenninger

Triangle Lake boys atop a large Douglas fir tree they loaded on a trailer. Gary Nenninger

enrollees engaged in work in both private and state-owned forests in Rhode Island. They built fire towers, truck roads for firefighting and logging, strung telephone lines, dug wells, worked on pest control and timber improvement, and built logging trails, shelters, and fireplaces. They helped develop a beach in front of the lake at Burlingame.

"Rhode Island CCC boys also worked in the Pacific Northeast. Short of manpower but not work in that area, the federal government decided to transfer 380 Rhode Island enrollees (two entire companies) to Salem, Oregon and Vancouver, Washington. While most of the conservation work that needed to be done was in the West, most of the unemployed were in the East. A total of 1,500 New Englanders were transferred across the country in October 1935.

"The selected corpsmen had to secure parental consent if they were under twenty-one. These boys, many from poverty-stricken families, began their journey from Fort Adams in Newport. They then boarded in Providence a state-of-the-art special train that included ten Pullman cars, four baggage cars equipped with kitchens, two cars carrying their equipment, and one hospital car staffed with a physician. The baggage/kitchen cars were stocked with enough food and wood for their six-day trek. They were led by twenty-six leaders and their assistants. The total cost of the trip per man to the federal government was $133.36. If a man's enlistment expired while in the West, the government provided transportation home.

"In 1935, [some of the members] of the 141st Company from Rhode Island, were transferred to Oregon. The young man from Warren traveled with his company to Oregon, where he served a maximum four consecutive enlistments and was honorably discharged on June 23, 1936.

"In Oregon, the Rhode Island boys were primarily involved in building and maintaining roads in privately owned forests. They built fire service guard stations at Walton, Greenleaf, and Alsea. They also built fire lookout towers, trails, and shelters. The CCCs from the 141st Company were absorbed into and became the 2108st

Company of CCCs. Its campsite was at Triangle Lake near the town of Junction City.

"After a little more than a year off, the enrollee from Warren re-enlisted in the CCC on September 7, 1937. This time he was sent to the 2130th Company, then located in the state of Wyoming.

"According to the National Archives historian Eugene Morris, it is difficult to ascertain with any degree of certainty why he was ordered there. Perhaps there was a manpower shortage or a need for a particular set of skills he had developed in the CCC. He could now drive a truck, operate a bulldozer, tractor and jackhammer, and weld and set explosives for demolition purposes such as moving boulders or removing tree stumps. He also learned a new skill, how to evade mountain lions. In any event, the young man from Rhode Island fell in love with Wyoming and tried to persuade his new bride several years later to move there, but she would have none of it.

"The Casper Chamber of Commerce persuaded the National Park Service to send Civilian Conservation Corps men, including the 2130th Company, to go to the Casper area in 1937. Some of the work performed by the CCC on Casper Mountain included, building bridges, improving roads, and reducing fire hazards. At Fort Casper they built parking areas, access roads, and a dike in the river.

"I did not get to know the Warren teenager well, as he passed away unexpectedly at a young age, when I was only nine-years old. But I still recall being mesmerized by his stories. The Teenager from Warren was my father, Leo Caisse. It has been a great source of pride to learn about his adventures and the environmental legacy he left in such far-flung places as Rhode Island, Oregon, and Wyoming."

The Triangle Lake rec hall where the boys played pool, checkers, cards or just read. Gary Nenninger

Peter Reilly
Camp Trask, OR

Peter Reilly giving a donation to Father Gary Zerr at Sacred Heart Parish in Tillamook, OR in July 2004. This was in thanks for all the parish had done for him and fellow CCC members while stationed at a CCC camp about 15 miles east of Tillamook during the 1930s. Olive & Herb Plep

The following story was an interview of a Rhode Island CCC boy, Peter Reilly, who worked at Camp Trask near Tillamook, Oregon. It was written by Ken O'Toole and published in the Headlight-Herald newspaper on July 27, 2004.

"Those Were the Days at CCC's Camp Trask" by Ken O'Toole

Peter Reilly's eyes lit up and his pace quickened earlier this month, as he retraced his steps from nearly 70 years ago at Camp Trask, where he arrived in October 1935, at age 18, with a group of 200 Civilian Conservation Corps recruits from Rhode Island.

The site about 15 miles east of Tillamook has since become Trask Park. Barracks, mess hall and outbuildings are all gone. Of the old bridge over the North Fork Trask River that Reilly remembered, a single abutment remains. The exuberant laughs and shouts of young men reprieved from Depression-era despair, are stilled.

Yet in his memories, the buildings were still new, the bridge was intact, and voices reverberated from across the decades.

A view of Camp Trask with the old bridge over the North Fork Trask River in the lower left. All of the buildings have been removed.[1]

Reilly eagerly read the Tillamook County Historical Society's plaque at the park that commemorates the contributions of the CCC to Tillamook. It notes that the CCC was "created in a period of severe economic depression," and that it "provided useful work and vocational training for unemployed single men and contributed much in the development and conservation of our country's resources, from 1933-1942."

In four or five trips back to the former CCC camp during the two-week visit from his home in Warwick, R.I., Reilly refueled recollections of a life-shaping experience, from age 18 to 20.

As his niece, Olive Plep of Pacific City and Portland, put it, "The CCC was emotional and physical salvation for him."

She explained that it gave him a chance to escape his rough life at home, to travel, learn responsibility, and save some money. It galvanized him for service in the military and set the course for a successful career as a painting contractor.

"The CCC, that was the foundation for him," she said. "It was like another world for these kids."

Reilly agreed, adding, "I could have stayed forever."

Now 87, he said his thoughts had often returned to Camp Trask. Over the years, he'd daydreamed of someday making this sentimental journey, but life always got in the way.

After CCC camp, World War II loomed as his next big adventure. He ended up in northern Alaska, where, as he put it, "the wind was so strong, it could bend the beam in a flashlight."

Then followed the years of making a living, then attending his ill wife until her death. More recently, he recovered from serious health problems of his own.

He figured, if he didn't make the trip now, then when?

"You'd better come out now," Plep had advised.

It was his first trip back to Oregon and Tillamook County since 1937 and his first jet flight. He even bought a new suit for the occasion.

In each of his visits back to the former Camp Trask with Plep this month, he tried again and again to find a huge boulder weighing maybe 70-some tons and big as a house, Reilly recalled that he had blasted from a hillside in the course of his duties as a "powder man" at the camp.

"You could just see the memories going through his head," said Plep, noting that her uncle recalled the locations of the buildings, and even the grease pit where they had tossed the fat from the camp kitchen.

Reilly remembers that first night, when the truck's flatbeds with benches and canvas tops carrying the boys lurched and jostled them along the road leading to Camp Trask and they spotted a bear. They'd never seen anything like that before. For sure, they weren't in Rhode Island anymore.

"That was the subject of the night," Reilly said.

Settling into camp life, Reilly learned to saw logs. Then a position in explosives as a powder man came up on a road-building crew. The several boys who'd had the dangerous job previously met with accidents because they "didn't take their jobs seriously," Reilly said. "That is how I got the job."

As for that elusive, big boulder, Reilly said they gave him a hammer and drill and told him to get that rock out of the path of a road that was being built. Well, it would've taken two weeks to break it up at that rate. Reilly had a better idea.

"So I put a charge behind it and rolled it right down the bank."

Seems like it should still be there, even after all these years, he figured. At that size and weight, where's it going to go?

Well, maybe it was blown up again later, Plep suggested. Reilly reluctantly conceded that could've happened, but he sure would like to have found that rock.

Camp life meant working an eight-hour day for $30 a month, with $25 of that sent back home to help relatives through those economically tough times of the mid-1930s. That left a little more than $1 a week spending money for when the boys made it into Tillamook.

"That was good money back then, when there was no money," said Plep.

Reilly remembers trying to make that money

An undated group photo of Camp Trask near Tillamook, Oregon.[2]

stretch. It helped that the boys could be trucked into downtown Tillamook to see a movie at the Coliseum Theater, and 10 cents would transport them into the flickering, two-fisted adventures of Gary Cooper and James Cagney.

A cup of coffee was 5 cents, and for another 5 cents, you could pick up a bag of Golden Grain, roll-your-own tobacco. Reilly chuckled at how readily he could still recite the Golden Grain slogan: "Good enough for anybody, cheap enough for everybody."

He is especially fond of the memory of those Sundays when he and the other boys were transported into Tillamook for Communion at Sacred Heart Catholic Church. They'd have to leave camp early for the service and miss breakfast, so the church would treat them to a hearty eggs-and-bacon breakfast.

During this month's visit, Reilly dropped by the church and made a generous contribution. He met several older women who recalled those times, as well. As one of them put it, probably with a smile and a certain glint in her eye, "We were kids in grammar school we remember you boys."

Sports were part of camp life, too. Reilly remembered when the team at the Catholic high school in Tillamook challenged the CCC boys to a basketball game. Their chant, reflecting the area's dairy industry, was, "Feed 'em the cheese! Feed 'em the cheese!"

Not to be outdone, the boys drew on their own camp occupations of clearing timber. They chanted back, "Feed 'em the ax! Feed 'em the ax!"

Some of the guys hitchhiked to Salem once to make some money picking hops. Reilly laughingly recalled that they learned yes, the hard way that the only way to make any money when you're being paid by the pound, is to start early in the morning, when the dew weighs down the otherwise light and wispy plants.

One shadow eclipsed these bright memories as Reilly recalled the dark-complicated young man who ventured into Tillamook once or twice with his friends from camp.

"He was real dark, but not black," Reilly said.

Certain people took notice.

"They filed a complaint, and they got the government to move him," Reilly said, shaking his head. "They had laws that if you weren't white, you couldn't be on the street after dark."

Reilly made the most of his two weeks in Oregon. His niece saw to that. They took in OMSI's Titanic exhibit, a picnic with the Oregon CCC Alumni Association in Salem, the fishing fleet at Garibaldi, Pacific City's Dory Days parade. And those four or five pilgrimages back to Camp Trask, where his life first began to show purpose.

"He kept looking for that boulder," Plep said.

As he and Plep walked around Trask Park a final time, Reilly seemed at last to have rekindled enough memories to warm him the rest of his days.

With a last look around, he said to his niece, "Let's go."

"He'd had closure," Plep said. "He'd done exactly what he wanted to do."

***

[Author Note: I never got to meet Peter but John Thrasher, Reference Librarian from the North Kingstown Library, helped me find his obituary:]

Peter Reilly, 88, of Timberline Road, Warwick died Thursday January 26, 2006 at Kent Memorial Hospital. He was the husband of the late Evelyn C. (Donahue) Reilly. He was born (approx. 1918) in Providence, a son of the late Mary Rose (Roy) and William F. Reilly. He was a life-long resident of Cranston moving to Warwick in 2000.

In his early years he was a member of the CCC serving at Camp Trask in Oregon. He also was an Army WWII Veteran serving in the Pacific Aleutian Islands.

After the war he worked as a painting contractor for the Rhode Island Hospital Trust Bank for 25 years. He then formed his own contracting firm for 10 years, retiring in 1981.

After his lovely wife Evelyn passed away, he realized his wish to revisit Camp Trask, spearheaded by his niece Olive [Plep] who had married and settled in Oregon. While there, he was able to visit many highways and cleared woodlands brought about by his CCC unit, a demolition regiment.

He is survived by Olive Plep's husband Herb and many nieces and nephews including Carolyn E. O'Malley, Barbara Lawton, both of Cranston, Olive A. Plep of Portland, Oregon and William F. Reilly of Warwick.

NOTES

Chapter 1 Rhode Island CCC Camps – Their History

1 Diane Galusha, Another Day Another Dollar: The Civilian Conservation Corps in the Catskills, Black Dome Press Corp., Hensonville, NY, 2009, 7.

2 Ibid.

3 Ibid., 7.

4 Ibid., 8-9.

5 http://www.nps.gov/archive/elro/glossary/roosevelt-franklin.htm.

6 Edgar Nixon, Franklin D. Roosevelt and Conservation, 1911-1945, Franklin D. Roosevelt Library; 1957, 3-4.

7 Galusha, 15.

8 http://www.nps.gov/archive/elro/glossary/great-depression.htm.

9 Arthur M. Schlesinger, Jr., The Age of Roosevelt, III, The Politics of Upheaval, Boston: Houghton Mifflin Company, 1960, 251.

10 George P. Rawick, "The New Deal and Youth: The Civilian Conservation Corps, the National Youth Administration, the American Youth Congress," unpublished Ph.D. dissertation, University of Wisconsin, 1957, 18-29.

11 "Message to Congress on Unemployment Relief. March 21," The Presidential Papers of Franklin D. Roosevelt, 1933.

12 John Salmond, The Civilian Conservation Corps, 1933-1942, A New Deal Case Study, Durham, NC: Duke University Press, 1967, 14.

13 Stan Cohen, The Tree Army, A Pictorial History of the Civilian Conservation Corps 1933-1942, Missoula, MT: Pictorial Histories Publishing Co., 1980, 6-7.

14 Ibid., 2.

15 NYS Conservation Department Annual Report, 1934, 141.

16 Mark Neuzil, "Roosevelt's Tree Army," The History Channel Magazine, November/December 2010, 57.

17 Salmond, 90-91.

18 Ibid., 33.

19 NYS Conservation Department Annual Report, 1934, 141.

20 Salmond, 34.

21 Franklin Folsom, Impatient Armies of the Poor, Niwot, Colorado: University Press of Colorado, 1991, 310-322.

22 Galusha, 41.

23 NYS Conservation Department, Annual Report. 1936, 140.

24 NYS Conservation Department Annual Report, 1942, 108.

25 Harper, 104, Salmond, 111.

26 NYS Conservation Department Annual Report, 1935, 170-171.

27 Galusha, 64.

28 "Youths, 17 May Enter the CCC," Plattsburgh Daily Press, September 27, 1935.

29 Salmond, 58-59.

30 Harper, 39-41.

31 Salmond, 59-61.

32 NYS Conservation Department Annual Report, 1936, 140.

33 Salmond, 68.

34 NYS Conservation Department Annual Report, 1937, 19, 134.

35 Ibid., 133.

36 NYS Conservation Department Annual Report, 1938, 126-127.

37 Salmond, 137-138.

38 Ibid., 176.

39 NYS Conservation Department Annual Report, 1939, 118.

40 Salmond, 200.

41 Ibid.

42 NYS Conservation Department Annual Report, 1941, 113.

43 Seventh Annual Report of the State Department of Agriculture 1933 to Seventh Annual Report of the Department of Agriculture and Conservation, 1941.

44 Perry H. Merrill, Roosevelt's Forest Army: A History of the Civilian Conservation Corps, Perry H. Merrill Publishing, Barre, VT, 1983, 170.

45 http://www.thesca.org/.

46 Galusha, 181.

Chapter 2 Camp Organization

1 Charles Price Harper, The Administration of the Civilian Conservation Corps, Clarksburg Publishing Co., Clarksburg, WV, 1939, 39-41.

2 http://www.ccclegacy.org/Camp_Roosevelt_68B9.php.

3 Salmond, 135-136.

4 Cohen, 46.

Chapter 3 Enrollee's Life in Camp

1 "The Conservation Corps, What It Is and What It Does," Civilian Conservation Corps Office of Director, Washington, D. C., June, 1939, 10.

2 Cohen, 47.

3 Hawes, 188-189.

4 Ibid., 189.

5 "The Conservation Corps, What It Is. . . , 8.

6 Hawes, 114.

7 Salmond, 51.

8 Ibid., 53.

9 NYS Conservation Department Annual Report, 1935, 170.

Chapter 4 Work Projects

1 Galusha, 102.

2 Harper, 65.

3 Ibid., 145.

4 Schenectady District Civilian Conservation Corps Area Yearbook, 1937, 79.

5 https://en.wikipedia.org/wiki/1938_New_England_hurricane

Chapter 5 Escoheag / Beach Pond

1 West Greenwich Rhode Island Directory Map, George E. Matteson, 1966.

2 The First Annual Report of the Department of Agriculture and Conservation, 1935, 81.

3 Third CCC District First Corps Area Yearbook, 1937, 182.

4 Escoheagan, March, 1936, 3.

5 Third CCC District First Corps Area Yearbook, 1937, 182.

6 Ibid.
7 Escoheagan, March, 1936, 4.
8 Third CCC District First Corps Area Yearbook, 1937, 182.
9 https://ridemgis.maps.arcgis.com/apps/webappviewer/index.
html?id=a2960d1a022e4dccaab14aa4a58f5d45
10 file:///E:/CCC%20Rhode%20Island/CCC%20RI%20Greene/
CCC%20RI%20Map%20Civilian_Conservation_Corps_in_
Exeter_RI.pdf
11 The First Annual Report of the Department of Agriculture and
Conservation, 1935, 96 & 98.
12 Ibid., 107.
13 Escoheagan, March, 1936, 1.
14 Ibid., 2.
15 Ibid., 6.
16 The Third Annual Report of the Department of Agriculture and
Conservation, 1937, 106.
17 The Second Annual Report of the Department of Agriculture
and Conservation, 1936, 106.
18 Escoheagan, Nov., 1936, 9.
19 Third CCC District First Corps Area Yearbook, 1937, 152.
20 Escoheagan, March, 1937, 1.
21 The Third Annual Report of the Department of Agriculture and
Conservation, 1937, 93.
22 Escoheagan, May, 1938, 13.
23 The Third Annual Report of the Department of Agriculture and
Conservation, 1937, 108.
24 Escoheagan, June, 1938, 6.
25 Escoheagan, March, 1937, 11.
26 Escoheagan, Nov., 1937, 12.
27 Ibid., 16.
28 Escoheagan, Dec., 1937, 4.
29 Escoheagan, Nov., 1937, 13.
30 Escoheagan, May, 1938, 9.
31 Ibid., 4.
32 Ibid., 9.
33 Ibid., 10.
34 Ibid., 13.
35 Escoheagan, June, 1938, 6.
36 Ibid., 8.
37 Escoheagan, June, 1938, 6.
38 Escoheagan, Aug., 1938, 10.
39 Escoheagan, May, 1938, 10.
40 The Fourth Annual Report of the Department of Agriculture
and Conservation, 1938, 16.
41 Escoheagan, May, 1938, 10.
42 Escoheagan, June, 1938, 12.
43 Escoheagan, May, 1938, 6.
44 Ibid., 13.
45 Ibid., 6.
46 Escoheagan, June, 1938, 5.
47 Escoheagan, May, 1938, 6.
48 Escoheagan, June, 1938, 8.
49 The Fifth Annual Report of the Department of Agriculture and
Conservation, 1938, 94.
50 The Fourth Annual Report of the Department of Agriculture

and Conservation, 1938, 103.
51 The Sixth Annual Report of the Department of Agriculture and
Conservation, 1940, 72.
52 Ibid., 76.
53 Ibid.
54 http://riparks.com/Locations/LocationArcadia.html
55 Escoheagan, Nov., 1937, 2.
56 Ibid., 8.
57 Escoheagan, Feb., 1938, 3.
58 Ibid.

Chapter 6 Greene / Mount Vernon (Foster)

1 Third CCC District First Corps Area Yearbook, 1937, 157.
2 The First Annual Report of the Department of Agriculture and
Conservation, 1935, 81.
3 Ibid., 96.
4 Third CCC District First Corps Area Yearbook, 1937, 155.
5 Ibid., 157.
6 The First Annual Report of the Department of Agriculture and
Conservation, 1935, 76.
7 The Wayfarer, Aug.-Sept., 1936, 1.
8 Third CCC District First Corps Area Yearbook, 1937, 157.
9 The Wayfarer, Nov., 1936, 3.
10 The Wayfarer, Aug.-Sept., 1936, 3.
11 Ibid.
12 Ibid., 6.
13 The Wayfarer, July 1936.
14 The Wayfarer, Aug.-Sept., 1936, 5.
15 The Wayfarer, July, 1936.
16 The Wayfarer, Oct., 1936, 2.
17 The Wayfarer, Nov., 1936, 2.
18 Ibid., 3.
19 Third CCC District First Corps Area Yearbook, 1937, 155.
20 Ibid.
21 Ibid.
22 Wayfarer, Jan. 1937, 3.
23 Ibid., 4.
24 Wayfarer, Feb., 1937, 3.
25 Wayfarer, Jan., 1937, 3.
26 Wayfarer, Feb., 1937, 3.
27 Wayfarer, Mar., 1937, 3.
28 Wayfarer, April, 1937, 4.
29 Third CCC District First Corps Area Yearbook, 1937, 157.
30 Wayfarer, May, 1937, 4.
31 Third CCC District First Corps Area Yearbook, 1937, 155.
32 Wayfarer, May, 1937, 2.
33 Wayfarer, July-Aug., 1937, 2, 4.
34 Ibid., 4.
35 Wayfarer, June, 1937, 4-5.
36 Third CCC District First Corps Area Yearbook, 1937, 155.
37 Ibid., 157
38 Ibid.
39 The Third Annual Report of the Department of Agriculture and
Conservation, 1935, 16.
40 https://ridemgis.maps.arcgis.com/apps/webappviewer/index.

html?id=a2960d1a022e4dccaab14aa4a58f5d45
41 Wayfarer, May, 1937, 5.
42 Wayfarer, Oct., 1936, 9.
43 Wayfarer, Nov., 1936, 9.
44 Wayfarer, May, 1937, 6.
45 Wayfarer, July-Aug., 1937, 4.

Chapter 7 Hope Valley / Arcadia (Richmond)

1 Third CCC District First Corps Area Yearbook, 1937, 159.
2 https://ridemgis.maps.arcgis.com/apps/webappviewer/index.
html?id=a2960d1a022e4dccaab14aa4a58f5d45
3 The First Annual Report of the Department of Agriculture and
Conservation, 1935, 80.
4 Third CCC District First Corps Area Yearbook, 1937, 159.
5 Ibid.
6 Ibid.
7 Check, Dec. 19, 1935, 3.
8 Third CCC District First Corps Area Yearbook, 1937, 159.
9 Ye Arcadia Scroll, March, 1936, 2.
10 Ibid.
11 Ibid.
12 Ibid.
13 Ibid.
14 Third CCC District First Corps Area Yearbook, 1937, 159.
15 Check, Dec. 19, 1935, 4.
16 Ibid., 2.
17 Ibid., 7.
18 Third CCC District First Corps Area Yearbook, 1937, 160.
19 Check, Jan. 19, 1936, 4.
20 Ibid., 2.
21 Ibid.
22 Check, Feb. 19, 1936, 7.
23 Third CCC District First Corps Area Yearbook, 1937, 160.
24 Check, Feb. 19, 1936, 9.
25 Check, Jan. 19, 1936, 3.
26 Ye Arcadia Scroll, March, 1936, 4.
27 Check, Jan. 19, 1936, 3.
28 Third CCC District First Corps Area Yearbook, 1937, 160.
29 Ye Arcadia Scroll, March, 1937, 1.
30 Ibid.
31 Third CCC District First Corps Area Yearbook, 1937, 159.
32 Ye Arcadia Scroll, Sept., 1937, 2.
33 Ye Arcadia Scroll, March, 1937, 2.
34 Ye Arcadia Scroll, March, 1937, 5.
35 Ye Arcadia Scroll, June, 1937, 2.
36 Ye Arcadia Scroll, Oct., 1937, 6.
37 Third CCC District First Corps Area Yearbook, 1937, 159.
38 Ye Arcadia Scroll, June, 1937, 2.
39 Ibid., 5.
40 Ye Arcadia Scroll, March, 1937, 5.
41 Ye Arcadia Scroll, Oct., 1937, 4.
42 Ye Arcadia Scroll, March, 1937, 5.
43 Ibid., 1.
44 Ibid., 5.
45 Ye Arcadia Scroll, June, 1937, 5.

46 Ye Arcadia Scroll, Oct., 1937, 6.
47 Ibid., 8.
48 Ibid.
49 Ibid., 7.
50 Ye Arcadia Scroll, Dec., 1937, 8-9.
51 Ye Arcadia Scroll, Dec., 1937, 6.
52 Ibid.
53 Ibid., 8.
54 The First Annual Report of the Department of Agriculture and
Conservation, 1935, 14.
55 Ye Arcadia Scroll, Jan., 1938, 4.
56 Third CCC District First Corps Area Yearbook, 1937, 159.
57 Ye Arcadia Scroll, Jan., 1938, 5.
58 Ibid., 6.
59 Ibid., 9.
60 Ye Arcadia Scroll, Feb., 1938, 4.
61 Third CCC District First Corps Area Yearbook, 1937, 159.
62 Ye Arcadia Scroll, Apr., 1938, 4.
63 Ibid.
64 Ibid.
65 Ibid., 6.
66 Ibid.
67 Ibid., 10.
68 Ibid.
69 Ye Arcadia Scroll, Sept., 1938, 4.
70 Ibid., 10.
71 Ye Arcadia Scroll, Apr., 1938, 8.
72 Ye Arcadia Scroll, Sept., 1938, 8.
73 The Fourth Annual Report of the Department of Agriculture
and Conservation, 1935, 16.
74 Third CCC District First Corps Area Yearbook, 1937, 159.
75 Arcadia Veteran, Oct., 1939, 9.
76 Sixth CCC District First Corps Area Yearbook, 1937, 30.
77 The Fourth Annual Report of the Department of Agriculture
and Conservation, 1939, 104.
78 The Sixth Annual Report of the Department of Agriculture and
Conservation, 1940, 70.
79 Third CCC District First Corps Area Yearbook, 1937, 160.
80 Check, Dec. 19, 1935, 1.
81 Ye Arcadia Scroll, March, 1936, 7.
82 Ye Arcadia Scroll, June, 1937, 4.
83 Ibid., 2.
84 Ye Arcadia Scroll, April, 1938, 9.

Chapter 8 Kent / Nooseneck (West Greenwich)

1 https://ridemgis.maps.arcgis.com/apps/webappviewer/index.
html?id=a2960d1a022e4dccaab14aa4a58f5d45
2 The First Annual Report of State Department of Agriculture,
1935, 12.
3 Ibid., 81.
4 Nooseneck Tattler, Sept., 1935, 4.
5 Nooseneck Tattler, Oct., 1935, 8.
6 Ibid., 3.
7 Ibid.
8 Ibid.

9 First Annual Report of State Department of Agriculture, 1935, 36.

Chapter 9 Putnam / Washington (Glocester)
1 Third CCC District First Corps Area, 1937, Yearbook, 81.
2 https://exploreri.org/trailmaps/RIDEM-George-Washington-Mgnt-Area.pdf
3 Third CCC District First Corps Area, 1937, Yearbook, 81.
4 Ibid.
5 http://www.riparks.com/History/HistoryGoddard.html
6 The Thirtieth Annual Report of the Metropolitan Park Commission of January Session 1934, 6.
7 Third CCC District First Corps Area, 1937, Yearbook, 81.
8 Ibid.
9 Ibid.
10 Ibid.
11 Ibid.
12 The Washingtonian, Dec. 16, 1935, 4.
13 The Washingtonian, Jan., 1936, 5.
14 Ibid., 11.
15 Ibid., 2.
16 The Washingtonian, Jan. 25, 1936, 8.
17 The Washingtonian, Jan. 1936, 3.
18 The Washingtonian, Jan. 25, 1936, 3.
19 Ibid.
20 Ibid.
21 The Washingtonian, Feb. 11, 1936, 6.
22 Ibid.
23 The Washingtonian, Feb. 22, 1936, 3.
24 Ibid.
25 The Washingtonian, Feb. 11, 1936, 5.
26 The Washingtonian, Jan. 25, 1936, 5.
27 The Washingtonian, Jan. 1936, 3.
28 The Washingtonian, Feb. 22, 1936, 6.
29 The Washingtonian, Mar. 6, 1936, 6.
30 Ibid., 8.
31 Ibid., 6.
32 The Washingtonian, Feb. 22, 1936, 7-8.
33 Ibid., 12.
34 The Washingtonian, Mar. 6, 1936, 8.
35 The Washingtonian, Mar. 20, 1936, 4.
36 The Washingtonian, April 10, 1936, 7.
37 The Washingtonian, April 30, 1936, 6.
38 The Washingtonian, June 3, 1936, 8.
39 The Washingtonian, July 15, 1936, 4.
40 The Washingtonian, Sept. 18, 1936, 5.
41 The Washingtonian, April 10, 1936, 4.
42 The Washingtonian, Feb. 22, 1936, 4.
43 The Washingtonian, Mar. 6, 1936, 5.
44 The Washingtonian, Mar. 20, 1936, 5.
45 The Washingtonian, June 3, 1936, 2.
46 The Washingtonian, Mar. 20, 1936, 12.
47 The Washingtonian, April 30, 1936, 6.
48 The Washingtonian, June 24, 1936, 9.
49 The Washingtonian, Sept. 18, 1936, 11.
50 The Washingtonian, Mar. 20, 1936, 3.
51 The Washingtonian, April 10, 1936, 5.
52 The Washingtonian, June 24, 1936, 3.
53 The Washingtonian, July 31, 1936, 8.
54 The Washingtonian, Sept. 18, 1936, 11.
55 The Washingtonian, April 30, 1936, 3.
56 Ibid., 4.
57 The Washingtonian, Sept. 18, 1936, 6.
58 Ibid., 7.
59 The Washingtonian, Nov. 31, 1936, 4.
60 The Washingtonian, July 31, 1937, 4.
61 The Washingtonian, June 3, 1936, 3.
62 Ibid.
63 The Washingtonian, Mar. 6, 1936, 4.
64 The Washingtonian, Feb. 28, 1937, 1.
65 The Washingtonian, Mar. 31, 1937, 2.
66 The Washingtonian, June 30, 1937, 2.
67 The Washingtonian, Feb. 28, 1937, 1.
68 The Washingtonian, June 30, 1937, 6.
69 The Washingtonian, July 31, 1937, 2.
70 Ibid.
71 Third CCC District First Corps Area, 1937, Yearbook, 81, 177.
72 The Washingtonian, Aug. 1, 1937, 9.
73 The Washingtonian, Mar. 31, 1937, 3.
74 Ibid., 4.
75 The Washingtonian, June 30, 1937, 3.
76 The Washingtonian, Aug. 31, 1937, 2.
77 The Third Annual Report of the Department of Agriculture and Conservation, 1937, 16, 94.
78 The Fifth Annual Report of the Department of Agriculture and Conservation, 1938, 16.
79 The Sixth Annual Report of the Department of Agriculture and Conservation, 1940, 71.
80 Ibid., 71, 76.
81 Ibid.
82 The Fifth Annual Report of the Department of Agriculture and Conservation, 1939, 108.
83 http://riparks.com/Locations/LocationGeorgeWashington.html
84 The Washingtonian, Mar. 6, 1936, 9.

Chapter 10 Westerly / Burlingame (Charlestown)
1 Third CCC District First Corps Area Yearbook, 1937, 79.
2 Ibid., 79.
3 Ibid.
4 Ibid.
5 Wahoo, Feb. 1937, 26.
6 Third CCC District First Corps Area Yearbook, 1937, 79.
7 The Thirtieth Annual Report of the Metropolitan Park Commission of 1935, 13.
8 Third CCC District First Corps Area Yearbook, 1937, 79.
9 The Thirty-first Annual Report of the Metropolitan Park Commission of 1935, 12.
10 The First Annual Report of the Department of Agriculture and Conservation, 1935, 76.
11 Ibid., 93.

12 Ibid., 113.
13 The Second Annual Report of the Department of Agriculture and Conservation, 1936, 113.
14 Third CCC District First Corps Area Yearbook, 1937, 79.
15 Ibid., 79.
16 The Third Annual Report of the Department of Agriculture and Conservation, 1937, 99.
17 Wahoo, Jan., 1937.
18 Wahoo, Mar., 1937.
19 Wahoo, June, 1937.
20 Third CCC District First Corps Area Yearbook, 1937, 79.
21 The Fifth Annual Report of the Department of Agriculture and Conservation, 1938, 15, 101.
22 The Fifth Annual Report of the Department of Agriculture and Conservation, 1939, 81.
23 The Fourth Annual Report of the Department of Agriculture and Conservation, 1938, 94.
24 Ibid., 104.
25 The Fifth Annual Report of the Department of Agriculture and Conservation, 1939, 107.
26 Wahoo, Aug., 1939, 11.
27 Ibid.
28 Wahoo, Oct., 1939, 4.
29 Ibid., 3.
30 Wahoo, Jan., 1940, 7.
31 Ibid., 8.
32 The Fifth Annual Report of the Department of Agriculture and Conservation, 1939, 116.
33 Wahoo, Jan., 1940, 7.
34 Wahoo, April, 1940, 3.
35 Wahoo, Jan., 1940, 8.
36 Ibid.
37 Ibid.
38 Wahoo, April, 1940, 2.
39 Ibid., 3.
40 Ibid.
41 Wahoo, June, 1940, 2.
42 The Seventh Annual Report of the Department of Agriculture and Conservation, 1941, 71.
43 http://www.riparks.com/History/HistoryBurlingame.html
44 Wahoo, August, 1939, 5.

Chapter 11 Woonsocket / Primrose (North Smithfield)

1 Third CCC District First Corps Area, 1937, Yearbook, 123.
2 Ibid., 123.
3 Ibid.
4 Winchell in Woonsocket, April 17, 1936, 3.
5 Ibid.
6 Ibid.
7 Ibid.
8 Ibid.
9 Ibid.
10 Ibid.
11 Ibid., 7.
12 Ibid.
13 Ibid., 8.
14 Ibid., 4.
15 Ibid.
16 Ibid., 5.
17 Ibid., 6.
18 Ibid.
19 Ibid.
20 Ibid.
21 Ibid.
22 Ibid.
23 Ibid.
24 Ibid.
25 Ibid., 7.
26 The Second Annual Report of the Department of Agriculture and Conservation, 1936, 106-107.
27 The Third Annual Report of the Department of Agriculture and Conservation, 1937, 105.
28 Ibid.
29 Ibid.
30 https://riskirunners.com/about-us
31 The Second Annual Report of the Department of Agriculture and Conservation, 1940, 73.
32 https://en.wikipedia.org/wiki/Diamond_Hill
33 Third CCC District First Corps Area, 1937, Yearbook, 123.
34 http://nhlr.org/lookouts/us/ri/mowry-fire-tower/
35 Third CCC District First Corps Area, 1937, Yearbook, 123.

Chapter 12 RI Boys in Other States

1 https://digitalcollections.lib.washington.edu/digital/collection/clarkkinsey/id/2735/
2 https://digitalcollections.lib.washington.edu/digital/collection/clarkkinsey/id/2715/
3 Second CCC District First Corps Area, 1937, Yearbook, 4.
https://vtstateparks.com/assets/pdf/coolidge-events.pdf
5 Second CCC District First Corps Area, 1937, Yearbook, 53.
6 Ibid., 51.
7 Ibid., 54.
8 https://vtstateparks.com/newdiscovery.html
9 Second CCC District First Corps Area, 1937, Yearbook, 55.
10 Ibid., 56.
11 Ibid., 112.
12 https://www.waymarking.com/gallery/image.aspx?f=1&guid=c79dd5f3-9fad-431b-8d77-b69b5ad26cab
13 Second CCC District First Corps Area, 1937, Yearbook, 111.
14 Ibid.
15 Ibid., 70.
16 https://www.youtube.com/watch?v=H3NzfwAOKLg
17 Second CCC District First Corps Area, 1937, Yearbook, 71, 126.
18 Ibid., 69.

BIBLIOGRAPHY

Books

Cohen, Stan. The Tree Army, A Pictorial History of the Civilian Conservation Corps 1933-1942. Missoula, MT: Pictorial Histories Co., 1980.

Folsom, Franklin. Impatient Armies of the Poor. Niwot, Colorado: University Press of Colorado, 1991.

Galusha, Diane. Another Day Another Dollar: The Civilian Conservation Corps in the Catskills. Hensonville, NY: Black Dome Press Corp., 2009.

Harper, Charles Price. The Administration of the Civilian Conservation Corps, Clarksburg, WV: Clarksburg Publishing Co., 1939.

Harpin, Mathias P. and Albro, Waite. In the Shadow of the Tree, West Warwick, RI: Pawtuxet Valley Preservation and Historical Society, 2003.

Hawes, Austin F. HYPERLINK "http://rqst-agent.auto-graphics. com/agent/SummaryPage.

Reports

Seventh Annual Report of the State Department of Agriculture 1933. Providence, RI.
The Thirtieth Annual Report of the Metropolitan Park Commission of January Session 1934. Providence, RI.
The First Annual Report of the Department of Agriculture and Conservation, 1935. Providence, RI.
The Second Annual Report of the Department of Agriculture and Conservation, 1936. Providence, RI.
The Third Annual Report of the Department of Agriculture and Conservation, 1937. Providence, RI.
The Fourth Annual Report of the Department of Agriculture and Conservation, 1938. Providence, RI.
The Fifth Annual Report of the Department of Agriculture and Conservation, 1939. Providence, RI.
The Sixth Annual Report of the Department of Agriculture and Conservation, 1940. Providence, RI.

NYS Conservation Department Annual Report, 1934. Albany, NY.
NYS Conservation Department Annual Report, 1935. Albany, NY.
NYS Conservation Department Annual Report, 1936. Albany, NY.
NYS Conservation Department Annual Report, 1937. Albany, NY.
NYS Conservation Department Annual Report, 1938. Albany, NY.
NYS Conservation Department Annual Report, 1939. Albany, NY.
NYS Conservation Department Annual Report, 1941. Albany, NY.
NYS Conservation Department Annual Report, 1942. Albany, NY.

Yearbooks

Schenectady District Civilian Conservation Corps Area Yearbook, Schenectady, NY, 1937.

Third CCC District First Corps Area Yearbook, 1937, Fort Devins, MA.

Newspapers

Check
Escoheagan
The Evening Bulletin (Providence)
Plattsburgh Daily Press
Providence Journal
Wahoo
The Washingtonian
The Wayfarer
Winchell in Woonsocket

Magazines/News Letters

"CCC Camp Designated a State Archaeological Preserve." Connecticut Woodlands, Spring, 2010: 21.

Neuzil, Mark. "Roosevelt's Tree Army," The History Channel Magazine, November/December 2010.

Pamphlets

"The Conservation Corps, What It Is and What It Does." Civilian Conservation Corps Office of Director, Washington, D.C. June, 1939, 10.

Letters

Franklin D. Roosevelt, Letter to James McEntee, March 25, 1942.

Maps

Rhode Island map: HYPERLINK "https://ridemgis. maps.arcgis.com/apps/webappviewer/index. html?id=a2960d1a022e4dccaab14aa4a58f5d45" \t "_blank" https://ridemgis.maps.arcgis.com/apps/webappviewer/index. html?id=a2960d1a022e4dccaab14aa4a58f5d45

George Washington/Pulaski Wildlife Management Area Walkabout Trail: HYPERLINK "https://exploreri.org/trailmaps/RIDEM-George-Washington-Mgnt-Area.pdf" https://exploreri.org/trailmaps/RIDEM-George-Washington-Mgnt-Area.pdf
Matteson, George E. West Greenwich Rhode Island Directory Map, 1966.

Others

Boden, Gary and Reynolds-Boothroyd, Sheila. The Civilian Conservation Corps in Exeter, Rhode Island HYPERLINK "http://www.yorkerhill.com/eha/Stories/Civilian_Conservation_Corps_in_Exeter_RI.pdf" http://www.yorkerhill.com/eha/Stories/Civilian_Conservation_Corps_in_Exeter_RI.pdf

Hilton, Ford. "A Brief History of Stone Ranch, East Lyme, Connecticut," unpublished biography in East Lyme Library History Room.

Rawick, George P. The New Deal and Youth: The Civilian Conservation Corps, the National Youth Administration, the American Youth Congress, unpublished Ph.D. dissertation, University of Wisconsin, 1957.

"Message to Congress on Unemployment Relief. March 21," The Presidential Papers of Franklin D. Roosevelt, 1933.

"Youths, 17 May Enter the CCC," Plattsburgh Daily Press, September 27, 1935.

Online Sources

Americorp Corporation for National & Community Service, HYPERLINK "http://www.americorps.gov/about/ac/index.asp"http://www.americorps.gov/about/ac/index.asp

Arcadia Management Area, HYPERLINK "http://riparks.com/Locations/LocationArcadia.html" \t "_blank" http://riparks.com/Locations/LocationArcadia.html

Camp Roosevelt Beginnings, HYPERLINK "http://www.ccclegacy.org/Camp_Roosevelt_68B9.php" http://www.ccclegacy.org/Camp_Roosevelt_68B9.php

Civilian Conservation Corps Legacy, CCC Brief History, HYPERLINK "http://www.ccclegacy.org/CCC_brief_history.htm" http://www.ccclegacy.org/CCC_brief_history.htm

Civilian Conservation Corps Legacy, CCC Facts, HYPERLINK "http://www.ccclegacy.org/ccc_facts.htm"http://www.ccclegacy.org/ccc_facts.htm

Eleanor Roosevelt National Historic Site Hyde Park, NY, HYPERLINK "http://www.nps.gov/archive/elro/glossary/great-depression.htm"http://www.nps.gov/archive/elro/glossary/great-depression.htm

Eleanor Roosevelt National Historic Site Hyde Park, NY, Franklin D. Roosevelt (1882-1945), HYPERLINK "http://www.nps.gov/archive/elro/glossary/roosevelt-franklin.htm"http://www.nps.gov/archive/elro/glossary/roosevelt-franklin.htm

Family Treemaker Genealogy, HYPERLINK "http://familytreemaker.genealogy.com/users/e/l/l/Thomas-A-Ellis-Aberdeen/WEBSITE-0001/UHP-0052.html" http://familytreemaker.genealogy.com/users/e/l/l/Thomas-A-Ellis-Aberdeen/WEBSITE-0001/UHP-0052.html

George Washington State Campground & Management Area Goddard Memorial Park HYPERLINK "http://www.riparks.com/History/HistoryGoddard.html" http://www.riparks.com/History/HistoryGoddard.html

Student Conservation Association, HYPERLINK "http://www.thesca.org/"http://www.thesca.org/

US Forest Service, HYPERLINK "http://www.fs.fed.us/about-agency/contact-us" \t "_blank" US Forest Service HYPERLINK "http://www.fs.fed.us/aboutus/history/chiefs/stuart.shtml" http://www.fs.fed.us/aboutus/history/chiefs/stuart.shtml

Wikipedia.org, HYPERLINK "http://en.wikipedia.org/wiki/Oak_Lodge" http://en.wikipedia.org/wiki/Oak_Lodge

ACKNOWLEDGEMENTS

I would like to thank all of the CCC men who shared the wonderful stories of their life and experiences in the CCC. Thanks, also, to the wives, children and friends who remembered the stories of their husbands and fathers and shared their stories, and photos, for this book; also the local historians and historical societies that shared photos and information.

To my wife, Lynn for her support and patience over the past six years of research and writing; to my children, Matthew, Kristy, and Ryan for encouraging and accompanying me on trips and hikes; to my parents, Martin M. and Joan, who instilled in me the importance of hard work and provided me with a college education that enabled me to achieve my goals. To my son-in-law Matthew Roloff who helped me with computer problems and to my granddaughters, Kira and Lydia Roloff, for going on research trips with me and to my new daughter-in-law, Jenna Podskoch for her encouragement.

To the following people I'd like to give a special thanks:

My dedicated editor, David Hayden, who has worked with me for over 20 years in editing my ten historical books. He was always there to correct and guide me through the writing of newspaper articles and this book. I never would have completed this book without his insightful questions and suggestions.

Mike Wilk who inspired me to help him search for his father's Rhode Island CCC camp. After he located it, Mike traveled with Al Klyberg and I and we found the other RI CCC camps in one day.

A special thanks to:

Amanda Beauchemin of Ford Folios who spent many hours and weeks doing an excellent job in the layout and cover of this book and to the support of her uncle Barry Ford.

Retired District NYS Ranger Paul Hartmann made most of the maps for this book.

Jordon Ford who helped me with my research at the UCONN Library for the RI CCC camp newspapers.

Albert Klyberg for his friendship and sharing his research on the Rhode Island CCC camps. Also, to his wife Beverly and son Kevin for their help in proofreading and photos.

For these family members for sharing their father and grandfather's CCC story: Betty Cesario, John MacDonald, Eileen Edel & Eileen Perkins, Colgate Searle, Donald Polaski, Leo Caisse, Robert Bisaillon, and Peter Godon.

Thanks to the Walter Pidgeon and Frank Fields' families who donated CCC photos to the RI Archives.

A special thanks to these two historians who shared their Rhode Island CCC boy's photo albums: Kathleen Duxberry for her Lorenzo H. Frisiello album and Larry DePetrillo for his John Cinq-Mars album. Also, to Gary Potter who shared his large collection of CCC camp photos. These photos were invaluable considering the scarcity of CCC photos.

Joan Sharpe, President of the CCC Legacy in Virginia for her research materials and proofreading.

Thanks to Janet Coit, Director of the Rhode Island Department of Environmental Management, for providing information and recommending staff members to help. Thanks to these administrators and employees for sharing photos and historical information: Bill Mitchell, RI State Parks Superintendent; Paul St. Pierre of Forestry; Forest Rangers Ed McGovern & Allan Waterman.

To these historical societies and members for sharing photos, research materials and proofreading chapters for their local camps: Edna Kent and Marie Sweet, Glocester Heritage Society; Sheila M. Reynolds-Boothroyd, President of the Exeter Historical Association and member Gary Boden; President Rich Keene and member Larry Smith of the North Smithfield Heritage Society; Ed Robinson, Foster Preservation Society; Richard Prescott & Lauri Arruda of the Hopkinton Historical Society; Stu Redish and Pam Lyons, Charlestown Historical Society; and Ellen Madison, Westerly Historical Society.

Thanks to these librarians for their materials and suggestions: Peggy Raposa of the Louttit Memorial Library in West Greenwich; John Thrasher and Tom Frawley, Reference Librarians from the North Kingstown Library; Gayle Wolstenholme, Glocester Manton Library.

To these town historians for their information, photos and proofreading: Edna Kent of Glocester & Chepachet; Sheila M. Reynolds-Boothroyd of Exeter; Stanley Hopkins of Foster; Stu Redish of Charlestown; Rich Keene of North Smithfield.

To Keven Breene, West Greenwich Town Administrator, for his historical information, CCC contacts and proofreading.

To Valley Breeze reporter Lauren Clem for her story about the Rhode Island CCC camps and my book.

Thanks to the following libraries who hosted my CCC talks that resulted in finding many CCC boys and their families: Westerly Library, Cross Mills Library in Charlestown, Central Falls Library, and Glocester Manton Library.

A special thanks to these organizations for hosting my CCC talks: Charlestown Historical Society, Westerly Historical Society and Hopkinton Historical Society.

Thanks to Janet Coit, Director of the Rhode Island Department of Environmental Management, and Christian McBurney, historian and author of "Small State Big History" for writing the blurbs for the back cover.

I thank you each and all for helping me make this historical record possible.

INDEX

More books from Marty Podskoch

The Adirondack Stories: Historical Sketches I & II tell interesting stories through the comic sketches of Sam Glanzman, well-known *DC Comics* and *Outdoor Life* illustrator. The Fire Tower books tell photo-illustrated stories that Marty gathered while traveling throughout the region, which led to the development of his Adirondack CCC Camps book detailing the area's growth after the Great Depression. He has also written about the CCC camps in Connecticut. He has also written two travel books: The Adirondack 102 Club and Connecticut 169 Club books where he now lives. These **autographed** books make perfect gifts for those who love the region's history.

Order yours today!*

Adirondack Stories: Historical Sketches	$20.00
Adirondack Stories II: 101 More Historical Sketches	$18.95
Adirondack Stories Two-Volume Set (includes vol. I & II)	$34.95
Fire Towers of the Catskills: Their History and Lore	$20.00
Adirondack Fire Towers: Their History and Lore The Northern Districts	$20.00
Adirondack Fire Towers: Their History and Lore The Southern Districts	*HARD COVER* $24.95
Adirondack Civilian Conservation Corps Camps: History, Memories, & Legacy of the CCC	$20.00
Connecticut Civilian Conservation Corps Camps: History, Memories, & Legacy of the CCC	$24.95 *HARD COVER* $29.95
Adirondack 102 Club: Your Passport & Guide to the North Country	*HARD COVER* $20.00
☞ *NEW!* Connecticut 169 Club: Your Passport & Guide to Exploring CT	*HARD COVER* $24.95

Podskoch PRESS

43 O'Neill Lane, East Hampton, CT 06424
podskoch@comcast.net   860.267.2442

*Book prices listed on this page do NOT include shipping and postage. Contact Podskoch Press for total price.